Damsels and Divas

Damsels and Divas

European Stardom in Silent Hollywood

Agata Frymus

RUTGERS UNIVERSITY PRESS
NEW BRUNSWICK, CAMDEN, AND NEWARK,
NEW JERSEY, AND LONDON

Library of Congress Cataloging-in-Publication Data

Names: Frymus, Agata, 1989– author.
Title: Damsels and divas : European stardom in silent Hollywood / Agata Frymus.
Description: New Brunswick : Rutgers University Press, 2020. | Includes bibliographical references and index.
Identifiers: LCCN 2019025129 | ISBN 9781978806085 (paperback) | ISBN 9781978806092 (hardback) | ISBN 9781978806108 (epub) | ISBN 9781978806115 (mobi) | ISBN 9781978806122 (pdf)
Subjects: LCSH: Motion pictures—United States—History—20th century. | Motion picture actors and actresses—United States—Biography. | Negri, Pola, 1899–1987. | Bánky, Vilma, 1898–1991. | Goudal, Jetta, 1891–1985. | Motion pictures—European influences. | Whites in motion pictures. | Femininity in motion pictures. | America—In motion pictures. | Silent films—United States—History and criticism.
Classification: LCC PN1993.5.U6 F765 2020 | DDC 791.4302/80922 [B]—dc23
LC record available at https://lccn.loc.gov/2019025129

A British Cataloging-in-Publication record for this book is available from the British Library.

∞ The paper used in this publication meets the requirements of the American National Standard for Information Sciences—Permanence of Paper for Printed Library Materials, ANSI Z39.48-1992.

www.rutgersuniversitypress.org

Manufactured in the United States of America

Dla rodziców

Contents

Damsels and Divas

Introduction

In 1992, a short article in the *New York Times* announced the death of a former silent movie star, Hungarian-born Vilma Bánky. What was remarkable was the timing of the obituary, which appeared over a year after the actress's demise. This was a result of an arrangement made by Bánky herself before her death; apparently disillusioned by the lack of interest from friends and press alike, the nonagenarian instructed her spokesman not to publish a notice of her death for at least a year. It was a bitter reflection of the feelings of a woman who nearly seventy years earlier had reigned as one of the most beloved stars of the Jazz Age, nicknamed the "Hungarian Rhapsody."[1] Bánky's popularity, as in the case of many other careers of the silent era, was matched in intensity by its briefness.[2] Indeed, her decline from global fame was as swift as her climb to it.

The verdict of posterity was not as generous to Bánky as it was to other silent stars, to her colleagues and friends, the likes of Rudolph Valentino, Charlie Chaplin, and Norma Talmadge. The latter figures have earned secure places within the domains of popular culture and academia, whereas Bánky remains virtually absent from scholarly analysis or historical memory. In a bid to readdress this scholarly bias, my task here is to analyze the star discourse of the 1920s as it pertained to Bánky and two other Hollywood performers of European origin, Pola Negri (figure 1) and Jetta Goudal. Their respective careers may have taken different turns, but what they have in common is that they all hailed from the Continent, and all offered useful case studies for the interrogation of ethnicity, nationality, and femininity in the climate of interwar America. Through the interrogation of their star personae—as depicted and informed by their on-screen presence, film magazines, fan letters, popular press, and promotional material—I aim to demonstrate some of the ideological tensions and instabilities of the culture that produced them. How was Europeanness constructed in

Figure 1. Orientalism abounds. German postcard for *Sumurun* (1920), released in the United States as *One Arabian Night*. Source: Ross Verlag, Berlin. Photo: Union Film.

their respective, studio-sanctioned images? What was the impact of whiteness and ethnicity on those constructions?

Stars

Every age has its heroines, and they reveal a lot about prevailing attitudes toward women in their respective eras. According to Jane Gaines, an influential commentator on stars in film history, movie players who achieve recognition have prominence in the social realm and their significance cannot be limited solely to the film industry. The construction of female stars is especially important, given their ability to illustrate the inner workings of patriarchy; what we say about famous screen actors is often a displaced form of the prevailing cultural ideology at large.[3] This dialectical relationship between star images and the dominant values, in which stars play a dual role in both reflecting and reinforcing certain societal norms, forms the basis of this project. In drawing on historical evaluations of the ideological changes of the 1920s, I aim to unpack and deepen our understanding of the notions of ethnicity, femininity, and class that underpinned the public narratives of the three actresses analyzed in my case studies.

Pola Negri, the subject of my first case study, came to prominence by playing roles of seductive, passionate women in German film productions; that typecasting continued after she embarked on her career in the United States in the early 1920s. The commercial success of the features she produced for Famous Players-

Lasky, including *Bella Donna* (1923) and *The Spanish Dancer* (1923), helped Negri secure her position in the upper echelons of the acting profession. The focus of the case study is the intersections between the images emerging from Negri's professional activity and the life that she led off-screen. I show how her star narrative was linked to a fear of uncultured immigrants and miscegenation, especially in relation to her highly visible romantic dalliances. In turn, and following Diane Negra's rationale, this established Negri as both a thrilling, exotic commodity on one level and a hazardous phenomenon on another.[4]

In the wake of cultural anxieties related to uncultured immigrants corrupting America, Negri became a figure of powerful political resonance; her romantic liaisons functioned to move her away from the revered ideals of assimilation. Beyond shining a light on the ideological climate of her era, the issues raised by Negri's celebrity status find uncomfortable resonance in the contemporary American landscape, in a country that was—to quote Tom Rice—"gripped by the corrosive forces of modernity, burdened by a fear of outsiders, and beset by a media-panic toward . . . *the enemy within*."[5]

The second case study is of Vilma Bánky, who signed a contract with Samuel Goldwyn's studio in 1925. To the American consciousness she was foreign, but still a fair-haired star, rising to the pinnacle of her fame through a fortunate wrench of fate. Being discovered by an independent producer marked Bánky as a real-life Cinderella, a narrative that worked in conjunction with her looks to establish her as a perfectly nonthreatening version of femininity. Racial logic inflated the national psyche, imagining whiteness as far more than a physical feature and more of a spiritual quality. Here, I illuminate several concerns adjacent to the concept of whiteness, particularly in the backdrop of the second wave of immigration. What did it mean to be a white foreign woman during that time? Who was considered to be the perfect embodiment of an assimilable émigré, and, most importantly, what were the ideological implications of whiteness in constructing that archetype?

In discussing the idiosyncrasies of her stardom, I utilize Richard Dyer's theory of whiteness as racially superior and therefore "invisible" as ethnicity.[6] The subject that interests me the most here is the complex mix of forces and conditions that equated Bánky with the embodiment of white womanhood, despite her European origin. To adequately illustrate the discursive forces at work in shaping Bánky's image, this chapter draws on a range of commentaries on the plight of women, feminism, patriarchal ideologies, and Americanization.

The aim of the third and last case study is to interrogate the characteristics of the image Jetta Goudal sustained throughout her film career, emphasizing notions of authenticity, exoticism, and the framing of female behavior as difficult. This exploration opens with questions relating to ethnic ambiguity, as Goudal was presented as both French and Asian, national/ethnic categories that have quite different resonances. The actress was launched into a stellar

Hollywood career as a French woman who embodied a sense of mystery, with nearly all press releases promoting her as a fierce character whose obscure background added to the sense of an all-encompassing enigma. What makes Goudal an outstanding figure is the fact that she sued three of the studios that contracted her services and was granted financial compensation on at least two and perhaps even all three occasions. Unfortunately for the further development of her own career, Goudal was eventually blacklisted by film producers and simultaneously continued to be portrayed as "the most temperamental actress that has ever been seen on screen."[7] Henceforth, I adhere to the line of argument advanced by Sean Holmes, who sees the ways in which the print media framed Goudal's position in her legal battles as deeply problematic.[8] Although I am generally not concerned with recovering the real woman behind the facades, I do contrast some of the biographical details of Goudal's life presented in court files and private correspondence, for instance, with the images popularized by the studios, in order to provide a poignant illustration for the fabricated nature of star personae.

There are several reasons why I found the narratives offered by Negri, Bánky, and Goudal to be suitable subjects for the undertaking of this scope. First, despite the proliferation of scholarly interest in silent cinema in the recent years, both Goudal and Bánky are virtually absent from the context of film history and are still waiting for an academic evaluation. With the notable exception of Diane Negra's study, the major works on Negri available in English, by Kotowski and Delgado, are biographical accounts aimed at the general reader, and as such fail to provide an insight into the construction of Negri's stardom.[9] A chapter on Negri from Jeanine Basinger's book *Silent Stars*[10] discusses the career trajectory of the star more broadly but does not place her in a transnational setting, nor does it analyze the idiosyncratic features of her persona across fan magazines in any depth. The only existing book on Bánky, *More Than a Dream: Rediscovering the Life and Films of Vilma Bánky* by Rachel Schildgen, is a tremendous biography that describes the life of the Hollywood star in detail, but it does not engage with the complex intricacies of representation that accompanied Bánky's portrayals in the popular media.[11] Jetta Goudal is perhaps the least-known star among the three, certainly in terms of academic coverage. Holmes's essay on the implications of Goudal's image as a temperamental diva, and the most recent work by Alan Robert Ginsberg, also exploring her troubled relationship with the studio system, are the only pieces of scholarship on the star to date that I am aware of.[12] Holmes's discursive elaboration of Goudal's problematic reputation in the 1920s provides a useful point of entry for investigating the regulation of female labor within the male-controlled power structure sustained in Hollywood.

A second reason for examining these specific leading female performers is that they each enjoyed periods of immense popularity with critics and audiences. Negri was lauded as a European revelation right from the outset of her tenure in

Hollywood, effectively setting a trend in the acquisition of continental stars by American production companies. Although signed to a small studio with no distribution arm, Bánky was, for a time, the biggest financial draw in Samuel Goldwyn's stock of stars. Arguably, Goudal was the star with the weakest box office appeal of the three, but she still had a big fan base and generated a lot of media interest. The narrative of stardom that pertains to these women reveals different ways in which American society was conceived in relation to ideas of Europeanness and ethnic heritage.

Another interesting aspect of the case studies developed in this book is that the lives of Negri, Bánky, and Goudal intersected with each other in many, often surprising ways. For example, in 1927 Bánky married Rod La Rocque, who was previously rumored to have had a romantic relationship with Negri, his co-star from *Forbidden Paradise* (1924). Fan magazines were adept at rendering Bánky's delicate, conspicuously white features in terms of their opposition to the aesthetic ideals represented by the dark, visibly exoticized Negri. Goudal and Negri, on the other hand, shared an ideological alliance with ideas of excess and exoticism,[13] particularly regarding their ostensibly problematic, unmanageable behavior on set. If the writers of *Photoplay* are to be relied on, Goudal was infamous for being very temperamental and difficult to handle; the same periodical characterized Negri as a volatile "tiger-cat," ready to fall into a fit of rage if she does not get what she wants.[14]

Methodology

Although I pay attention to the specificity of Negri's, Bánky's, and Goudal's cinematic roles, the textual analysis of their on-screen heroines is not the only, or even the main, element of this project. In his seminal study of stardom, Dyer argues that star phenomena are constructed across a variety of texts that go well beyond one actor's oeuvre, and encompass all publicly available information on the given performer.[15] In approaching my case studies, I follow Dyer's lead and adopt what is now the most prominent methodological model within the field of star and celebrity studies. I thus examine the kinds of public personae that emerged from contextual and cultural artifacts of stardom, and especially in the pages of the most popular film magazines of the 1920s, such as *Photoplay*, *Picture Play*, and *Motion Picture Classic*. At times, the information provided by such publications is supplemented by features circulated in the popular press or local newspapers, as well as historical documents in the form of court records and private correspondence.

I also situate my work in the context of more recent debates about female stars. In particular, I use the multidisciplinary framework for studying star texts that Negra established in her monograph *Off-White Hollywood*. She describes this as a multivalent method drawing "from the fields of film studies, women's studies, American studies and critical ethnic studies."[16] While the methodology I implement here mirrors Negra's, it also builds on postcolonial theory, developments in the field of fan studies, and academic evaluations of fan magazines of the 1910s and 1920s, authored by Gaylyn Studlar, Shelley Stamp, and Michael Williams, among other scholars.[17] I found Studlar's rich body of work, and her analysis of the intersections between exoticism, consumerism, and female moviegoing, of remarkable value. My debt to Negra extends beyond the adoption of her methods, as her detailed chapter on Negri has become a crucial scholarly examination of the star as a cultural phenomenon, remaining to this day one of the very few in-depth studies of any of my chosen film performers. I follow Negra's evaluation of the star's precarious position in regards to whiteness, authenticity, and Americanization.

In the introduction to the edited volume on the film exchange between America and Europe, Andrew Higson and Richard Maltby assert that the well-documented international mobility of film personnel between 1920 and 1939 indicates the commercial, as well as cultural, potential embodied by Europe.[18] Taking their argument as a starting point, my aim was first to determine the iconographic and ideological considerations that made the process profitable and, second, to investigate how discursive parameters of Europeanness played out in practice, reflected and enhanced in the personae of the stars I selected for this analysis.

In researching the wider sociocultural landscape of the period, I used a number of critical and historical formulations—developed, for instance, by Lois Banner—pertaining to women's struggle for social and political autonomy in the 1920s. In mapping the mechanics that governed the movie industry during the decade, I relied on crucial contributions to the field by Richard Koszarski and Janet Staiger.[19] Dyer writes about the importance of audiences in creating star images while also directing attention to the idea that the meanings inherent in a star image can resonate differently with different demographics.[20] Although this audience-based approach is important, it is not part of my focus here. Instead, the study is largely limited to the portrayals of stars produced by the movie industry, especially through various movie publications, occasionally including an opinion expressed by a fan letter to one of those periodicals. As a project, the book aims to sketch the contours of the dominant public representations of Negri, Bánky, and Goudal, drawing on the most coherent features of their personae that emerged across a variety of platforms. Although I acknowledge the multifaceted nature of star phenomena, as well as their dependence on the people that consume them, an analysis of how audiences engage with those constructions of female stardom falls outside my scope.

Film periodicals reached the apex of their popularity in the early 1920s, when the circulation of *Motion Picture Magazine* alone exceeded 400,000 copies a month. *Picture Play* could boast half of that figure.[21] Clearly oriented toward female readership, they combined film reviews and star gossip with coverage of the latest fashions and advertising for beauty products, ranging from hair dye to freckle-removing creams. Working in close allegiance with studio executives, who supplied such publications with studio-sanctioned gossip, fan magazines constituted the most crucial avenue through which star personae were commodified for wide circulation. As such, they are incredibly useful resources for film scholars and historians alike, in both illustrating the promotional discourse on stars and placing it firmly in the wider ideological frameworks of the decade. On a wider scale, the book offers a study of fan culture of the 1920s and its interactive mechanisms.

While this research concentrates on the ideas of stardom propagated by fan magazines, I have occasionally extended the remit of this investigation to the accounts published in the pages of the popular press—namely, but not exclusively, the *New York Times*, the *Chicago Tribune*, and Utah's *Ogden Standard-Examiner*. This decision was, again, of a pragmatic nature, as many of the events related to Goudal and Negri were not discussed explicitly or were merely alluded to in the fan publications. In those instances, the news press offered a wealth of detail that was impossible to access simply by reading *Photoplay* and its ilk. To supplement my understanding of principles governing the star system, I consulted various archival manuscripts, including studio-generated documents. Many of the sources I draw on in my study of Goudal's career—for instance, predominantly private correspondence and telegrams—came from the extensive collection of materials gathered in the Jetta Goudal Papers and the extensive collection held at the Margaret Herrick Library in Los Angeles. In choosing the films for textual analysis in this volume, I focused on (but did not limit myself to) features that are still extant. Otherwise, I center my attention on star vehicles that enjoyed a significant commercial or critical success, or those that were effective in mirroring certain dimensions of off-screen images of its leading stars.

Ethnicity and Americanization

Conceptually, the discussion contained within this volume is centered on two elements of American culture that I consider particularly influential, specifically the concept of white femininity and its relationship to Americanization. In that respect, my analysis operates as an extension of Negra's work on American society and émigré picture players, in which she argues that the public personae of certain female European stars functioned to enhance the perception of America as a global power.[22] In an era that emphasized homogenization over cultural diversity, cinema exerted a powerful influence, acting as a propagator of the dominant middle-class ideology.[23] Clearly, the United States is a society that, at its very core, is built from an immigrant populace of varying religious and national backgrounds. It is therefore important to note that my use of the term "American" throughout this work pertains to the white, Anglo-Saxon, protestant elite (so-called WASP) and the values they upheld.

Because ethnicity is impossible to separate from inscriptions of gender, I wish not to interrogate these terms as exclusive power structures but, rather, work to show how different dynamics of representation interact with one another to create meanings that focus on my chosen stars.[24] I see gender and ethnicity as elements of one's identity that overlap, creating a distinctive form of disadvantage.[25]

My framing of ethnicity as a social construct separate from, yet supported by, the theorization of race requires a brief explanation here. Whereas race is broadly understood as a wide category that encompasses people of similar skin color and national background, I discuss ethnicity as a narrower subcategory, often lacking the distinctive visual parameters of racial categorization. In seeing race and ethnicity as artificial notions, I frame the latter as more fluid, given that ethnicities constantly re-invent themselves in modern settings "in response to changing realities both within the group and the host society."[26] For instance, the predominant logic of the early twentieth century imagined Magyars, Spaniards, and Italians as ethnic groups vastly inferior to Anglo-Saxons, Germans, or Scandinavians. Common lore at the time promulgated the assumption that immigrants occupying the highest realm with the internal hierarchies of whiteness were more likely to emulate the protestant ideals of hard work and restraint in their own behavior.

All three star texts under scrutiny here are represented by Caucasian, racially white women. The variances in their national heritage and appearance—namely, hair and eye color, makeup, costuming, and resulting casting tendencies—and the ways in which such features were elaborated by the contemporary press, marked them as ethnically different from each other, in a sense that Bánky was seen as a near-perfect evocation of whiteness, whereas Negri and Goudal were not. I see the politics of ethnicity as having a strong bearing on the representation of class, as foreign women were often presented in juxtaposition to whiteness, upper-middle class, and restraint, instead signifying the promiscuity associated with lower classes. I deploy Edward Said's *Orientalism* and Dyer's *White* to critically navigate my way through these issues.[27] Sean Redmond, Lola Young, and Tim Bergfelder are other scholars whose work I found of great use in unpacking the specificities of exoticism and its repercussions for star personae.[28]

Although ethnicity constitutes an integral facet of one's private identity, the ethnic identities of stars do not rely purely on the racial heritage they were born with. As noted by Ian C. Jarvie, star ethnicity is an amalgam of their "real" ethnicity, the alleged ethnicity of their star persona, and the ethnicity they most often embody in their films.[29] The intersection of these three notions is particularly fascinating in relation to Negri, Goudal, and Bánky, whose respective ethnicities were often not aligned with each other. For example, Pola Negri was born to Polish parents in Congress Poland, but her constructed off-screen ethnicity had more to do with being a Gypsy than a Slav. In her star vehicles, Negri often portrayed characters of Spanish or Italian descent; in *East of Suez* (1925) she was even cast as half-English, half-Chinese.

Female stars have importance as vessels that facilitate the circulation of concepts of femininity, ethnicity, and identity,[30] which helps to shape and develop socially sanctioned modes of behavior. As such, star studies can conceptualize the leading film players of an era as signifiers of something that goes beyond the simple combination of star publicity and on-screen appearances. To quote Michaela Krutzen, "Biographies of stars must be biographies of society."[31]

What makes the process of interpreting film performers of the past challenging is their immersion in discourse that is politically, socially, and culturally far removed from our own. But this is precisely the reason why popular star myths of bygone eras are so fascinating to contemplate. In being distant to one's own ideological milieu, they can also be formulated as concise, closed narratives, because "with the death of the star," as Williams suggests, "the phantasmatic nature of stardom becomes more vivid."[32] The nature and especially the allure of stardom as a cultural institution was reflected on by one reader of *Picture Play*, who wrote of Rudolph Valentino in 1928, after the idol's tragic death: "Rudolph Valentino was a very ordinary Italian. I mean him no disrespect, for indeed, I was one of those fans who adored his silver shadow, but in the interest of truth one must say that the substance was far less alluring than the shadow."[33] This book concentrates on the silver shadows thrown by three remarkable European women whose stars shone briefly, but very brightly, on the firmament of 1920s Hollywood.

CHAPTER 1

Pola Negri and Romance

"Ah Love! It's Not for Me"

William K. Everson points out that the acquisition of European filmmakers and actors was one of the ways in which Hollywood set about strengthening its image as an international cultural center at the beginning of the 1920s.[1] Pola Negri was one of the first continental stars recruited through Hollywood's fascination with Europe. She came to the United States in late 1922 at the invitation of Adolph Zukor, a producer who recognized the artistic and, most significantly, financial advantages that Negri's star appeal could generate for his company. From the start of Negri's career in Hollywood, fan magazine discourse established her in the context of what was viewed as her exotic disposition. "Pola Negri is highly emotional in private life as well as on the screen. She never spares herself," declared an article in May 1922.[2] Negri's publicity painted a portrait of carnal vitality and intensity that could befit only a continental star. In the words of one columnist, the star "walked into Hollywood with the hauteur of an empress."[3]

By populating the pages of the fan press, numerous romantic endeavors worked to increase Negri's star value while concurrently enhancing her connection to the notion of a European diva. In keeping with Diane Negra's argument, the romantic relationships in which Negri engaged formed the most important extratextual source of her stardom, since they "literalized the myth of the vamp."[4] Liaisons with the most influential people in the industry came hand in hand with a critical commentary depicting the star as a passionate diva; indeed, one of the earliest mentions of her antics in the American fan press referenced her alleged romantic involvement with Charlie Chaplin, whom she met during his visit to Europe.[5] Negri's career undulated alongside a series of affairs with the most desirable actors of the era: after her stint with Chaplin, she was briefly linked with Rod La Rocque and, most notably, with Rudolph Valentino. Those affairs, however, placed her beyond the spectrum of respectable femininity, eventually restricting her professional prospects. As a female foreign celebrity, Negri was forced to negotiate some of the most trenchant ideological assumptions of the period about what was acceptable in terms of the performance of ethnic and gender identity in America.

Because the dominant Western discourses equate love with the most intimate aspect of one's personal identity, and because the private lives of movie players are constituted as a site of truth, romance can be seen as the most truthful locus of star identity.[6] As a result, fans' acknowledgment of the manufactured nature of star images was partial, often not extending to the romantic relationships of their idols. To the readers of *Photoplay* and *Motion Picture Classic*, Negri was at her most authentic in seduction, courtship, and heartbreak. This chapter examines the ways in which Negri's exuberant love life blurred the lines between cinematic diegesis and public discourse. It argues that Negri's romantic endeavors connected her to the vamps she portrayed on screen, simultaneously validating her eastern European ethnicity. As a woman who was—to use Negra's term—"off-white," Negri became synonymous with an unsuppressed female desire that stood in stark opposition to ideas of white virtuousness.[7] In a period of increased interest in tabloid journalism, Negri's off-screen conduct gave credibility to the characters she created in her work, and the compatibility between these two types of representation effectively turned her into a hazardous commodity. She was, as such, caught between the "old" and the "new" world, an outsider who had infiltrated and worked her way inside the American nation.[8]

Charlie Chaplin

In order to examine how Negri's love life was articulated, I briefly outline some concerns that correspond to film magazines' initial handling, and eventual commodification, of such matters. Upon their emergence in the early 1910s, the first film-oriented publications paid little attention to the off-screen lives of movie players, largely limiting their discussion to upcoming productions and casting decisions. From 1914 onward the leading periodical of this type at the time, *Photoplay*, started to extend its gossip pages to include business matters, such as lawsuits, studio finances and star salaries, although it still managed to steer away from writing about the intimate relations of the major movie players.[9] More overt acknowledgment of star couplings dates back to 1917, the year in which *Photoplay* published its eponymously titled spread "Who Is Married to Who."[10]

Gradually, the focus of fan press shifted to circulating private information relating to extrafilmic personalities, and revealing personal likes and dislikes of the stars, as well as their prospective fiancées and spouses. In providing a steady supply of what they presented as fascinating private details of stars' lives, these magazines secured the loyalty of their readership. In its heyday, the studio system focused on off-screen star personae to a greater degree than European modes of film promotion; the Hollywood publicity machine was invested in endorsing its leading players as people who had interesting private lives.[11] By the mid-1920s, fan magazines were adept in disclosing not only who was married to whom but also—to quote Martha Gever—"who is dating and maybe sleeping with whom."[12]

In February 1922, when Negri arrived in Hollywood, Chaplin was at the height of his artistic success, having recently directed *The Kid* (1921), his first full-length feature. In the book detailing his trip to Europe, *My Trip Abroad* (published in 1922), the English comedian recounted his first meeting with Negri at the Palais Heinorth in Berlin, calling her "divine" and "the loveliest thing he has seen in Europe."[13]

As in the case of the other romances conducted by Negri in the years ahead, there seems to be no consensus as to whether the affair grew organically or whether it was simply a matter of clever publicity designed by Famous Players-Lasky as a form of investment in its newest contract player. Notwithstanding, the Negri I analyze here is a constructed persona rather than a biographical entity; it is the type of information that circulated about her that interests me, not whether it was factually accurate.[14] Given Chaplin's huge international fame, his rumored relationship with Negri inevitably received a lot of media coverage (figure 2). By directing her attention to the nation's most eligible bachelor, Negri substantially bolstered her market value and was soon commanding headlines herself. *Picture Play* reported that the king of comedy was reluctant to discuss the nature of his involvement with the European actress. After being asked about Negri by Elza Schallert, a gossip columnist, Chaplin's face allegedly turned red: "He had met his Waterloo, and he thenceforth became as silent as a sphinx on the subject of feminine pulchritude."[15]

The short-lived affair was conducted in a whirl of speculation, with announcements of engagements quickly followed by supposed quarrels and splits. A press conference held at the Del Monte Lodge on January 28, 1923 was used to announce Chaplin's plans to wed Negri, although in early March numerous outlets quoted the actor as saying that he was too poor to afford a wedding ceremony. Negri's publicist, in response, issued a statement declaring that "the happy days are dead" and that "it's all over."[16] The subsequent reunion piqued the interest of the fan press, with many commentators painting Negri as highly emotional and therefore incapable of keeping her private affairs to herself.

In the account provided by Harry Carr, when Negri planned to end her relationship with Chaplin she decided to use the public media to let the world know of her intentions by paying for an eight-column headline in all the most popular papers.[17] By June, Negri allegedly claimed Chaplin was irreversibly unsuited to matrimony.[18] The promotional aspect of all these actions did not go unnoticed, with *Picture Play* reporting that "[Chaplin's] supposed engagement to Pola Negri netted the romantic young couple millions of dollars' worth of advertis-

Figure 2. The pair in the popular press in 1923: *Buffalo Enquirer*, January 18.

ing."[19] These attributions betrayed a sense of extravagance and eccentricity that became entrenched in Negri's star text, and further framed her in the context of her temperament. In epitomizing a continental, semi-exotic demeanor, the actress "identified with the world of passion, with strong affect."[20] To quote Jeannine Basinger, "The idea was that Pola Negri, a European diva, was out of control, an egomaniac."[21] In many ways, this narrative was emblematic of the wider trends in star publicity, with fan magazines actively generating controversy to engage their readers.

Rod La Rocque

Negri's private antics relied largely on taking an active sexual interest in men, which intersected with aspects of her portrayals on the silver screen. The compulsion to draw her life according to the outlines of her performances surfaces more sharply in the narrative treatment of her character in *Forbidden Paradise* from 1924. It fed into the tendency to view Negri's private persona as that of a flirtatious woman interested in sexual conquest. "Pola actually is the Czarina," contended the *Exhibitor's Trade Review*, "and no one will deny it."[22] Here, I analyze the narrative of the film and the way in which its promotion conflated the seductive character of the czarina with Negri's off-screen qualities.

Early in the film, a group of revolutionaries attempts to topple the monarchy of a fictional Balkan state by assassinating the empress. "Let's put an end to a [*sic*] female rule! It's shameful to have to obey a woman—especially that kind of woman!" proclaims the leader of the revolt in addressing his followers. Luckily, a young officer, Alexei Czerny, witnesses the speech and comes to the czarina's rescue. She repays him not only by increasing his rank to captain but also by inviting him to spend the night with her. Albeit humorously, the plotline promulgates the assumption that women of power use their influence for the wrong reasons, such as to facilitate their promiscuity. At first, the man is torn between the advances of the powerful and sexually confident czarina and the desire to remain faithful to his fiancée, caring and loyal Anna (Pauline Starke). Soon enough, he trades his initial reluctance toward Negri's character for passionate love, "only to discover that he is the latest in a long line of royal consorts."[23] This painful realization is executed in classic tongue-in-cheek fashion for which Ernst Lubitsch's direction is so celebrated: the empress stages a banquet attended by a number of officers, all of whom wear the same medal she has presented to Alexei after they became lovers. Unable to bear his disgrace, the captain falls into madness and threatens to kill Negri's character. "All the guards are gone, you are on my mercy," he declares. The dynamic between the pair is reversed once more due to a dramatic turn of events, with the czarina's loyal servants getting back to the castle just in time to save her life.

Alexei receives a death sentence for the attempted assassination, but the generous empress grants him his freedom. He leaves, happy to go back to Anna, his sweetheart, but the czarina wastes no time mourning their relationship. The two women are representative of the patriarchal archetypes of good girl and bad girl, wife and seductress, and the tension between them culminates in the final image of Anna as "a nurturer, comforter [and] a forgiver of sins,"[24] in opposition to the czarina and her unbridled eroticism.

Of course, the czarina's "punishment" here is largely symbolic, and she does not mourn the loss of Alexei for too long. The last scene shows a Spanish ambassador waiting for an audience with the czarina. "I have to warn your excellency that her majesty hates any negative appearance—especially in a moustache. For the good of your country I would advise you to curl your moustache upright," advises one of the servants. The diplomat follows the suggestion and, immediately, the czarina is smitten.

It has to be noted that Anna's success in regaining Alexei's affections has nothing to do with her actions—in fact, she is absent from the narrative progression of most of the film—and everything to do with the selflessness of her act and the manner in which she thereby epitomizes a behavioral model that women should aspire to. The end of *The Forbidden Paradise* can also be read as a comment on the gendered ideals of being white, whereby whiteness is affirmed by men if they suppress their sexual desires and by women if they exhibit none.[25] As argued by Richard Dyer, the sex drive in white women constitutes a symbolic fall from whiteness, "a disturbance of their racial purity."[26] "The model of a white woman is the Virgin Mary, a pure vessel for reproduction who is unsullied by the dark drives that reproduction entails."[27]

Staying faithful to Lubitsch's aesthetic strategy, the motion picture heedlessly appropriates a variety of historical fashions and architectural styles, exhibiting an "untroubled lack of discrimination in the staging of the past."[28] Sergio Delgado attests to the positive reactions that surrounded the film, writing that the reviews of the film were arguably the best in Negri's entire American career. The picture attracted nothing but praise, with the critics contending that the reunion between Negri and Lubitsch had long been overdue.[29]

The role also gave its chief star the opportunity "to exchange steamy looks and open-mouth kisses with Rod La Roque,"[30] which naturally caused rumors regarding the nature of their relationship off-screen. *Photoplay* observed that "Rod La Rocque continues to be the most favored of Pola Negri's suitors," adding that both parties claim their romantic involvement "isn't serious." "But for the present it seems to amuse Pola sufficiently. It's impossible to imagine Pola Negri without a love affair. Not permanent, possibly, but hectic for the time being."[31] Challenging the idea that the relationship is romantic in nature, one column declared that the friendship is bound to benefit La Rocque, who—lacking certain pose and finesse—will be able to develop more refinement simply through association with Negri, his European colleague.[32] Alternating positions toward these stars facilitated construction of a contentious debate, further activating magazine readers.

As with the liaison with Chaplin—and various romantic dalliances that followed soon after—it is unclear to what extent Negri's involvement with La Rocque was part of Zukor's promotional tactics, and to what extent it was a genuine reflection of her private desires. Both Scott Eyman and Rachel A. Schildgen assert that the publicity generated by the rumored couple relied on an actual (although short-lived) romance involving the two stars.[33] Eyman goes on to point out it was Negri who insisted on casting her current lover in the part of Alexei Czerny.[34] The evidence for the Negri/La Rocque relationship can be pinned to one main source, a letter written by Goldwyn's assistant to one of her friends: "After her affair with Chaplin cooled off and Rod La Rocque was bewitched, if she didn't have the audacity to bring Rod to the very same apartment—in fact in the very same bed—where she previously had Chaplin. . . . However, that is Pola for you—brazen. If I had been Rod I would have left her then and there—but the poor fool was only a toy in her hands and let himself be juggled about as she wished and utterly helpless."[35]

Between rumors of engagements and elopements, the fan press spotlighted Negri as a woman who enjoyed looking for new romantic pursuits. On one level, this narrative activated the idea of a creature of temperament and passion, "continental to her fingertips,"[36] and thus surrounded by men willing to succumb to her every desire. Additionally, in the eyes of the public, flagrant displays of affection were much more popular among foreign stars than among the naturally more reserved American stock of actors: "We shut ourselves and our feelings so closely inside. Perhaps that is why we find imported romance more thrilling than home-grown, because foreign players are not afraid to depict emotion and passion frankly."[37] *Picture Play* reported that La Negri did not limit her efforts in seduction to her work colleagues; she was as successful with unnamed Peruvian ambassadors and millionaire tennis champions as she was with the shining stars of the silver screen.[38] Shortly after breaking her engagement with Chaplin, for instance, Negri attended the re-opening of the Coconut Grove nightclub in Hotel Ambassador accompanied by Bill Tilden, one of the most celebrated tennis players of the period.[39]

Negri's bohemian image was authorized as she continued to voice her views on her inability to settle down: "I do not believe in marriage. It is not for me. I am selfish. No, not selfish, for I have sacrificed everything for love. . . . Freedom comes before anything. I am a Gypsy, just like my father."[40] With the reoccurring gypsy trope, Negri was attributed to ideas of independence and free-spiritedness, concepts that run counter to the main current of traditional American culture during this period. In another magazine report, Negri questioned the sanctity of marriage, or at least supported optional divorce; staying in an unhappy relationship is "a barbarous cruelty," she claimed, and one ultimately working "against the ultimate happiness of the human race."[41]

Gaylyn Studlar points out that in their commentary on the relationships of stars, fan magazines aligned themselves with patriarchal models of female subjectivity.[42] In seeking to channel women into normative modes of conduct, editorials abstained from discussing romantic liaisons in more depth, unless the participants were either engaged or married.[43] Within that rhetorical framework, Negri's comments had the capacity to spark alarm. Described by *Photoplay* as being "in and out of engagements with a rapidity of Houdini from handcuffs,"[44] Negri was something of an eccentricity in the world of happily married wives and searching-for-love singles. Her sexually emancipated conduct taxonomically differentiated her from the highest ideals of white femininity and the principles of self-restraint, purity, and modesty. The intrinsic link between ethnicity and gender is therefore reflected in the star discourse that represented Negri as a symbiosis of multiple transgressions—namely, alleged ethnic difference, female independence, and overt (thus deranged) sexuality.

Rudolph Valentino

From the late spring of 1926, the press coverage devoted to Negri became dominated by the descriptions of her intense affair with Rudolph Valentino. Supposedly, the two fell in love at first sight after meeting each other at a party thrown by Marion Davies, a mutual friend.[45] Louella Parsons, a gossip columnist, gave herself credit for introducing the pair. By Parsons's admission, Valentino asked her for the favor: "Introduce me to Pola Negri. I saw her last picture and I think she is fascinating. Can't you arrange for her to come to one of Marion's parties?"[46]

There were significant parallels in the image of Negri and her new suitor, in a sense that the notion of being temperamental and exotic, so integral to Negri's allure both on and off screen, was also supported in relation to Valentino's persona. Indeed, their star narratives were so aligned that some press reports claimed that Negri's part in *The Spanish Dancer* was written with Valentino in mind, and that it was intended to be released under the title of *The Spanish Cavalier*.[47] Lea Jacobs sees this as particularly poignant: "If any female star of the early 1920s could have filled Valentino's shoes, it would have been Negri."[48] Valentino's representation was that of a swarthy, passionate Italianness that was, much like Negri's identity, mutable. At once primal and sophisticated, his continental facade suggested cultivation, on the one hand, and exoticism, on the other.

According to the critical evaluation of Valentino's persona developed by Studlar, the studio system consciously placed him within romanticized narratives of the Middle East or the Old World to cater to the female desire for Orientalism, in which he could hide "what some might have interpreted as exciting sexual promise, but others regarded as dangerous foreign bestiality."[49] To many contemporary observers, Valentino posed a threat to national womanhood because he seduced American women into rejecting the simple but good-hearted American man.[50] "Rudolph Valentino makes our pulses throb madly to the tune of his lovemaking,"[51] noted one fan magazine, actively contextualizing the masculine allure held by the performer for female audiences.[52] In a very similar vein, *Picture Play* outlined Negri's non-Anglo-Saxon appeal in describing her as "a wild cat . . . who doesn't calculate."[53]

Stars like Valentino and Negri demolished the puritan vision of prewar conventions, creating a highly sexualized star quality where impulsiveness, boisterousness, and fieriness were put on a pedestal. To quote Joe Franklin, "smouldering sex appeal" was their stock in trade.[54] Thus, as Stacey Abbott elaborates, these exotic images were simultaneously constructed as desirable and dangerous, which reflected an ambiguity toward modernity.[55] Negri—particularly when paired with Valentino—offered new, opulent pleasures while instantaneously corresponding to the creation of new moral dangers, such as excessive consumerism, overt sexuality, and interethnic mixing.

As an item, Valentino and Negri encapsulated a mixture of temperament and passion that attests to the appeal held by European decadence within the American discourse of the period. They were often spotted dancing at The Sixty Club, a popular destination among the Hollywood elite. On one such occasion—which is a telling example of how the star system sought to overwrite on-screen images of stars with their personal antics—they wore matching outfits inspired by Spanish culture, with Negri dressed as a dancer and Valentino posing for photographs as a toreador, dressed in the costume he wore for the filming of *Blood and Sand* (figure 3).[56] According to the description given by *Photoplay*, they won first prize in a contest for the most beautifully dressed couple: "They wore Spanish costumes, both in cloth of gold, and they certainly looked stunning. When they took to the floor together and did a glorified tango together they were a sensation."[57] Many stars and starlets of the period participated in upscale costume parties and other "carnivalesque events" in which they were able to showcase Orientalized versions of themselves.[58] Alexander Walker explained the popularity of costume balls among the Hollywood elite in terms of the fantasy element they contained: "Stars who spent their working lives playing roles seemingly could not exist without the same sort of stimulus in their social lives." Fancy dress parties thus extended their film parts into their after-hours.[59]

Some commentators, such as David Bret, have suggested the Negri/Valentino relationship was again no more than a series of publicity stunts, a marketing rationale aimed at increasing their respective box-office appeal.[60] However, personal correspondence in the Margaret Herrick Library suggests otherwise. Letters written by Valeria Belletti, who held a position as Samuel Goldwyn's secretary at the time, suggest Negri's romantic involvement with Valentino was in fact genuine.[61] Real or not, the relationship enhanced the image of the actress as a paragon of irrationality and romance and further anchored her within a narrative of extravagance.

Negri and Valentino's life together was painted as a constant whirl of luxury, where roses, wine, and sunsets over the Hollywood hills come together in perfect harmony. Valentino spared no expense in pampering the new object of his desires. According to *Photoplay*'s report, the Italian actor sent Negri a tribute of orchids worth $1,000 to congratulate her on the opening of her new picture *Good and Naughty* (1926).[62] The magazine alleged that Negri disregarded social convention in being just as openhanded by sending her beloved "a huge mass of red roses on a giant frame, taller than his head and twice as long."[63] This is not to say the passionate union was viewed as completely devoid of pitfalls. Two months before Valentino's death, one columnist stressed the unstable nature of Negri's

Figure 3. Negri and Valentino wearing Spanish costumes at The Sixty Club. Source: *Cine-Mundial*, September 1926, 718.

affection by suggesting that "her romance with Rudolph Valentino is blasted. Some one [*sic*] quotes her as having said that she is through with men forever, and will live only for her art in the future. But she may decide that, after all, her major art is flirtation."[64]

Valentino's Death and Funeral

Valentino visited New York in mid-August to promote his latest vehicle, *The Son of the Sheik*, but was hospitalized on August 15, due to a perforated ulcer in his abdominal cavity. Despite undergoing immediate surgery, the condition proved to be fatal, claiming Valentino's life eight days later. Reactions to the sudden death of the star at the pinnacle of his popularity visualize the breadth of his short-lived fame.[65] An estimated 50,000 to 75,000 onlookers gathered in front of Frank E. Campbell Funeral Chapel on Broadway, where Valentino's body was deposited,[66] with men and women fighting so desperately to catch a last glimpse of their screen idol that the glass window they were pressing against fell outward, shattering to pieces on the heads of those unfortunate enough to be standing close by.[67] The police were unable to control the ensuing havoc; over one hundred people suffered injury and several had to be hospitalized with broken limbs and bruises.[68] The *New York Times* reported that members of the public were forbidden from attending Valentino's bier on August 26, and that 200 police officers were put on duty to prevent further riots.[69]

Maintaining that she was engaged to Valentino at the time of his death, Negri appointed herself chief mourner and spent over $2,000 on an extravagant arrangement of red roses and white blossoms that spelled her first name.[70] She repeatedly emphasized her deepest affection for her tragically dead fiancé, telling the *New York Times*, "My love for Valentino was the greatest love of my life; I should never forget him. I loved him not as one artist might love another but as a woman loves a man."[71] Negri's personal conduct at the funeral did not pass without furor in the daily press, with most accounts dismissing her grief-stricken behavior as an overly dramatic performance. She allegedly swooned and fainted, and even threw herself at the coffin, to the dismay of other attendants.[72]

"She wept, she wailed, she clutched her long black hair," wrote Parsons, describing the intense grief exhibited by the star. "She fell on her knees crying to high heaven to let her die, too. Never in her most scenery-chewing moments as an actress did Pola stage such a performance as she put on before Marion [Davies] and me."[73] Undoubtedly, this type of behavior exceeded the normative models of bereavement accepted by WASP American culture, which emphasized self-control and suffering in silence.[74]

Recognizing the complexity contained within the representation of femme fatale and her agency, Mary Ann Doane provides a useful reformulation of the figure,[75] which effectively sheds new light on representational schemes pertaining to Negri. In Doane's critical evaluation, the femme fatale is a carrier of tragedy who confounds agency and subjectivity with the very lack of these attributes. In a sense, her power is independent of consciousness and, therefore, is beyond her own, rational control. This reading resonates with the force embedded within accounts of Negri's romantic history, where she often appears as a victim of powerful, mysterious forces; consider a piece from *Photoplay*, for instance, citing the actress: "Always I have sought love, and always there have been disappointments. I am a fatalist. I believe in my star. It is my fate to be unhappy in love."[76] In the words of one of her contemporaries, Myrtle Gebhart, "Pola has simply got the habit of falling in love. She thrives on it, calling love 'one of the crosses a woman has to bear.'"[77] "Love at firs' sight is nossing [*sic*] but suffering," she revealed, rather fatalistically, in another interview.[78] Taken together, as Negra discussed, interviews of this kind testified to the deadly effect she exercised, unconsciously, on her lovers and positioned Negri in parallel with the femmes fatales of the fin de siècle.[79] Effectively, the star image blurred the lines between diegesis and discourse, or between art and life, with the death of Valentino serving as yet another enhancement of that fatal narrative. It proved La Negri could not be loved back, or at least was not destined to enjoy her happy ending.

After the New York funeral, Valentino's body was shipped to Los Angeles to be laid to rest in Hollywood Memorial Park. The studio issued extensive instructions regarding the journey to the West Coast, making sure that Negri was accompanied by a "good publicity man" to document her mourning.[80] Arguably, the producers saw this as a real-life opportunity to engage with the tragic femme fatale type known from Negri's publicity to date, although they failed to predict the consequences this larger-than-life act would have on the evolution of her image. On one level, Negri's actions authorized the link between exotic ethnicity and hysteria, adding veracity to the image of a passionate diva. Thus, to cite Charles J. Maland, the way she behaved during the funeral of the movie icon "planted some of the seeds of acrimony among the public that would grow and later blossom."[81] Consequently, Negri's demeanor was viewed as overblown and lacking good taste.

Prince Serge Mdivani

On May 5, 1927, in Seraincourt, France, Negri wed a Georgian socialite, Prince Serge Mdivani (figure 4). The information came as a shock to the public given its time frame: the ceremony took place a mere nine months after the sudden death of Valentino. The fact that Negri openly disrespected the codes of mourning made her even more susceptible to public scrutiny, as even the most ardent of her fans started to question the authenticity of the emotional outpouring she

Figure 4. Negri and Mdivani on the day of their wedding. Source: *Sunday News*, July 10, 1927.

displayed after losing her fiancé. If Delgado's account is to be relied on, the box office returns for Negri's newest venture *Barbed Wire* (1927) plummeted because of the antipathy she faced; ticket sales dwindled as soon as the news of the wedding entered the public domain.[82] "The American Valentino cult was determined to ruin me for daring to live a life that was not completely dedicated to the memory of Rudy," declared Negri in hindsight, years after her marriage to Mdivani had ended.[83]

Liaisons with European aristocracy, both real and presumed, attested to the extraordinary nature of American film idols, elevating them to the highest echelons; Gloria Swanson's marriage to a French nobleman in 1925, which allowed her to use the title of the Marquise de la Falaise de la Coudraye, is a case in point. Although contract players of the period were expected to engage in a series of romances to increase their visibility, this manner of female representation, as Virginia Wright Wexman attests, contradicted the revered ideals of marriage and long-term monogamy.[84] In this respect, the preferred magazine formula was filled with conflicts: some controversy generated readership, but a radical subversion was out of the question; in the end, periodicals paid obeisance to patriarchal ethos. As the interests of publicity were not entirely compatible with socially sanctioned patterns of behavior, the star discourse had to restructure the tales of passionate affairs to fit the patriarchal paradigm. One of the ways in which it chose to do it was to underscore the romantic notion of one single "great love" in a star's life, a love that came to an abrupt and often tragic end, "destroyed as a result of death, 'career pressures,' or some other impediment."[85] This logic had already governed some elements of Negri's narrative, particularly in reference to the positioning of her relationships with men before she emerged as a Hollywood icon. Numerous local newspapers across the country, including the *Billings Weekly Gazette*, recounted: "Rudolph Valentino was mentioned. Miss Negri clutched her throat. 'Please!' she whispered. 'That is a very sacred thing to me. I will not discuss it.'"[86]

The same report addressed her as "princess," causing vehement opposition in the star who preferred to remain known as Miss Negri, regardless of her new marital status. What is more, the way the newlyweds met entered public knowledge, sparking additional controversy. They were introduced to one another at Mdivani's brother's wedding to Mae Murray, which Negri had attended with Valentino at her side, with the matinee idol serving as the best man. Interestingly, an interview published in the pages of the *New York Times* as well as a short feature published by the *Motion Picture Classic* stated that Mdivani and Negri were old friends and that the star had known her future husband since the age of fourteen.[87] No historical evidence supports the claim the two knew each other before starting their courtship, however; even Negri's biography fails to mention the alleged long-standing friendship. Taken together, such information might be viewed as produced in an effort to neutralize the negative ideological implications of their union.

In one of her works on Mary Pickford, Studlar argued, very poignantly, that the popular discourse worked with the notion that Pickford's happy marriage to Douglas Fairbanks was something of a payback for her troubled childhood in a poor family.[88] Hollywood's fascination with their love focused on the rhetoric of fate repaying Pickford for past misfortunes, seemingly to draw public attention away from the scandalous fact that they started their romantic involvement when they were both still married to their respective partners. In a comparable fashion, the relationship between Negri and Mdivani was contextualized in some quarters as a cure for heartbreak and a well-deserved respite, thereby reconciling Negri's figure with a more conservative vision of womanhood. "Ah, no one had more tragedies in life than I," Negri was cited as saying in *Motion Picture Classic*. It was further reported that she met Mdivani at "one of those moments in life when life seemed darkest."[89]

By showing the star in that light, the publicity attempted to displace the specter of scandal related to Valentino's death by encouraging a rather different response to Negri's private trajectory. Here, she invites compassion, not condemnation. Still, accounts of this nature could do very little to repair the damage done to Negri's reputation under the circumstances, as even the staunchest defenders felt she betrayed Valentino's memory. The inherent failure of this narrative can be understood as a consequence of the strong associations with the vamp persona that Negri already had at this point in her career, prior to commencing her relationship with Mdivani. Pickford's image, on the contrary, linked her to Victorian morals and lack of sexual agency, which was crucial in terms of successful reframing of the scandal.

Picture Play published a regular column titled "What the Fans Think," which encouraged readers to either criticize or give praise to their favorite movie players. Many opinions expressed in that forum disapproved not only of bad scripts and casting but also of stars behaving badly off-screen. In January 1928, for example, Edith Perrin defended Negri by saying that everyone's grief deserves to be respected, regardless of external conditions.[90] The following issue of the magazine published a passionate counterargument to Perrin's suggestions. Written by a fan identified as E.G., the letter argues that the American public is understanding toward "real" mourning but it can't sympathize with insincere grief:

> We are a straight-thinking reasoning people who are not taken in by an actress who sheds copious tears over her fiance's death one year and prances merrily to the altar the next. As a nation, we are more than sympathetic, but we have not yet reached the point where we cannot distinguish between real and simulated grief. I lost all patience when I read passionate defenses of Miss Negri. . . . And now we are expected to sympathize with frail broken flower because death has

> robbed her of one man and forced her to get herself another. It is a slap at the public's intellect. Pola Negri is, in one respect, right. Real love is not for her.[91]

Editorials, on the other hand, were more restrained in passing moral judgment on Negri's behavior. A month after Valentino's funeral, *Motion Picture Classic* suggested, somewhat subtly, that "the death of Valentino, and the reactions of the public and the profession give rise to many cynical thoughts and conclusions which are better kept in the mind than committed to paper."[92] In July 1927, *Photoplay* took a stance in the trials and tribulations of Negri by describing her exhibition of weeping and swooning as damaging to the images of other screen stars, generally chastising her demeanor. "It is no wonder," it declared, "that the public is ready to label all film stars as *temperamental freaks* if the excesses of the few received so much coverage in the media."[93] Nonetheless, the article steered away from directly accusing Negri of insincerity, merely suggesting the star should consider keeping her emotional trauma in the private sphere, instead of reliving it in the spotlight. Despite noting that Negri's grief may have been genuine, *Photoplay* invited condemnation on the part of its readers: "'The world does not know my grief,' she [Negri] moaned to the reporters in September. 'Red roses for passion,' she cries gaily to them in the springtime, and her wedding is a fete for the French journalists."[94]

Richard DeCordova argues that the 1920s witnessed a shift in the limits of star discourse, and that the discussion of off-screen star personae relied as much on a fascination with scandal as it did on a revulsion by it, so by engaging with more problematic aspects of star behavior, fan letters sent a powerful message about what lies beyond the lines of respectability and what can or cannot be socially sanctioned.[95] Conforming to Dyer's view, this is the primary function of stars: to provide vehicles for discussion of sexual and familial issues and to reinforce normative standards of behavior.[96] Studlar suggests that popular fan magazines remained conventional in offering little commentary on more scandalous subjects; such events might however be alluded to sometime after their occurrence, thereby adopting a general strategy of relying on the pre-established knowledge of their readership.[97] It was the daily press, not the fan magazines, that thrived by supplying its readers with controversy.[98] *Picture Play*, for instance, mentioned the wedding four months after it took place, suggesting that the new Mrs. Mdivani might be leaving Hollywood life in a year or so, but it did not discuss matters any further.[99] A year later, the same publication became more outspoken in accusing Negri of creating a false persona to get more publicity: "She so seldom says anything real," it claimed, while pointing out that staying true to oneself does not attract much media interest. "Her love affair with Rudolph Valentino and her subsequent picturesque grief over his death—with her very becoming widow's weeds and her tragic, haunting eves all followed so soon by her joyful marriage to a handsome foreigner."[100]

Paradoxically, the critique most commonly leveled against Negri was that she allowed herself to be dominated by romantic passions and her mercurial nature, instead of concentrating on her acting career. Nevertheless, it was specifically the star's torrid love life that filled the pages of film magazines, playing a crucial part in the promulgation of her vamp image by discursively reinforcing her links to both the Orient and the Old World. "There is not an actress on the stage or screen who has taken more paint to air her frequent love affairs than has Pola Negri," wrote one disgruntled reader of *Picture Play.* "We are constantly confronted with her latest amours: we are continually hearing her impassioned protests, *Ah love! It is not for me!*"[101] In creating a desire for controversy, the star system was responsible for catapulting Negri to great popularity while, simultaneously, constituting a reason for her fall into even greater disfavor. The star's loves, wrote Gladys Hall, run like a gamut "each hectic and each publicized." Several months after Negri "trailed widow's weeds across the continent,"[102] she was already finding solace in the arms of her current husband.

Mdivani's rumored financial problems, alongside accusations of using a fake aristocratic title, brought Negri another setback in terms of public image. "Is Prince Serge Mdivani, newlywed husband of Pola Negri, film star, a bogus prince?" asked *Hollywood Vagabond*, claiming that "a noted Slavic genealogist had been employed to trace the lineage and that no evidence had been uncovered in Russian archives that substantiated the princely title."[103] The article suggested that Mdivani was outraged by the appearance of rumors questioning his heritage and sought to redress the matter in court. In any case, Negri's association with Mdivani generated negative responses, which can be credited to the slippage between aspects of Negri's private peregrinations and her life on-screen.

An account penned by a different columnist in the same year highlighted how little attention Americans paid to aristocratic titles, which stands as an indictment of how, at the dawn of the Depression, the public started to turn against values associated with highbrow versions of Europe. It presented Serge Mdivani as someone caught between being a snob and an old-fashioned oddity.[104] Second, the union Negri formed with the prince refused to conform to the dynamic favored by the patriarchy, with the husband as the breadwinner and the wife as a domestic goddess. Negri's ambitious nature was often played out as problematic, particularly given that the dominant ideology maintained that "when a woman becomes too successful to take second place to a man, she forgoes her chance at love and marriage—and happiness as well."[105] A number of articles published in this period alluded to Negri's impressive earnings, while the *Chicago Tribune* framed Mdivani's decision to enter matrimony in terms of financial gain, subsequently emphasizing the value held by aristocratic status for his wife.[106] According to the view promulgated by the popular and fan press, Mdivani's career as a businessman played second fiddle to Negri's professional occupation, and, at least for *Motion Picture Magazine*, such role reversal within marriage could only cause frustration:

> The Prince is trying so hard to create the impression that he is a stern business man! . . . Yet, I'll wager he never has a client who doesn't ask a question or two about Pola. This must be annoying to a gentleman whose primary interest during business hours is supposed to be real estate and investments. It's really too bad. Every man who *is* a man wishes and expects to be the head of his house. Leadership is his divine prerogative. When he barters off his birth right in marriage, even to one of the world's most beautiful women, he finds that her charm cannot take the place of his lost self-respect, and that her fame is a ball and chain to him.[107]

Even Negri herself supposedly described her husband as willing to make great sacrifices for the sake of his wife's art, and yet asking nothing of her in return.[108] As stated by one of the daily papers, Negri went as far as to dismiss the rumors suggesting she intended to leave the acting profession behind in order to settle down and confine herself to the role of wife in the immediate future.[109] Hence, the media coverage of Negri's marriage contrasted with the normalcy ascribed to the traditional gender dynamic within marriage. Another press feature reported that David Mdivani, Negri's brother-in-law, was arrested for speeding in Santa Monica. When filling out a form at the police station, he put down "husband" as his occupation. "He is the husband of Mae Murray, and the brother of Serge M'Divani [*sic*], whose occupation is likewise that of being a husband of Pola Negri."[110]

Americanization

It is important to note that Mdivani was yet another man in a series of high-profile foreign-born lovers that prevented Negri from fully integrating into American culture. This dynamic provided a point of contrast between Negri and Vilma Bánky, a subject of another case study in this book. Bánky's marriage to Rod La Rocque, American citizen, highlighted her image as a star willing to be assimilated into American society. For the 1920s nationalist discourse, Americanization was a variant of assimilation in which the immigrants joined the "imagined community," in Benedict Anderson's sense, by appropriating the ideology and behavioral patterns deemed "American."[111] While the reality of existence of such a homogeneous culture has since been disputed, it can be argued that the term "American," at least in the time period in question, came to signify the idealized vision of the white, Anglo-Saxon, protestant model. By entering a relationship with another eastern European, Negri confirmed she was either incapable or unwilling of being assimilated into the social fabric of America, and would rather sustain her connections to nobility and Old World values than foster stronger links to her adopted home country. Americanization was, to paraphrase Russell A. Kazal, a direct journey to modernity, and Negri failed to purchase her ticket.[112]

At the same time, this trajectory exemplified a failure in earlier attempts to promote Negri as an aspiring American subject. Negra points out that at the dawn of her American career, the star offered comments that reflected the concept of the American Dream: "Always America has been my dream from the time I was a child in Poland. . . . It's like heaven to which people go for eternal happiness."[113] Magazine features such as "Pola Swears Allegiance" and "Uncle Sam's Adopted Children" were tailored to represent the actress as willing to partake in assimilation, understood as a process of entering a society "made up of groups clustered around an Anglo-American core."[114] These efforts, nevertheless, were soon replaced by a discourse that underlined cultural difference, as well as Negri's liaisons with foreign men. In May 1928, *Picture Play* carried an article discussing foreign players and their intention—or lack of thereof—to take American citizenship.[115] Many players from abroad, it argued, decided to shed their immigrant identity and become American citizens in order to recognize and cherish the affluence and opportunities given to them in the New World. The article frames such acts as admirable gestures of gratitude in the pluralist American setting. The magazine reported that, despite "taking out American papers" upon the completion of *Bella Donna*, Negri failed to follow through with her declarations to swear allegiance to the United States: "So at present Pola is Georgian. Yet who knows what she will be next?"[116]

Accounts such as this one looked askance at Negri's attempts at Americanization, implying they were driven by a need to generate publicity rather than a sincere desire to thank the United States for its hospitality. The tendency to castigate movie players for lack of American patriotism reverberated on the national stage particularly loudly in 1928, when the country was on the cusp of an economic downturn. That year's fan discourse witnessed heightened criticism of the popularity of foreign players. One moviegoer maintained that "we do not have to import the French mademoiselle, the Spanish sénorita or the Italian signorina in order to attain real temperament, acting or beauty. . . . The patriotic Americans should have 'America First' for their slogan. The boys and girls of our country should be favored first, last and always."[117]

Some fan commentary suggested that Hollywood favored continental players over their American counterparts. Writing about Alma Jean Williams—a New Yorker who used to perform under the pseudonym Sonia Karlov—*Picture Play* ridiculed the extreme popularity of foreign actors: "Broken accents were popular in Hollywood. Weren't there Garbo and Negri and Banky, and Corda, and De Putti? Nobody heard of a foreigner treading the extra's weary path. Only the home-grown product was trampled—and by the alien."[118]

The narrative structure of another of Negri's films, *A Woman of the World* (1925), adhered to the discourses of nationality inherent in her off-screen persona. Based on Van Vechten's novel *The Tattooed Countess*, the film tells the story of Elnora Natatorini, an Italian countess who, faced with heartbreak, decides to journey "to the other side of the world" in search of consolation. She arrives in Maple Valley, a small town in Midwestern America, where she stays with her cousin. Negri's heroine "exudes glamour and mystery with her long cigarette holder, luxurious chinchilla wraps, and a butterfly and skull tattoo on her arm"[119] and naturally causes havoc within the members of the puritanical community, who initially consider her to be an affront to public sensibilities. Wearing chiffon and satin, Elnora connotes a sense of bohemia and sophistication at odds with her new surroundings. In one of the early scenes, she scandalizes the district attorney to the point where she is asked to leave Maple Valley. "We don't want loose women from other towns here . . . and I'll give you twenty minutes to get back from where you came." "Pardon, Monsieur," replies the woman with her trademark nonchalance, "you allow *so little* time—I come from Italy."

Initially, Elnora's flamboyant behavior manages to startle and alarm the sheltered residents, scandalized by the fact she smokes and drinks. Despite inhabiting a drastically different social milieu, the countess is generous and accepting toward the townsfolk; eventually, she is repaid with the same kindness. Walker writes of the heroine of *A Woman of the World*: "It is true that [Negri] keeps her dignity and can master a baleful power. . . . But while the film never makes her look ridiculous, which is a considerable victory on her part, it does something worse. It makes her look *passé*. It leaves her exoticism stranded in a hick town; and the analogy with her Hollywood career is hard to resist."[120]

In a sense, the picture provided Negri with an opportunity to comment on certain national aspects of her stardom, as the main theme of the culture clash can be seen as indicative of her personal struggles to adjust to the requirements of American society. Yet, unlike Negri's off-screen ideological trajectory, the film ends happily with the heroine successfully integrating herself into the local community through marriage. Whereas Elnora discards the guise of exoticism in favor of domestication, the Negri star persona remained deeply immersed in the world of luxury and nobility, associated with her continental aura.

Conclusion

Negra articulates how fatalism, transgression, and loss entered the dramatic formula of Negri's love life. "Accounts of Negri's romantic history testified again and again to her destructive force, describing her morbid influence as inevitable," which "added extratextual support to the filmic construction as fortune-telling gypsy and . . . also discursively reinforced her connections with Old World values."[121] Cast in this light, the star system gave credence to the idea of Negri as representing primitive and eternal femininity. In addition, as Negra argues, the ideological resistance to change represented by Negri's national identity was paralleled by the rise in wider trends that displaced the immigrant Other in favor of a "good girl" type, a symbol of modernity and American purity.[122] Sweet, all-American blondes such as Janet Gaynor entered the star pantheon, effectively ending the reign of the vamp.[123] Moreover, with the advent of talking pictures Negri started to appear old-fashioned, as her acting style refused to assimilate to new technological developments. Apparently deliberate dismissal of convention and patriarchal norms made Negri a transgressive figure with disruptive connotations; this image was only reinforced in 1926, when her life was turned into magazine fodder. Because of her conspicuous exhibition of grief over Valentino's death, and the marriage to Mdivani that followed so soon after, the star had to bear the brunt of public ostracism.

While Negri was turning into a preeminent fixture in the Hollywood pantheon, *Photoplay* and its ilk ran several articles that emphasized her willingness to become "a full-fledged American."[124] The standardized star narrative that came to be mobilized by fan discourse was also connected to larger nationalist concerns. Simultaneously, the romantic liaisons she was entangled in functioned in tandem with her ethnicity to move her away from the ideal of assimilation. In a way that seemed to run in parallel to the experience of the countess of *A Woman of the World*, the star firmly belonged to Europe, a continent represented as the arena of aristocracy and thereby unequal opportunity and unearned privilege. Unlike Elnora, though, she did not marry an American man and, by proxy, refused to shed her old identity. The nucleus of antipathy formed in the aftermath of Valentino's funeral kept growing after Negri's highly publicized marriage to Prince Mdivani. These actions, paired with the broader factor of shifting tendencies in on-screen acting, heightened Negri's transformation into an epitome of foreignness and contributed to her withdrawal from the limelight. The image that stemmed from the star's reputation as a vamp, nurtured by the rumors concerning her private life, had catastrophic implications for the progress of her career.

CHAPTER 2

Pola Negri as the Vamp

"TEMPTATIOUS POLA ASSAILED PICTURE CITADEL BY STORM"

Tony Guzman categorizes the 1920s as the most important period for the exhibition of European films in the United States, with foreign movies breaking onto American screens to enjoy great artistic prestige.[1] Not surprisingly, this cultural exchange was not greeted warmly by studio moguls who were reluctant to share their profits with companies overseas. In this highly competitive environment, *Photoplay*'s article on foreign film input attests to the popularity enjoyed by Negri's three vehicles among other German productions: "The entire German industry has produced so far as America is concerned," the author declared, "one 100 per cent financially successful picture—*Passion*—three or four mediocrely successful pictures—*The Golem*, *Gypsy Blood*, *One Arabian Night*—and several failures, such as *Hamlet* and *Deception*."[2] Ernst Lubitsch, who directed Negri in six feature films in Weimar Republic, followed in her footsteps by arriving in Hollywood in December 1922.[3] At this point, the pair enjoyed their status as two shining stars of German cinematography, familiar to American moviegoers from such artistic collaborations as *Gypsy Blood* (1918), *Passion* (1919), and *One Arabian Night* (1920).[4] The majority of theaters in this period, at least in the urban landscape, were local venues attended by immigrant spectators; the European populace too could have an impact on sustaining Negri's success. Frederick C. Luebke generalizes that German nationals who settled in America after the Great War were "somewhat better educated, more highly skilled, and more urban" than those migrating at the dawn of the century.[5]

This chapter explores the assumed relationship between star persona and private life through an investigation of Negri's portrayals in *Passion*, *Gypsy Blood*, and *One Arabian Night*—the three German productions that catapulted her to fame in America—and the four pictures she made shortly after joining Famous Players-Lasky in 1923; *Bella Donna* (1923), *The Cheat* (1923), *The Spanish Dancer* (1923), and *Shadows of Paris* (1924).[6] Here, I move from an investigation of the issues that arise from the portrayal of Negri's love life to her on-screen work. In accordance with the bolstering rhetoric of star discourse, Negri's roles were frequently assumed to be a window into her unique personal sensitivity, a reflection of her true self. In the pages that follow, the roles Negri played in these films are compared to the public image of the private life of "La Negri," as constructed by the star system. How can we understand her cinematic representations, and how did they inform the construction of Negri's private persona?

Most of Negri's early Hollywood narratives share a common denominator in positioning the star as a dangerous seductress who uses sex to achieve her goals. In particular, the vamp roles she plays in *Passion*, *Gypsy Blood*, *The Spanish Dancer*, and *Shadows of Paris* act as beacons of social mobility. Some scholars have noted the changing nature of the vamp archetype, pointing out that few of Negri's vehicles labeled her overtly, allowing ample room for maneuver between the notion of agency and female virtuousness.[7] In *Passion* and *The Spanish Dancer*, for instance, she is portrayed not only as a sexually aggressive, upwardly mobile woman but also as one who uses her influence in good faith to save the lives of her lovers. But if Negri's filmic appearances grew more complex and nuanced, gradually outgrowing the vamps of her early career, the narrative of Negri's off-screen life remained static.

Lubitsch's Films: *Passion*, *Gypsy Blood*, and *One Arabian Night*

Originally produced under the title of *Madame DuBarry* for Universum Film-Aktien Gesellschaft (UFA), *Passion* was the first German film screened in the United States after the Great War. Although met with critical and financial acclaim upon its American release, it was also accompanied, as Graham Petrie puts it, by "cries of alarm and outrage from American producers who saw their livelihood threatened and from patriots who felt it was far too soon to forgive and forget where German culture was concerned."[8] To steer clear of anti-German prejudice, the historical epic was initially marketed as an Italian production starring "Poli Negri."[9] Despite those political concerns, the interest generated by Lubitsch's film was so high it played over five times a day in the lavish Capitol theater. The film premiered on December 12, 1920 and screened for two weeks, a nearly unheard of (if not record-breaking) run at the time.[10] One journalist quoted an estimated 305,000 attendees during its initial fortnight.[11] *Motion Picture Magazine* marveled over the unexpected success of the feature, calling it "a bolt from the blue," and, in praising its artistic merit, branded the director as the European answer to D. W. Griffith.[12] Indeed, the financial success of *Passion* prompted major studios to invest in foreign product: by the end of 1921, Famous Players-Lasky alone had imported 129 German features for redistribution.[13]

The plot revolves around Jeanne, a dressmaker's assistant who ascends from a working-class background to a position of power in the French court as the king's mistress. In the course of the film, the seamstress seduces the proletarian Armand, but soon enough exchanges him for a new lover in the person of Don Diego, who is then replaced by Count DuBarry. *Passion* provides an early illustration of the tendency to cast Negri as a woman who uses sexual means to achieve upward mobility and whose engagement in a series of affairs gradually expands her political influence, culminating in a liaison with the most powerful man in France, Louis XV. Throughout the film, she exerts agency over her desirability and uses it to meet her own ends. Taken at face value, the closing scene of the film, where the protagonist is taken to the guillotine, provides an example of the culturally popular theme of punishing women for their transgressive actions. Yet, Lubitsch's picture is enriched with aspects that make it differ from the standard vamp narrative, particularly in relation to where the audience's sympathy is placed. First and foremost, Jeanne is not portrayed as the epitome of female duplicity but rather as an outsider positioned beyond the conventional power structures, who succeeds in clawing her way to the top, regardless of her background.

Nicholas Smedley contends that Lubitsch was well known for catering to female tastes and that he wanted his audience to identify with the film's protagonist despite her shortcomings.[14] According to this line of argument, Jeanne's plight is not the story of a vamp so much as the tragic tale of a woman who reaches the highest echelons of society but attracts resentment for doing so. Once at the very top, she is never safe. Even though the protagonist might be thoughtless and capricious, she is not a predatory villainess in the tradition of Theda Bara's *A Fool There Was* (1915). The multidimensionality of Negri's part did not go unnoticed in the fan press, with *Picture Play* stressing its resistance to simple typecasting: "An American actress would have made Du Barry either a pretty flirt or a plain everyday 'vamp.' Pola Negri makes her a real superwoman."[15]

In fact, *Passion* manages to avoid essentialism in regard to all of its main characters, including Armand and Louis XV, who are presented as neither inherently good-natured nor evil. The nuances of Jeanne's relationship with Armand, the first man in her series of romantic pursuits, also point away from reading her character purely in terms of so-called vamping exploits. Thus, as soon as she gains serious influence at the French court, she uses it to spare the impulsive Armand from being executed for murder. The king agrees to pardon her supposed cousin, which leads Jeanne to test the boundaries of her power by asking for another favor, a request that Armand be promoted to the position of palace guard. Upon learning that the infamous Madame DuBarry is responsible for saving him—and that she is, in reality, his former beloved—Armand tries to persuade her to run away with him and start anew. It is clear that DuBarry continues to care for Armand, despite the fact she refuses his offer. In terms of their relationship, Jeanne is not, then, "the cynical and heartless woman she appears to be," as her actions stand at odds with the idea of how a vamp should behave.[16]

In his evaluation of Lubitsch's take on French history, Thomas Elsaesser divides the film into two parts.[17] Whereas the first is concerned with Jeanne's conquests and is very playful and comedic in tone, the second conforms to the perceived notion of German cinema of the period as "gloomy" and "anxiety-ridden."[18] The reckless abandon with which Jeanne pursues each of her consecutive lovers adds another dimension to the way the first half of the film represents her. Scott Nye discusses how "sexuality is her key tool, but one she only leverages with a playfulness that keeps her in control. Each successive lover is her playmate, but she decides when playtime is over."[19] Flattered by the attention she gets from men, she treats her suitors in a flirtatious yet very childlike way, which is exemplified in a scene where she tries to decide whether she would rather spend her Sunday with Armand or Don Diego. Faced with the dilemma, she counts the bows on her bodice to make the decision.

In a scene depicting her first meeting with Louis XV, Jeanne exhibits "coy skittishness"[20] as she kisses him, jumping onto his lap (figure 5). Her unusual position in terms of agency is reflected here by visual means, with Negri's body initially located above her suitor's, as she sits on the arm of the chair. Most importantly, she initiates the encounter and remains in charge throughout. Actions like this demonstrate that she is no mere object of desire but someone who, cramped by no inhibitions, takes great pleasure in desiring her men. As countess DuBarry, Negri constantly alternates between sexual confidence and joyful childishness, emanating primitive, almost crude physical appeal. Nye argues that it is her flirtatious nature, not an appetite for power, that motivates the sexual adventures of Negri's character.[21] Consequently, he sees Jeanne's elevation to the position of royal consort not as her highest achievement but rather as one of the many consequences of her extravagant, self-indulgent lifestyle. At the end, *Passion* takes a sharp melodramatic turn that highlights the role of history in intervening with the lives of ordinary humans. Madame DuBarry has to die because she associated herself with the king, and thus became a representative of the most hated bourgeoisie. His downfall marks her own.

Gypsy Blood was Lubitsch's second collaborative effort with Negri to be distributed in American theaters. Even though it did not achieve the impressive box-office results of *Passion*, it was similarly lavished with praise by critics. Again, the film attracted some anti-German sentiments; according to *Picture Play* it was deemed not safe for public presentation in Los Angeles after the recent mob attacks that took place in relation to the screening of *The Cabinet of Dr. Caligari* (1921).[22] Based on Prosper Merimée's famous novella *Carmen*, *Gypsy Blood* operates as a simple tale of love and betrayal. It tells the story of Carmen,[23] a woman gone astray whose primary pursuit is to lead a decent man to damnation; and thus, it lacks the multilayered qualities of the protagonist of *Passion*. The film opens with Don José, a sergeant in the Spanish army, who returns home on leave

Figure 5. Madame DuBarry flirts in *Passion* (1919).

to visit his fiancée and family. During his stay, a gypsy girl is arrested for pulling a knife on one of her colleagues in a cigarette factory, forcing Don José to intervene. From their first meeting Carmen is determined to seduce the handsome cavalryman. Negri's characterization is bold in the descriptions of sexuality that run beyond the bounds of bourgeois respectability; she is a signifier of lechery traditionally linked to the lower classes, and to gypsies in particular.

Despite Don José's initial contempt, he soon falls under Carmen's malevolent spell. The infatuation marks a downward spiral for the man who, after being demoted to soldier, kills his superior in an act of jealousy and becomes an outlaw. Soon enough—to Don José's growing despair—Carmen finds herself a new love object in a young bullfighter. Fueled by greed and desire, Carmen fails to exhibit any signs of compassion, swiftly moving from one male victim to the next. The story ends tragically when the betrayed soldier cannot bear his disgrace, killing his unfaithful lover and himself.

As a temptress of the silver screen, Carmen is, to paraphrase Jess Sully, a potent amalgam of fears and preoccupations, at once threatening and enthralling.[24] In his book *The Romantic Agony*, Mario Praz links the archetype of the fallen woman with an Oriental repertoire and subsequently identifies Carmen as the first mass-produced femme fatale within popular culture.[25] Phil Powrie's interpretation correlates with these assumptions, suggesting that the narrative conflates Spanishness with Andalusia, the most southern part of Spain, because the region bears a mark of Arab culture.[26] If one accepts the validity of his argument, one can engage with the iconography of Carmen through the lens of postcolonial theory, where she is highly sexualized precisely because of her association with the Orient.[27] Carmen represents the living embodiment of active, sexually promiscuous, nonwhite femininity. Her figure is particularly problematic because she crosses many boundaries, not only through questioning patriarchal values in her usage of sex for personal gain but also through personifying an ethnic hazard.

No work of fiction exists in a cultural vacuum. In her scholarship on divas of the Italian silent screen, Joy Ramirez explains that the aesthetic codes contained within the stories of cinematic femmes fatales were influenced by the "decadent sensibility that preceded them in art and literature" and the increasing popularity of grotesque imagery in the late nineteenth century.[28] Many early moving pictures derived their themes from Gustave Flaubert's *Salammbo* or Oscar Wilde's *Salomé*.[29] Ewa Kuryluk identifies the origin of femme fatale as a trope that attempts to rediscover ancient mythologies, as artists of the fin de siècle became fascinated by the spiritual, pagan universe with the mystical dimension it seemed to give to female sexuality.[30] Both political and social contexts in the 1920s have changed since the promulgation of that imagery at the turn of the nineteenth century, stripping the femme fatale of its complexity and imbuing it with new, if not more simplistic, meanings.

Powrie discusses how the popularization of what he terms the "Carmen narrative" goes hand in hand with the re-emergence of public concern about the growing independence of women.[31] The "Carmen" films, he argues, appear "in cluster" every time in history when the patriarchal paradigm is under scrutiny, as a reflection of the changing political climate. Indeed, the historical period under discussion here witnessed a number of societal shifts, mainly in relation to the visibility of women in the public sphere. The ratification of the Nineteenth Amendment in the United States in 1920 granted women the right to vote, which, alongside the increase in numbers of female workers, was viewed by the defenders of traditional gender roles as a threat to the status quo.

Within the context of the beginning of the decade in America, then, Carmen, the classic cinematic vamp, could be fashioned as a response to the fears of untamed social mobility and perceived changes in the position of women. The image of the infamous dancer communicated the castigation of uncontained female desire, offering a fantasy world where, as Sabine Hake advocates, "it was still possible to indulge in an unrestrained gender essentialism."[32]

All cultural texts adapted from Merimée's novella take a moralizing stance toward the titular protagonist, using her tragic fate as a means to re-establish and highlight the patriarchal order. *Gypsy Blood* does it with particular poignancy, with one of the last intertitles proclaiming: "So runs the tale. But some say she did not die . . . *for she was in league with the Devil himself!*" Negri's heroine is constructed as Other, in terms of sexuality, class, and nationality; ultimately, aspects of her identity as a gypsy, outlaw, and woman with sexual agency work in conjunction with each other to legitimize her death.[33] In seducing Don José, Carmen corrupts a man who represents Western civilization. Driven by passion rather than staid, rational thinking, Carmen becomes a woman whose refusal to adjust to rigid limitations of sexuality stands in opposition to the American way of life, to purity and civilization. Seen against the backdrop of new forces of modernity, such as the second wave of immigration in the United States, at a time of "widespread and often irrational hostility toward foreign influences,"[34] the plot of *Gypsy Blood* gained new resonance on American screens.

Richard Dyer suggests that, especially in relation to silent film, the filmic performance of stars is taken as revealing their off-screen personalities.[35] Film historians studying the late 1910s and early 1920s agree that it was not until the early 1930s that the public freely accepted the distinction between the private lives of the stars and the ones they lead on the celluloid, as studio publicity in the 1920s sought to authenticate a homogeneous consistency between a player's perceived private life and their professional persona.[36] The issues that unfold in the arena of stardom are reliant on the careful negotiation between what a star represents on-screen and who she or he is presumed to be behind closed doors. In that respect, Negri had the capacity to encapsulate the threat inherent to the women she portrayed in her work. According to the paeans that resounded through fan magazines, she was nothing short of outstanding in the role of Carmen, because her capricious off-screen persona was aligned with the personality of the character. "It has already been said that Negri is highly emotional," wrote Maximilian Vinder in *Photoplay*. "Not only is this so in her work but she is intense in her private life. She never spares herself."[37]

If the general discourse of the era was to be believed, the cinematic apparatus had the capacity to detect all pretense and artifice; thus, a true star had no choice but to "be herself" and bare her soul in her performance if she intended to become a movie sensation.[38] This rhetoric of not simply acting but rather revealing oneself in front of the camera was widely applied to Negri, a "vehement and volcanic" performer who made the "illusion a perfect one, being at all times Carmen, not an actress trying to be Carmen," as chronicled by the *Exhibitor's Herald*.[39] Such strategy proposes that the primary objective of good casting goes beyond simply finding a talented performer; instead, it depends on finding someone whose personal traits are convergent with the role, someone who, as Barry King characterizes it, is "a self or personality" that can behave on cue.[40] Looking back at her body of work in 1926, Negri named Carmen as one of her favorite roles to date, and one of the most immersive screen opportunities she was offered, saying, "I understood her. I loved her. I was her. It was like playing an organ with innumerable stops. Every emotion could be touched upon."[41]

What is more, the magazine discourse established Negri in the context of her non-Anglo-Saxon origin, which at once explained the intensity of her performance and again encouraged a narrative conflation between her personal identity and that of Carmen. *Variety* commented on the incandescent sexual appeal of the film's main character, while the *New York Times* described Negri's role as that of a "magnetic, unmoral animal, a free-living, free-loving savage of capricious appetites and a consuming zest for satisfying them."[42] One press feature argued that equally outstanding dramatic results could not have been achieved by an American actress, because she would have been too concerned with looking attractive in every scene of the film. Negri, on the other hand, did not have to look beautiful at all costs: "If she had to rave, she raved; if she had to laugh or, cry, she laughed or cried. AND she didn't care whether the emotion made her look pretty or ugly. She delivered the goods."[43] The reviewer of *Photoplay* found Negri's creation superior to the previous screen incarnations of the eponymous heroine because of her earthy, uncultivated behavior: "None of your silk-stockinged Calves and Farrars, this cigarette girl. None of your fringed-shawled beauties with rouged cheeks and cherry lips."[44] The depiction of Negri's on-screen endeavor offered by *Picture Play*'s columnist spoke of her in similar terms, as a "disreputable, low-down and rowdy gypsy girl. Her clothes are in atrocious taste, her finery is shabby, and her morals are unquestionable. That is to say, they are unquestionably bad. Miss Negri doesn't try to look pretty, play to the camera, or attempt to be alluring. She simply gives a marvelously faithful picture of a vulgar, ignorant and wanton gypsy girl."[45] Functioning as an indication of star quality, opinions of this kind implied that Negri's unique way of being supplemented her film heroines with a sense of authenticity. Her personality, the article suggests, shone through her screen performances, endowing Negri's version of Carmen with real, down-to-earth sexuality, hard to attain by other means.

Undoubtedly, the narrative treatment received by Negri's protagonist in *Gypsy Blood* was crucial in sketching the contours of her star image in Hollywood

Figure 6. Negri in *Gypsy Blood* (1918). Source: Photochemie, Berlin, no. K. 2849 and K. 2850. Photo: Union Film.

(figure 6). It has to be noted, however, that the period was typified by typecasting, which was as much a cultural phenomenon as it was an economic one, driving the commodification of the chief movie players, orchestrated by the studios. The Ideal Cast Contest, run by the popular *Motion Picture Magazine* in the late 1910s and early 1920s, offers a particularly poignant illustration of the widespread use of "types" in classifying film stars. The publication encouraged its readership to choose their favorite movie personalities, while also providing a set of categories (leading woman, leading man, villain, and vampire) for each player to fall into. The ever-changing results were published in subsequent issues of the magazine. In the October 1921 installment of the contest, Theda Bara was voted the best "vampire" of the screen, receiving 681 votes; second place was occupied by Louise Glaum with 351 votes, followed by Negri, scoring 162 votes.[46] Thus, the contest and its results indicated how the German star entered continuous cultural circulation as a vamp figure in American discourse months before coming to the country under contract to Famous Players-Lasky.

Nevertheless, *Passion* and *Gypsy Blood* were not the only films imported to the United States by First National to catapult Negri to international fame. In September 1921, American audiences were given the chance to see Negri in *One Arabian Night* for re-distribution. The film was not heralded by critics to the same extent as *Gypsy Blood*, also failing to hold the box office appeal of its predecessors.[47] However, the subject matter of the film should grant it at least a brief mention. A product of Weimar culture, the motion picture indulged in the creation of a completely fictional Arab world that drew freely from a variety of Orientalist tropes, including slavery, indulgent harems, sheiks, and seductive belly dancers. Both the geographical setting and the historical period represented here defy even loose definitions. As Edward Said argues in his canonical work on the depiction of the Middle East, such lack of specificity is exemplary of the discourse promulgated by the Western culture.[48] In alluding to conventional representational traditions, *One Arabian Night* is populated with Arab women marked as "objects of sexual desire by their seductive dresses and dances," on the one hand, and with "barbarous and violent men" who "purchase women to add to their harems," on the other.[49]

McCormick describes the somewhat convoluted narrative trajectory of the film as "two interwoven subplots focusing on two female roles, the dancer (played by Negri) and the harem favorite Sumurun (Hasselqvist)."[50] Executed with plenty of comic relief and some intense drama, the story focuses on Sumurun's blossoming love for a carpet merchant, Nur-Al Din, and her subsequent fall from favor as the sheik's preferred consort. Upon hearing a man whistling at Sumurun's window, the sheik orders her to be killed, although he later chooses to spare the young woman's life. Following the advice given to him by a slave trader, the sheik goes to the city to find a new addition to his harem. The pursuit ends successfully when he watches a sensual dance performed by Yannaia, Negri's character. McCormick sees Negri's portrayal as one of the most transgressive elements of the tale, in the sense that the dancer uses her physicality to exploit the structures of power and, like the character of Jeanne in *Passion*, "sleeps her way to the top."[51] What associates Yannaia closely with the characterization of Jeanne goes beyond their obvious ideological agendas and participation in upward mobility, extending to the playful manner in which they both engage with their romantic conquests. After she is brought to the palace bedchamber, Yannaia makes the sheik chase her for a while before beckoning to him and letting him carry her to the bed. In the next scene, we see her awake, with her companion asleep. Looking out the window, Negri notices the sheik's son and starts to flirt, encouraging him to come up to her. The aura of mischievousness that underpins the portrayal of the dancer—which comes to the fore in that short sequence—is representative of Lubitsch's work, but it was largely absent from Negri's American vehicles thereafter.

Yannaia's subplot concludes with the dancer being stabbed to death by the sheik, who, after learning of her exploits, becomes overwhelmed with jealousy. In return, Yeggar the Hunchback, a supporting character portrayed by Lubitsch himself, avenges Yannaia's death. Film scholars suggest that the tragic elements of the film's closure contrast in tone with the rest of this lighthearted feature, and lack credibility and effectiveness as a result.[52] In any case, the death of the dancer does not appear to be designed as a parable or a moral indictment, but more of a tragic coincidence in this otherwise uplifting, vibrant pageant. By the end of *One Arabian Night*, the sheik—an autocratic political leader—is dead, so the women of the harem are free from their brutal oppressor. Despite the overall lightness in the film's tone, American press drew heavily on the archetype of the fallen woman in promoting Negri's involvement in the picture, suggesting that her dancer "cares for nothing but bewitching the hearts of men and arousing jealousy."[53] *Picture Play* described Yannaia's rise within the internal hierarchies of the harem as "meteoric," simultaneously underlining the fact that her doings end in tragedy.[54]

There is a great deal of intensity to Negri's screen work. Visibly indebted to theatrical tradition—Negri was re-creating the role of Yannaia from a previous stage production of the same title[55]—she moves expressively, using exaggerated gestures, either rolling her eyes in displeasure or breaking into fits of manic laughter. Pamela Robertson Wojcik criticized the apparent myopia of star scholarship that focuses on the extratextual construction of a given star, as well as on "fandom, type, and ideological meaning without necessarily attending in any exact and descriptive way to what the actor does on screen to produce him or himself as a type."[56] While the approach integral to this analysis draws from the methods established by star studies, and indeed focuses on stars as texts, I agree with Robertson Wojcik that screen performance has significance in manifesting itself in the star personae. In Negri's case, the exaggerated elements of her acting style do reveal something about Negri the vamp and are thus worthy of further interrogation. Mary Ann Doane historicizes physical hyperbole as a common acting strategy for silent players, who, being unable to use their speaking voices, had to rely on "gestures and the contortions of the face," often to results that contemporary viewers find uncanny.[57]

Yet, theorizing silent cinema as an incomplete medium because of its lack of synchronized sound—and ascribing one, universal type of acting to all actors of the silent era—is clearly a generalization. Joy Ramirez suggests that heavy pantomime was popular in portrayals of vamps, where heightened dramatic effect, heavy makeup, and exotic costumes overdetermined the star's "role as dangerous woman, in effect using her iconicity to transform her into spectacle and the personification of desire."[58] Overtly stylized performance is thus consistent with vamp iconography. *One Arabian Night* exhibits a proclivity to shoot most of Negri's close-ups from a high angle, looking down on her from above, a technique that effectively singles her character from the rest of the women in the community and also enhances the dynamism of her performance in the dancing scenes.

Displays of highly mannered acting skills were important in building on Negri's star image, overplaying such attributes as mischievousness and flamboyance. In films directed by Lubitsch, Negri's acting functions not only to reinforce the confidence displayed by Jeanne and Yannaia; it also adds to the comic vein in the director's signature blend of sexual tension and comedy. The predatory, hypersexual elements of Negri's on-screen characterizations—especially that of Carmen—were to be magnified during the American stage of her career. Whereas Negri of *Passion* and *One Arabian Night* is a coquette, Negri of the Paramount era revives the danger of the vamp type, which becomes apparent in the publicity stills, where she "glances sidelong at the camera," adopting regal, remote, and often "suggestively threatening" poses.[59]

Framing Labor

Before I move to the discussion of Negri's oeuvre in Hollywood, I would like to investigate the social and national conditions that influenced her publicity in the early days of American fame. Being a product of "the fervid Berlin theater,"[60] Negri carried the connotations of Europe and high culture, which played predominantly to middle-class sensibilities and facilitated film producers in fighting the social stigma that depicted moviegoing as a working-class entertainment. Simultaneously, she was imbued with the aura of exotic otherness and the connotations of unrestrained female sexuality. The financial potential of these associations must have been evident to Adolph Zukor, a film producer who had made forays into European culture as early as 1912; he partially financed *Queen Elisabeth*, which starred a prominent actress of the French stage, Sarah Bernhardt. In 1922, Zukor articulated his objectives in nurturing the cultural capital of moviegoing by writing to Bernhardt: "You were the first great artist to lend her genius to our art. Your example . . . gave the motion picture industry the impulse that has raised it to the place of the most important spectacle in the world."[61]

When Zukor started to lay plans to invite Negri and Lubitsch stateside in the same year, he was careful to avoid anti-German sentiments, still rife in the States in the aftermath of the Great War. In a telegram sent to another executive producer, Zukor advised arranging separate arrival dates for Negri and Lubitsch, to minimize their potential negative impact. The telegram read: "Would be very bad from all angles bring over more than one at a time. Should leave reasonable period between to avoid propagandist criticism and be sure make no promises."[62] The document has poignancy in revealing the tensions that permeated American culture at the time in relation to European influence: although international mobility was actively encouraged by "the capital of moviedom,"[63] it was treated with a degree of caution by conservatives, if not actively frowned on. Economic developments are often at odds with prevailing social attitudes; Hollywood's desire for making profit by creating a global film product somehow went against the grain of American xenophobia.[64]

For Anne Helen Petersen, the narrative of rebellion and resilience that became central to Negri's biographical profile also worked to manufacture sympathy "and, in the process, deflect from any xenophobic protests of a *foreign import*."[65] As Negra points out, fan magazines initially promulgated the idea of Negri as a woman of strong principles and work ethics, rather than simply a European diva.[66] James R. Quirk's introduction to a biography of "the magnificent Negri" published in *Photoplay* during these initial stages of her Hollywood career focused on the obstacles she had to overcome on her way to stardom.[67] This type of publicity drew from the American doctrine that saw hard work and regulation of the self as vital in achieving professional success,[68] and helped establish Negri as a positive figure in public milieu despite the potentially negative associations she had with Germany, even though she was of Polish, not German, origin.

Negri was born as Barbara Apolonia Chałupiec in a Warsaw slum, and her childhood was an impoverished tale worthy of a genteel melodrama.[69] A young's girl desire to be noticed worked in conjunction with natural agility to grant her a scholarship to a prestigious ballet school, although press accounts do not agree as to the location of the institution; some list the Warsaw Imperial Academy of Dramatic Arts, and others point toward Moscow or even St. Petersburg.[70] Much of Negri's early Hollywood publicity claimed she was subjected to some of the most rigorous dance training in Russia, where she was forced to perform submerged in three feet of snow, but where she also operated in the highest social orders, drawing the attention of the royal family.[71] Not surprisingly, there is little to no evidence to support such embellished accounts. Upon returning to her home country, she was put under a two-year contract with Poland's first major film studio, Sfinks, to moderate success.[72] In 1917, the twenty-year-old actress left the war-shattered Polish capital for Berlin, where she starred in approximately twenty film productions over the next five years.[73]

In emphasizing the role of perseverance, Negri's biographical meta-narrative made a direct reference to one of the most enduring myths of American "business civilization," as Roger Butterfield calls it,[74] the fantasy of "rags to riches" at the heart of the American Dream. Diana Anselmo-Sequeira calls these sorts of texts "collective lessons to the transformative power of perseverance and ambition, characteristics that always undergirded the protean narrative of self-reliant . . . young civilizations such as America."[75] One of the noteworthy elements of Negri's story, as imagined through a variety of discursive practices, is its strong reliance on agency rather than providence; indeed, the former tends to constitute the core of female success stories. The continuous assertion of hard work and talent is what sets Negri apart from other star personae such as Vilma Bánky, whose elevation to the Hollywood summit is credited mainly to serendipity rather than to natural predisposition or tenacity.

The press accounts of Negri's life story functioned both as testimony to the extraordinary abilities of stars and, on a national level, as almost fairy-tale descriptions of American society at large, where one can rise to great heights regardless of one's background.[76] Ernst Lubitsch commented on the latter aspect of this social paradigm in his interview for *Motion Picture Magazine*, where he spoke highly of the wealth opportunities given to newcomers in the American film industry. The practice of hiring previously unknown players for major film roles was, in his opinion, unheard of back in the Old World, and would certainly "strike a European producer dumb with horror." An opinion of such nature paints Europe, or at least its film industry, as a place where rigid power structures are still in place, effectively excluding it from the narrative of modernity, rupture, and change. Lubitsch concluded the interview by asserting that Hollywood taps "new sources of power and genius," while "in Europe, the gateway of opportunity is narrow and difficult."[77]

By the mid-1910s, fan magazines had developed proficiency in supplying the public with star biographies, usually embellished with vivid depictions of poverty, class struggle, and personal metamorphosis that struck a balance between the ambitions of the performers and sheer luck. Like many other star texts, Negri's story promised that anyone could move up to the highest societal order, provided they had good character, talent, and charisma. A recurrent trope in the texts on Negri re-imagined her pre-Hollywood existence as a life of sacrifice and suffering, where all aspects of the story come together to paint a colorful picture of Negri the artist who had to go through hardship to achieve greatness. The reliance on one's own labor in this narrative effectively removed the star from the realm of the vamp and her financial exploits, albeit temporarily. This trend soon intersected with a discourse that exemplified Negri as a temperamental diva, criticizing her for failing to meet the high standards of American film production. In the same year, William McKegg observed that Negri's mood swings created a tense atmosphere on the set of *The Cheat*; Negri "was like a tigress, holding at bay the entire Lasky lot. No one knew just what to do."[78]

What this illustrates is that Negri's publicity in the mid-1920s started to build on the notion of temperament and represent her, to use Sean P. Holmes's words, "as a highly strung volatile performer who was prone to fits of irrational rage."[79] This characterization lay at the core of Negri's image as a European diva, "continental to her fingertips," and provided a reflection on her German roles. After all, she became one of the icons of Weimar Cinema by portraying independent women of strong sexuality and, to use Jeanine Basinger's phrasing, "animal magnetism."[80]

Bella Donna and *The Cheat*

In casting his new acquisition in the role of Bella Donna, a young woman who exerts her charms on men for financial gain, Zukor cemented the image of Negri as a performer specializing in vamp parts, a woman of destructive potential (figure 7). Even the name of the character is telling, as it means "beautiful woman" in Italian but is also the name of a poisonous plant. The widely awaited American debut placed the star in the context of the East, a semi-mythical setting that awakes gripping passions in women and men alike. *Bella Donna*'s publicity drew a picture of an escapist fantasy drenched in romance and glamour, where "proud Pola meets the appraising, brilliant eyes of the Oriental potentate."[81] Negri's heroine accompanies her husband, Nigel Armine, an English engineer, on his journey to Egypt, where she quickly demonstrates the capricious and ever-changing nature of her affection by falling in love with Mahmoud Baroudi, a masterful sheik.[82] Developments back in England work against Armine's financial interest, and when Bella Donna finds out her spouse has lost his fortune, she realizes he is no longer of use to her. She decides to poison him. However, not only does her vicious plan come to a halt, but her lover turns his back on her. Once again, the character played by Negri is plummeted into misfortune to provide a moral lesson. Betrayed and left on her own, the now antiheroine wanders into the barren wasteland of the desert to meet her tragic, but anticipated, destiny. In the end, to use *Picture Play*'s summation, "when she is scorned and reviled by every one [*sic*], there is little illusion of beauty left."[83]

Naturally, Famous Players-Lasky was invested in comparing the quality of its product with Negri's Lubitsch-produced vehicles, claiming that "Bella Donna . . . differs from her previous foreign-made productions as a sparkling Tiffany diamond differs from the dull paste imitation."[84] Advertising material emphasized the idea that the picture was superior to Negri's European films, owing to excellent production facilities offered by Hollywood and "all the resources that only Paramount can supply."[85] Critics, nonetheless, could not come to a consensus regarding *Bella Donna*, and opinions as to whether it was tailor-made for Negri's talents varied. *Motion Picture Magazine* preferred her European productions over her first American feature, noting, nonetheless, that "Bella Donna is so fascinatingly interwoven with her personal color and magnetism that you are robbed of any acute critical faculty soon after she appears on the screen."[86] *Variety* thought that the film was well appointed and that Negri looked better than she had in her German films,[87] while *Photoplay* provided a much more negative verdict. "Will we ever again see the bedeviling DuBarry or the vivid, seductive Carmen?" asked the columnist.[88]

As far as Negri herself was concerned, according to the account given by Richard Koszarski, the initial excitement she felt about entering the biggest film market in the world in 1922 was soon eclipsed by reservations she had regarding the quality of her scripts and "Hollywood's backwater culture."[89] By her own admission, Negri had doubts about the one-dimensional character of Bella Donna, fearing that the role might not give her enough room to showcase her acting versatility and that it might cause her to be typecast as a vamp. "I didn't like *Bella Donna* myself. My imagination of the role was so

Figure 7. Advertising for *Bella Donna* (1923). Source: *Motion Picture News*, February 10, 1923.

different!" she reportedly said. "But I allowed myself to be persuaded. They said to me, 'Ah, but American audiences are different! You will not succeed unless you adapt yourself to our ways.'"[90] These doubts were, in hindsight, understandable.

While receiving some critical acclaim, the film's depiction of racial issues, and the ensuing portrayal of low female morals, was deemed scandalous in conservative quarters. In Texas, these themes culminated in the picture being banned from distribution within the boundaries of the state. Pittsburgh's Ku Klux Klan criticized Negri for becoming a threat to the high ideals of white womanhood, calling *Bella Donna* "a revolting play."[91] What the Klan saw as particularly degrading was the film's depiction of an erotic fascination between a Western woman and an Egyptian man who eventually spurns her.[92] Such beliefs were not as extreme as they might appear to us nowadays, considering that some respectable figures—including feminist Charlotte Perkins Gilman—spoke in favor of nativist ideology, underlining the role played by women in maintaining racial purity to "cleanse the human race of its worst inheritance."[93]

The outrage provoked by the cinematic misdoings of Bella Donna was not diminished by the fact that, by the end of the film, the chief protagonist is punished for allowing herself to go astray. Her engagement in an extramarital, interracial affair results in death; hence, the story is problematic in its concurrent rehearsal of both "the empowerment and the containment of female desire."[94] Interestingly, and somehow unexpectedly, the film also attracted criticism from the black community, with one commentator noting, "If Miss Negri were American she could join the Ku Klux Klan. Now she can only entertain it and make it believe it is right."[95] In the view of the *Baltimore Afro-American*, the principal plot of *Bella Donna*—as well as the plots of two other films starring Negri[96]—is that of "the hare-brained, love-struck woman . . . and the motif of profitable relation of races, the white races as [*sic*] against some other darker group. Sometimes she loses in her game of love, but most often she drags the flag of white superiority in the mud only to hoist it in great triumph when the dark man might be thoroughly humiliated."[97] In falling for Baroudi, the Oriental subject, Negri's heroine attempts to transcend the binary relations between the West and "The Other." Subsequently, she is castigated for undermining the cultural paradigm. Thus, the narrative closure of the film impacts the variety of its possible readings, giving priority to the principle of restoring the natural order.

Negri's second American film, released in the same year as *Bella Donna*, was *The Cheat* (1923), a remake of Cecil B. DeMille's production from 1915, this time directed by George Fitzmaurice. Negri portrays Carmelita, a South American socialite disowned by her family for marrying below her status. Being in the throes of a gambling habit, Carmelita finds it impossible to live on her husband's modest salary and decides to take advantage of a loan offered to her by Rao-Singh, a crook posing as an Indian prince.[98] When the heroine seeks to repay her debt, Rao-Singh demands sexual favors and brands her a cheat with a hot iron crest. Mariusz Kotowski describes the story of *The Cheat* as essentially a reworking of that of *Bella Donna*, and it is easy to see the parallels: "A society woman betrays her husband as she falls for some smooth-talking scoundrel, and she is consequently abandoned to fend for herself in a series of life-threatening situations. The audience watches her drag herself through the dirt, never doubting she deserves punishment."[99]

In the evaluation penned by Janet Staiger, the main narrative function of the cinematic vamp was to test the self-control of the male.[100] In that respect, Carmelita can be considered as representative of the type. The publicity materials for the film indicate, however, that the female imaginary it offered was much more complex. Despite starting off as a quintessential predatory woman who undermines men and the symbolic order, Carmelita manages to redeem herself, regardless of her wrongdoings: "*The Cheat* has a happy ending. Pola Negri plays (for the first time in her career) a *sympathetic* role, a character that the audiences will take to their hearts. Her temptations and struggles, her little weaknesses, and in the end her strength of character based on real, honest love, will hold audiences in a spell of enchantment."[101]

The material circulated by the studio upon the film's release identifies Negri's role as that of a "lovable heroine . . . torn between her love for her husband and the attractions of this millionaire rival."[102] Positioning Negri in the middle of a romantic triangle was a narrative device previously utilized by *Gypsy Blood* and *Bella Donna*. Simultaneously, the promise of "a happy ending" works in tandem with the positive description of Negri's new screen character to signal a departure from the narrative pattern established in her previous films.

Like *Bella Donna*, *The Cheat* capitalized on the image of active sexuality associated with Negri by placing the star within a plot of deception and romance. Both films also fed into the rich symbolism of the Oriental villainess by linking their heroines with a duplicitous Arab and a bogus Indian prince, respectively.

Overall, Negri's first American vehicles allowed her to commit a series of symbolic transgressions and painted her on-screen characters as women who dared to cross the boundaries of traditionally passive female sexuality and defy the rigid boundaries of social distinction. Yet, even when films directed by Lubitsch appeared to deploy comparable narrative strategies, they also had a certain tongue-in-cheek quality and humor that was absent from the characterization of Negri in her first features produced in Hollywood. Undoubtedly, the heroines of her German films were capable of taking matters into their own hands and—while often lacking a strict moral code—were still portrayed as complex characters with which moviegoers might identify. The apparent superiority of the Lubitsch portrayals might, to some measure, be explained by the fact that the plots of *Passion* and *One Arabian Night* are governed by female desire but remain open in positioning female spectators as their assumed audience. In comparison, the Negri of *Bella Donna* and *The Cheat* is a universal but one-dimensional type compromised for American consumption, a woman "driven *by* the plot rather than *driving* the plot."[103]

The Spanish Dancer and *Shadows of Paris*

Both *Bella Donna* and *The Cheat* met with only moderate financial success, which prompted the studio to search for a screenplay that could prove as popular among the moviegoing public as one of Negri's German productions.[104] The star initially hoped to work under the direction of Lubitsch, her frequent collaborator, on the set of her third feature for Famous Players-Lasky. However, the idea had to be aborted due to the director's commitments in directing *Rosita*, a film starring Mary Pickford, for another production company.[105] Interestingly, *The Spanish*

Dancer—the vehicle the studio settled on as Negri's next film—and *Rosita* were adapted from the same literary source, the opera *Don César De Bazan*, which naturally invited critical comparisons. The majority of critics dismissed Pickford as unable to create a Spanish atmosphere on the shadow screen, favoring Negri's portrayal as more fiery and, hence, more authentic. *Motion Picture Classic* provided an interesting deviation from the rule, suggesting *Rosita* is superior to *The Spanish Dancer* simply because the former feature was directed by a man of European heritage: "Ernst Lubitsch knows more about Kings and their retinues and European people than our American directors. That is natural. He was born a European, and for years he knew the sophistication of the Continent."[106]

The publicity still for *Rosita* depicts Pickford smiling, with her blonde locks creating a halo-like structure above her head. The dress she wears is very simple, and with no jewelry or visible makeup, she can hardly connote the typical image of a seductive dancer (figure 8). In constructing its heroines, Hollywood relied on familiar typology recognizable in literature, theater, and popular entertainment: fair, white features symbolized moral superiority, whereas dark hair (usually paired with heavy makeup) signified more carnal appeal, an earthy and dangerous version of womanhood.[107] This ideological rationale underpins the juxtaposition of publicity stills from the rival productions of *Rosita* and *The Spanish Dancer* published in the pages of *Motion Picture Classic*.[108] To reference Dyer's discussion of whiteness, Pickford constructs an extreme representation of an angelically glowing white woman, suggesting virtuousness and moral superiority.[109] In technical terms, the backlighting serves to emphasize the famously blonde hair of the actress, which would have looked too dark otherwise. Metaphorically, it sustains the visual fantasy of white femininity.

Negri's interpretation of the same character favors excess over Pickford's simple, natural look and carries strikingly different connotations. She looks decidedly more confident, if not slightly sinister, in comparison with Pickford's happy-go-lucky appeal. As one columnist rhapsodized, "[Negri] has the same soft and beautiful ferocity [as a tiger]. She has the same sleepy air of seeing everything out of watchful half-closed eyes that are looking at nothing."[110] The star of *The Spanish Dancer* is shown adorned by a plethora of heavy accessories, with her hair partially covered by a turban, a potent visual symbol of Hollywood's version of Orientalism, and wearing Negri's trademark, dark lipstick. By accentuating her raven-black hair and kohl-rimmed eyes, studio-driven publicity connected her to the visual tropes of the vamp archetype, heavily slanted toward an Orientalist image.

Set in seventeenth-century Spain, *The Spanish Dancer* is the gripping tale of Maritana, a gypsy dancer enmeshed in a series of intrigues in a Spanish court. Upon first meeting her soon to be lover, Don César, Maritana entertains him by reading his fortune on tarot cards, only to learn that the man will soon become penniless after crossing swords with a younger man. Even so, to use the words

Figure 8. Two versions of a Spanish senorita. Mary Pickford in *Rosita* (1923) and Negri in *The Spanish Dancer* (1923). Source: "In Comparison," *Motion Picture Classic*, November 1923, 48.

of Kotowski, "as the dancer looks the nobleman in the eye, they feel a mutual attraction, theirs to pursue if they should ever meet again."[111] The encounter is followed by a series of unfortunate events in which Don César is stripped of his possessions and sentenced to death for killing a man in a duel. In the meantime, Negri's heroine is asked to perform for the queen, finding herself in the midst of shifting political alliances between Spain and France. Don Salluste, a scheming courtier, comes up with a plan that aims to use Maritana's appeal to win him favor with the king. As the story unfolds, Maritana "saves the situation and manipulates the matters so that . . . the King is so pleased he gives the couple [Maritana and Don César] his blessing and restores Don César's estates."[112]

There are several narrative similarities in the portrayals of the heroines of *Gypsy Blood* and *Spanish Dancer*, especially with regard to their occupations as dancers. During the silent film years, especially from 1916 to 1926,[113] Hollywood appropriated a broad imaginary of Orientalist tropes, and having a gypsy dancer as a leading character brought some of these associations home. Dance reproduces an imagined vision of the East in encompassing all the qualities that allegedly make it inferior to the Occident: femininity, corporeality, and nonlinguistic communication.[114] For Studlar, certain forms of dance have the capacity to create a sense of liminal identity because they represent a desire to escape the constraints of bourgeois domesticity.[115] What comes to the forefront in this formulation is the act of transgression embedded in female performers who defy traditional gender roles by removing themselves from the domestic sphere, entering the public one. What separates Carmen from Maritana, though, is the sense of agency the former exerts over her own performance; while Carmen uses dance as a tool to gain influence over men, Maritana falls victim to the scheme set by the malicious Don Salluste, who utilizes her to meet his own ends. In *The Spanish Dancer*, Negri's heroine is not driven by an insatiable appetite for power; rather, she acts out of devotion, not malice.

Dance—in folk tales, a skill unique in its ability to move a dancer from the lower to the highest societal strata—is integral to the stories of Maritana and Carmen. Similar narrative threads were also interwoven into the early, extravagant accounts of Negri's off-screen existence, which suggested that she once used to perform for the last emperor of Russia, Czar Nicholas II, even receiving personal gifts from Czarina Alexandra.[116] Her elegant dancing was met with so much admiration at the royal court that the czar and czarina became personally acquainted with Negri and welcomed her to their inner circle.[117] In all likelihood, stories like this were a complete fabrication, as there is no evidence to support the claim that Negri came into contact with the Russian royals.

Visually, Maritana and Carmen constituted a destabilizing ethnic presence; dressed up in traditional gypsy garb, with swirled skirt and bangles, Negri became an elegy to sexual temptation. Her characters offered a telling illustration of how ethnicity is leveraged in the depiction of female sexuality. Still, it should be noted that in terms of discursive function, Maritana does not signify as much of a disruption to the male-centered paradigm as Carmen does. The key distinction between the two characters lies in the fact that Maritana's love for a man is genuine, which effectively spares her from the punishment inflicted on Carmen. Paraphrasing Negra, *The Spanish Dancer* offers a narrative recuperation of the vamp, where Negri's character is neither a vision of purity nor a caricature of feminine evil: "Here, rather than destroying her lover, she rehabilitates him."[118]

According to the critical evaluation provided by Marcia Landy, the trajectory of change that Maritana goes through is framed in positive terms, because rather than being driven by a selfish desire to turn herself into a royal consort, her major motivation is to save her beloved. In that respect, she does not comply with the vamp type, as her character does not remain fixed through the course of the narrative and, instead, is allowed some room to grow. Yet, the nuances of this cinematic portrayal did not influence the perception of Negri's off-screen image. "Her persona," argues Landy, "is consistent with the tendency of the film to present her transformation from a gypsy to an aristocrat, thus stressing her love and devotion to the dashing Don César."[119] In his history of representations of working-class characters in American film, Steven J. Ross explains how this was a popular dramatic formula in silent films that touched on issues of social mobility. Seen through the prism of Hollywood, any struggle (whether personal or societal) could be solved through love; and true love was strong enough to break down any class barriers.[120]

Another point of intersection between Carmen and Maritana refers to their ethnic identities as gypsies. Being a gypsy within the realm of Western culture means having a distinctive culture and traditions, albeit no homeland nor national territory to call one's own. The figure of the gypsy thus precedes and foregrounds that of a twentieth-century immigrant, in terms of suggesting a contamination of the American nation and a consequent inability to assimilate into it. Historically, there is a long-standing association between Romany gypsies and the practice of fortune-telling, which places them outside the discourses of humanism and rationality, some of the most crucial aspects of modern American society. In addition, the associative web of "gypsy" ethnicity links it to the northern regions of the Indian subcontinent, which places it in close alliance with the notion of the Orient and in juxtaposition to whiteness. Gypsies that emerge from different cultural texts are presented as "essentially a [*sic*] consistent, natural, real, eternal, stable and static phenomena,"[121] which again aligns them with the dominant cultural image of the Oriental subject, also seen as eternally fixed. To quote Said, "The very possibility of development, transformation, human movement—in the deepest sense of the world—is denied the Orient and the Oriental."[122]

Carmen and Maritana were hardly the last of Negri's characters whose stories were set in Spain. As evidenced by the *New York Times*, Negri came to specialize in parts requiring her to embody Spanish women,[123] which of course comes as no surprise given the strong links between Spain, the Arab world, and a vibrant dance culture. All elements so integral to the representation of Spain in Western imagination worked to turn it into a semi-Oriental setting and, therefore, a perfect backdrop for the exploits of the vamp.

Aligning itself with a typical pattern of metamorphosis and upward class mobility, the plot of *Shadows of Paris* follows Negri as Blackbird, a brazen dancer of the Parisian underworld[124] who, upon learning her lover and fellow gang member has been killed on the battlefield, assumes a new identity. No longer "a queen of crooks" but a Polish countess[125] named Claire, she enters the highest strata of society to eventually marry Raoul de Gramont, the prefect of police.

At times, the woman struggles to leave her old life behind and visits her old haunts unbeknownst to her husband. One such escapade ends in Blackbird meeting her former sweetheart, whom to this point she presumed dead. When she receives her old companion adorned with the finest silks and jewels, the thief in him awakens. This, in turn, makes the heroine see the Apache for what he really is: a criminal of debatable morals rather than the love of her life. The film ends with Claire's regeneration, enacted through her devotion to a man of wealth and position. She sinks into Gramont's arms as she confesses her shameful connections to the demimonde.

Shadows of Paris opens with a scene showing Negri wearing a tight bodice, an ungainly checked skirt, and a feathered scarf and hat. The film signals her rise to prosperity, and dual identity, mainly through the use of costume; Blackbird/Claire re-assembles the same outfit every time she enters her old habitat, dressing in Parisian haute couture to perform the role of a wealthy wife. Emmanuelle Dirix writes about the sexual associations of feathers in both American and French culture, where they had long been integral to music halls and vaudeville performance.[126] Wispy feathers, particularly ostrich and marabou, constitute a characteristic blend of vulgarity with a touch of glamour. Their cultural connotations "mirrored that of those who wore them: they were too close to prostitution for comfort."[127] In the words of Stephen Gundle and Clino Castelli, "Feathers, furs and even fabrics with leopard print not only harnessed the magnetism of the Orient, but testified to character as being more primitive and closer to nature."[128] Ideologically, animal fabrics are Westernized artifacts of exoticism that inextricably link female character to nature and primitivism. This typified mode of representation, with its associations between women and animals, was an important component of vamp iconography, extended in *Shadows of Paris* to the narrative layer of the film. Claire's original name, after all, is Blackbird, which cements the link between the animalistic and what is considered deceptive, if not downright evil.

"Here at last the star has come into her own," wrote *Motion Picture News* in relation to *Shadows of Paris*, "a role which fits her like a proverbial glove and into which she throws all the fire, temperament, passion and emotional ability which we saw in those early successes that brought her to the attention of the American public."[129] Reviewers located part of the drawing power of this intense story in the fact that it effectively resurrected what they saw as the most congenial role for Negri, presenting her as the sultry type familiar from *Passion* and *Gypsy Blood*.[130]

Daughter of a Gypsy

Fan discourse suggested that Negri shared many psychological characteristics with her filmic incarnations: she was a free-spirited woman unwilling to settle down and, like Carmen and Maritana, described herself as a gypsy (figure 9). The star system responded to the surge of public interest in Negri's past by promoting her as the daughter of a gypsy and a Polish aristocrat. "My father was a Hungarian gypsy, the handsomest man I have ever known, dark, fiery and daring. From him I inherit restless temperament," Negri was cited as saying in an interview given to *Photoplay*.[131] Statements such as this continued to authenticate the exotic ethnicities incarnated by Negri on celluloid. In other words, she was able to elicit the passion of a gypsy dancing girl because *she was one* herself.

A biographical note published in *Motion Picture Classic* also claimed that Negri's father was a gypsy, adding that her real name was Apollonia Chalupez, although "she was once the Countess Dombski."[132] Another press feature revealed that the future Hollywood star was raised single-handedly by her mother in great poverty. Her father was a political activist and a creative soul, "a gypsy violinist involved in a political uprising" whose absence was magnified in almost all biographical accounts of her life.[133]

The sudden disappearance of the father figure from the young Negri's life was assumed to take a great toll on her emotional well-being, effectively romanticizing her past while simultaneously reinforcing the idea of feminine vulnerability. One press account blurred the lines of demarcation between the private and the public life of the star in suggesting that before Negri came to recognition she used to earn her living as a dancer in Poland and Austria.[134] Her act was brought to an end by the outset of the Great War, forcing Negri to look for refuge in Berlin.[135]

On another level, the border-crossing nature of the actress was often associated with eastern Europe, which was becoming increasingly more central to the stereotype of the fallen woman at the beginning of the century. Indeed, Praz is of the opinion that beside the widely understood space of the Orient, the vamp archetype could be placed in Russia, symbolically incarnating the body of a Slav woman.[136] At the end of her career in 1931, Negri recalled that she found it particularly hard to adapt to the Anglo-Saxon way of expressing emotions, because,

Figure 9. Epitomizing the vamp on the cover of *Picture Play* in July 1924.

as a Slav, she naturally lacked restraint.[137] Fan discourse attributed Negri with a myriad of ethnicities, which built her within the parameters of exoticism and further aligned her with the imaginary of the vamp.

Other components of Negri's screen portrayals—particularly those related to the gypsy archetype—were presented as concurrent with her private life. For instance, Maritana's occupation as a fortune-teller stands as a potent trope of irrationality, which was also carried from Negri's films into her private life. Harry Carr reported that because of her profession and cultural background, Negri was intensely superstitious: "One day she saw an ornament on one of the sets that looked to her like a peacock—the jinx of all jinx signs known to the theater world. She ordered it down. When the prop man refused to obey in the absence of the director she flew into a wild rage. She tore the set half apart to get at the offending gewgaw. She threw it on the floor so hard that it broke in two, despite the fact it was made of cast iron."[138]

Motion Picture Magazine published a series of stories describing the star as immensely superstitious, accentuating the affiliation between Negri's alleged ethnicity and the concept of irrationality.[139] In a similar vein, Myrtle Gebhart argued that superstitions and lucky charms were incredibly popular among the employees of the studios. "Film folk have pet hoodos [*sic*], and I went on a still hunt to discover their luck charms, just what place superstition plays in their life and work—and found some very laughable and human idiosyncrasies," she wrote in "Their Streak of Superstition," published by *Picture Play*.[140]

Shortly after Negri's retirement from Hollywood, Walter Ramsey of *Motion Picture Magazine* pointed to ethnic and national identity as relevant in terms of one's propensity to be irrational:

> Negroes are the most superstitious people in the world. And next come the actors. . . . Foreign actors even carry their old-country superstitions into Hollywood. It seems that in Poland the sign that means good luck is a little pig. Or in a pinch, even the squeal of a pig is the last grunt in good fortune. Hollywood has just lost her most famous Polish actress, but it is a matter of history that she never started a picture until a live pig had been turned loose to spread good luck all over the set. And how those little pigs used to spread good luck is also a matter of more-or-less common knowledge.[141]

The aptly titled "Vampires I Have Known" described Negri as "one of the most fascinating and dangerous sirens on the screen" who exceeded the convention of the day by embracing the most emotional of behaviors.[142] "Ah Pola! A very pirate of a vampire, indeed, flying into gorgeous rages, laughing with her head thrown back in irresistible abandon, weeping great tears," claimed the feature, adding that "everything for Pola is inevitable. She is a fatalist."[143] While press mentions of this nature initially worked to support Negri's exotic publicity, the resulting tension constituted one of the reasons for her inability to establish a lasting career within the American context. And of course, as Negra points out, "this sort of Old World fatalism that permeated press characterizations of Negri contrasted sharply with the energetic ideas of American capitalism."[144]

The interviewer of *Movie Weekly* reported that it is impossible to predict Negri's behavior, because "she is always electric, volatile—you never know quite what she may do."[145] "Compared with the garden conceits of Hollywood, hers is a passion flower among dandelions," wrote Herbert Howe at the beginning of the 1930s, again emphasizing the temperament of the Polish star.[146] Thus, Negri conformed to the formula that placed her in opposition to the hegemony of white, Anglo-Saxon, protestant culture,[147] characterized by Donald H. Roy as "sober, reserved, frugal (Puritanical), legalistic (contractual)."[148] To an extent, the emphasis that Negri's publicity put on her irrational conduct created a representation of womanhood paralleled by the first roles Negri portrayed for American audiences in *Passion* and *Gypsy Blood.* Just like Carmen, the star connoted passion rather than rational, staid thinking; she was not constructed in line with the existing patriarchal paradigms. As such, she became a potent signifier of foreign values, a signal of lurking trouble that mobilized multiple fears about threatening the status quo.

Beauty

While much magazine coverage was given to descriptions of the physical appearance of female players, editors devoted even more attention to discussions that linked physical appearance to certain mental attributes. In 1923 *Motion Picture Magazine* offered its readers an insight into the inner lives of screen personalities by contemplating the shape of their respective noses, claiming that the slanting flatness of Negri's features reveals "a dare-devil, pleasure-loving temperament—one fond of excitement and violent contrasts." The shape of Negri's nose indicated she was "vital and wild, with executive ability and a keen sensitivity to art" and "a strong, domineering woman."[149] According to *Photoplay,* which ran a similar column, part of Negri's uniqueness lay in her Oriental beauty that did not conform to dominant American standards.[150] In contextualizing her looks, the article defined the star as a phenomenon of nature more than a human being; the vamp femininity was thus encoded as an excess of uncontrolled, fierce passions:

> When I visited Europe four years ago the most thrilling sights that met my eyes were the volcanoes Etna and Negri. Etna was inactive whereas Pola never was. So to her I awarded the willow plume of adjectives. . . . Pola's beauty is the beauty of suggested drama. It is the Orientale. It is the barbaric throb of drums in hot-scented jungles by moonlight. It is a volcanic flame with the enchantment of threat. Green eyes, slumberous dilating tigress eyes, in a face as white as Moscow winter beneath the night blackness of her hair. Savage, threatening Cossack beauty that knows no law. Pola's is the dagger beauty of barbaric splendors.[151]

This depiction is exceptionally striking when compared with the lexicon employed by Howe to describe some of the other "most beautiful women of the screenland." His description of blonde Swedish star Greta Nissen plays on ideas of whiteness: "A snow maiden dancing out in the midnight sun with the color on her hair, Greta Nissen is the Norse exquisite. The glory of morning, the clarity of a bell, the loveliness of a lily swaying in dawn."[152] Negri's beauty, then, was represented in terms diametrically opposed to the ideals of white womanhood. She was as captivating as she was dangerous. Myrtle Gebhart's article also compared the star to a volcano, calling her "Madame Vesuvius" and "a barbaric, elemental force."[153] A letter written by one of Negri's admirers used analogous terms, describing the Polish actress as the embodiment of a rare personality, "deep, mysterious, charming, burning with the fires of Vesuvius one moment and peaceful as a calm sea the next."[154]

In the same breath with which many accounts cherished Negri's temperamental appeal, they also criticized her for failing to conform to the conventional visions of femininity. Howe's list of the ten most attractive Hollywood actresses, which included Negri, ignited a debate that spanned across the pages of *Photoplay* for several months.[155] In January 1926, Margaret Reid objected to the presence of foreign-born talent in the ranking. "Aren't the standards of beauty in Europe entirely different from that in this country?" she asked rhetorically, adding that Negri "would be simply a typical Polish girl, maybe a beautiful one in Poland but not in here."[156]

In addition, the dichotomized relationship between different types of white looks and opposing moral qualities echoed the period's approach toward issues of ethnicity.[157] *Picture Play* made a poignant observation in suggesting that screen vamping has long been the domain of the dark-haired woman that has "to be poisoned or knifed to let the blond leading lady get the guy."[158] Following a similar pattern, Reid's letter makes a clear distinction between the "vamp" types, represented by Pola Negri, Barbara La Marr, and Nita Naldi, and that of American-born, typically blonde leading ladies. The former "fall short of beauty by the American standard, too, because they do not look natural, and an American beauty must be natural. Who ever saw anybody look like them?"[159] Such reasoning reverberated with the cultural dynamic that equated "real" female beauty with purity and inner virtue. At large, xenophobic sentiments found a reflection in the opinions of moviegoers who saw European actors as essentially too foreign in appearance or manner of acting to be eligible for a comparison with the American stock of players. "I realize that American actors fit best in America. Certainly, the average American audience can best understand and appreciate their interpretation of characters," argued one letter chosen by the editorial board of *Picture Play*.[160]

Another issue that comes to the forefront in the discussion of Negri's beauty is her strong aesthetic tie to makeup, which informed the origin and further development of the vamp iconography. Her dark hair and eyes rendered her as belonging to suspicious, morally devalued ethnic groups, while the vivid makeup she wore firmly placed Negri in the discourses of artifice and transformation.[161] In her critical evaluation of the history of the American beauty industry, Kathy Peiss argues that the dominant ideology has always placed makeup outside the truthful exemplification of social integrity, "identifying cosmetics with disrepute and deceit, a debased female and non-European 'other.'"[162] This is particularly true in regard to the cultural landscape of the 1920s, when the spike in the popularity of color cosmetics had been treated with suspicion everywhere but in big metropolitan areas, such as New York and Chicago. The growing demand for face paint was a phenomenon largely limited to young, single women living in large urban centers, and it was not until the late 1920s that it entered the mainstream. In the rural parts of the country, conspicuous makeup remained associated with wanton women and continued to be viewed as morally dubious. In her film portrayals, Negri sported a sensual look that relied heavily on cosmetics; with emphasized dark eyelids and carmine lips, she contrasted sharply with the idealized vision of natural female beauty. Furthermore, the constant cultivation of modern beauty practices framed Negri as an excessively produced and self-regulated body, which reinforced her link to seduction, the urban landscape, and commodification.

Such visual strategy is embedded not only in extratextual sources of Negri's stardom but also, for example, in the character of Baroness Gerda Wallentin, portrayed by her in *Three Sinners* (1928). Gerda's blonde hair has no relation to traditional virtues of white femininity, outlined in relationship to Pickford's angelic looks beforehand. Instead, it is a "chemically acquired, counterfeit blondness"[163] that implicates the heroine in an aggressive embrace of personal marketing (figure 10). The aesthetic language of cinema upheld a tradition that connected artificial blonde to perverse sexuality, to prostitutes and chorus girls; it is notable that Alla Nazimova wore a platinum wig to portray Salomé, the wicked temptress, in the film adaptation of Oliver Wilde's *Salomé* from 1923.[164]

Especially throughout the late 1920s and 1930s, hair bleaching connoted cheating, as the practice attempted to "misrepresent the wearer's true self," writes Pam Cook.[165] Indeed, the association continued to reach unprecedented heights toward the end of the 1920s, and it resonates with the characterization of the baroness, who bleaches her hair—if not to disguise herself, then to start a new life—having just abandoned her husband. *Three Sinners* puts low connotations of platinum blonde in motion through Gerda's occupation as a hostess in a gambling den, further building on Negri's expertise in portraying characters of the underworld. Fan magazines played a pivotal role in promoting Negri as a woman who actively endorses artifice in her performance of femininity and constructs herself, to use the term coined by Negra, as an "excessively produced body" in private life.[166] *Photoplay* indicated that the star was solely responsible for the spreading popularity of "the clown make-up" among female moviegoers.[167] *Picture Play* too blamed the star for bringing conspicuous makeup into fashion. "The dead-white

Figure 10. Negri in the publicity still from *Three Sinners* (1928). Source: *Picture Play Magazine*, October 1930.

make-up that swept the country" relied on draining "one's face of all natural color" and covering it in a thick layer of powders, complete with carmine lips.[168]

Androcentric society places women in a paradoxical position, at once crowning them for the prerogatives of beauty and then constantly challenging them to find the right balance between caring for their looks and not appearing too concerned about them. Especially in connection to ethnic whiteness, an ideal woman is a creature of moderation, someone who stems away from artificiality and whose physical appearance is an extension of inner virtue. Thus, by highlighting the role of Negri as a self-produced commodity, excessive use of makeup located her outside the discourse of respectable femininity. When the star is presented as a woman enthusiastically engaged in the pursuit of beauty, she is deemed worthy of contempt, becoming a distorted, extreme figure.

Many film scholars have observed that acting styles began to shift at the end of the 1920s, producing more nuanced and subtle performances, and an understated way of acting rather than the extended gesturing and rapid movement associated with actors such as Negri.[169] In this respect, the strong association with the vamp typology, lauded by Negri's fans in the early 1920s, made her look passé within the changing cultural landscape, a point exemplified by a letter published in one fan magazine in 1929:

> What Pola began in Germany she continued in America, and yet she failed. What, then, is the tragedy in her career? It is in the following things: too much love fire, too much passion, blood, and flesh in the primitive thing called love. Such a feeling has outlived itself in life and could not stay long on the screen. People nowadays criticize more or less all the actions of themselves and others. Spiritual demands and human interests have changed our tastes and emotion to a considerable degree. For better or worse, nowadays one even loves with the mind. Look at life, at modern literature, the contemporary stage—does the primitive Pola Negri love have a place there? This primitive love fire, the emotional way of portraying it, makes us put Pola Negri in the first rank of all great actresses of past screen traditions.[170]

The Negri emerging from this letter is a figure of excessive emotion and melodrama, no longer appealing to the taste of American moviegoers, who were growing increasingly more attuned to nuance in performance style and in the expression of emotion. Deemed "a great actress of past tradition," Negri was axiomatic of the vamp type and, by extension, hardly compatible with the new fashion of restraint.

Conclusion

The act of signing Negri to Famous Players-Lasky was designed to capitalize on her pre-established "astounding success in celluloid in the United States."[171] From her arrival on the American shores in 1922—a high water mark for the popularity of her German productions—the Negri star persona continued to be rooted in the notion of an active and independent, thus threatening, version of womanhood. *Bella Donna*, her American screen debut, subsumed the star into the vamp narrative already familiar to her fans from the portrayals of *Gypsy Blood* or *Passion*. With her wicked intentions and the power to lure decent men to their doom, one cannot affiliate Bella Donna with the playfulness typical of the heroines of Negri's German oeuvre. Here, she signified a disruption in the patriarchal paradigm, first as a woman who is sexually active, and second, as one marked by ethnic difference.

With the advent of the women's rights movement and the second wave of immigration, the early 1920s were a time of cultural upheaval. Witnessing a flux of newly emerging concepts relating to the position of women in capitalist society, these wider social shifts formed a turning point in the evolution of the femme fatale as a theme in visual arts. Initially a complex reworking of ancient legends and the story of Salomé, discourse at the time utilized the notion of the female vampire to express ideas concerning voracious female sexuality and the threat of foreign impact on the middle-class, protestant values.[172] Hence, some of Negri's films can be analyzed in the light of increasing promulgation of those fears. Ultimately, the feature that links Negri's characters in *Passion*, *Gypsy Blood*, *Bella Donna*, and *The Cheat* is the ease with which they employ personal means to enter higher social rankings; the likes of Carmen use sex in exchange for status and evince no guilt. Many of Negri's heroines had to be castigated for their audacious transgressions—often by the ultimate punishment, death. While Bella Donna wanders into the desert, never to return, Carmen's jealous lover stabs her to death. These tragic endings illustrate the consequences of forsaking traditional values in favor of sexual liberation. They stand as an indictment of attempts to cross the boundaries of ethnicity, class, and patriarchal order.

On the surface, Maritana from *The Spanish Dancer* accorded Negri a narrative position similar to her part in *Gypsy Blood*, with both characters marked as "other" threefold, by virtue of being Spaniards, gypsies, and dancers. Still, instead of representing "a poison that . . . infects the man's system and causes him to consider evil actions,"[173] Maritana saves her beloved from his reckless life of gambling and fighting, and aids his escape from captivity when he is about to be seized for debt. *Moving Picture World* wrote that "Pola Negri has the dash and the fire of old and better opportunities along these lines than in some of her other pictures. She gives a splendid performance,"[174] with *Photoplay*'s critic declaring that "she is again La Negri of *Passion*. She has shed the veneer of sophistication and has reverted to the primitive woman type."[175]

The discursive connection between certain actors and characteristic types of female representation put women at risk of becoming passé once the type they portrayed was no longer à la mode. Although Negri's new films tended to slowly dissociate her from the vamp stereotype, the star system was invested in incorporating intertextual components of her earlier performances in her off-screen image. Most importantly, Negri's private persona lacked the multifaceted quality of her cinematic incarnations, and several visual features—such as Negri's trademark look of white face paint and heavy lidded, kohl-rimmed eyes—worked in tandem with extrafilmic texts, successfully integrating her star image into the vamp narrative. In keeping with Negra, the actress problematized colonial ideology because her publicity contrasted with and challenged ideas of American morality and empire.[176] Ancillary texts endeavored to support the portrayal of Negri as a foreign import and a carrier of irrationality, galvanizing conflict between old-world fatalism and modern ideas of American living.

CHAPTER 3

Vilma Bánky and Whiteness

"THE ALMOST PERFECT ANGLO-SAXON TYPE, MORE ENGLISH THAN THE ENGLISH"

The early 1920s witnessed a spike of interest in the import of European stars to Hollywood. The vogue started with the arrival of Pola Negri, the subject of the previous chapters, who signed to work for Famous Players-Lasky in 1922 with her German director, Ernst Lubitsch. Ginette Vincendeau and Alastair Phillips observed how the film studios started to hire talent scouts to keep a constant watch on successful stage and film actors on the Continent.[1] It was in this cultural landscape that Vilma Bánky, a young Hungarian actress, signed a contract with Samuel Goldwyn, an independent producer, in March 1925. In introducing Bánky to American audiences, Goldwyn's publicity department fabricated a highly sentimentalized narrative of discovery, which continually emphasized the role of fate and destiny in her lucky break. I analyze how fan magazines shaped Bánky's star image by placing her within this Cinderella narrative, and identify the most crucial components of her star persona during her tenure at Goldwyn's studio.

This chapter also explores the ideological value of Bánky as an epitome of idealized, passive femininity through aesthetic means that accentuated her conspicuously pale or white features. The discourse of whiteness found its most active shape in the description of Bánky's appeal in film periodicals, as exemplified by a letter written by one of her fans: "The beauty among beauties is Vilma Bánky. . . . Of a sweet and shy disposition, Vilma is in every sense an ideal woman."[2] I investigate how the dramatic retelling of Bánky's life worked in tandem with her films to construct her as lacking agency, and thus, to portray her stardom as a perfect embodiment of white, nonthreatening womanhood. The sudden but short-lived popularity she achieved testifies to the appeal of such a star image. In fact, Bánky's assimilation into the fabric of American society went smoothly because she personified ethnic qualities that were considered highly respectable.

The Cinderella Myth

In her discussion of the Cinderella myth and its relationship to early cinema, Diana Anselmo-Sequeira points out that by the late 1910s the fantasy of metamorphosis governed the American screen.[3] To Anselmo-Sequeira, the narrative of female stardom and magic transmutation was just one of many developments transplanted to cinema from the stage; it became a powerful story in which the tutelage of the motion picture moguls substituted for the "happily ever after" with a prince. The star system repackaged its stars as everyday Cinderellas who were given their chance because of the transformative action of a male producer.[4] In 1918, *Photoplay* wrote of "Cinderella . . . girls who . . . became famous overnight when their good fairies led them into the magic light of the Kliegs."[5] The tale of Cinderella was incorporated into the lives of many movie stars of the 1920s, forming a base for the biographies of such prominent actors as Mary Pickford, Mabel Normand, Colleen Moore, and Clara Bow.

On one vantage point, such success stories were aligned with the format of the film periodicals, which often urged women to participate in beauty contests and commercial searches for new, aspiring movie performers—activities that extended the promise of a Cinderella-like transformation to their readership.[6] Bow's star phenomenon was inadvertently anchored to such fantasies, as her own journey to Hollywood started with her participation in the Fame and Fortune Contest organized by *Motion Picture* in 1921.[7] Less directly, magazines appealed to the aspirational beliefs of change and self-improvement—often unrealistic—in offering advice on how to emulate screen idols through adequate fashions and beauty regimens. Therefore, one might unpack Cinderella stories as more than an attempt to narrativize the role of female performers in patriarchal society, and extend them to a form of activating strategy, foregrounding fans' participation in the star culture.

An anecdote concerning the first meeting between Bánky and Goldwyn, as circulated by the fan press, carefully played out this Cinderella scenario. In the early months of 1925, Samuel Goldwyn embarked on a search for his own version of Greta Garbo, who had recently been brought to America by his business rival, Louis B. Mayer.[8] It was during the journey that took Goldwyn from Berlin to Budapest that the producer met Vilma Bánky, "one of the most noted beauties in Central Europe,"[9] and asked her to join his stock of stars. Aileen St. John-Brenon wrote about the encounter in 1928, suggesting that Vilma's "type" and potential were immediately recognizable: "Mr. Goldwyn saw her in Europe, decided that her type of romantic beauty expressed the perfect embodiment of wholesome womanhood, and persuaded her to sign her name on a dotted line."[10] According to Goldwyn, he saw a postcard depicting Bánky while strolling through the Hungarian city of Pest (now part of Budapest) and, being struck by the star potential of the young, fair-haired woman, became determined to contact her.[11] Such recounting demonstrates how white female Europeanness could function as a commodified, saleable form of heritage in the American context. After days of fruitless searching, Goldwyn's efforts to find Bánky eventually reached the actress; she then managed to arrange a dinner with the producer, just hours before he was destined to board a train and leave the country for good.[12]

It was by emphasizing the role played by pure chance in Bánky's rise to the Hollywood top that enabled the studio to position her as a modern-day incarnation of Cinderella. In his critical evaluation of Cinderella as a literary trope, Rob Baum asserts that "what we worship in her is not what she is but what she gets; by subscribing to the myth of Cinderella, we sustain our collective female belief in wealth, beauty, and revenge."[13] Indeed, the parable is useful in demonstrating the potential of all females, no matter how disadvantaged, to be successful in life. It is a vision where obstacles are overcome by a higher power and magical patronage. For Baum, the bewildering persistence of the tale has significance as a projection of possibility; yet, it does not provide an example of how to navigate the world in order to succeed, because Cinderella's agency is absent. In accepting the validity of this view, one can begin to unpack Bánky in parallel terms, as a mere pawn in the game of fortune rather than a driven and autonomous individual. Notably, Bánky was portrayed as a girl lucky enough to be saved from her dull livelihood by a perceptive producer. In equating the star with a gem that is waiting to be discovered, the Cinderella narrative reduced her own sense of influence and agency, romanticizing what was primarily an economic and cultural appropriation of the attractions of Europe by the American film industry.

Although framed mainly in positive terms, Bánky's "lucky break" was, supposedly, revealing of the unfair rules that governed the movie acting business. In that respect, it attracted a degree of minor criticism attributable to her foreign origin. For Tamar Lane, "there have been many picture celebrities who have ridden to fame on mad luck, but Vilma Banky takes the Grand Prix, the Futurity Sweepstakes and the Kentucky Derby for getting all the breaks in her favour."[14] Lane's article discussed how, in granting a starring role to a virtually unknown young actress, the studio system denied the same opportunities to other equally talented—and perhaps more experienced—individuals. She lamented that in "her very first entries, and in the course of a few months," Bánky was presented to the public alongside Ronald Colman and Rudolph Valentino, a stellar cast that many aspiring actresses could only dream of. This type of outlook was not only a reflection on the inner workings of the star system but also an indication of xenophobic sentiments prevalent in popular culture. In the late 1920s, when the vogue for foreign stars was on its wane, moving picture magazines started to mock the demand for émigrés, asking, if only hypothetically, whether native-born stars were not good enough for the American public. The film industry was, according to fan publications, much more accommodating to non-Americans: "Nobody heard of a foreigner treading the extra's weary path. Only the home-grown product was trampled—and by the alien."[15]

Much about Bánky's ascent to prominence positioned her in relation to foreign stars of established international fame who—in the words of *Picture Play*—arrived in Hollywood with "regal manner and queenly condescension." Bánky, in contrast, held no assumptions or great expectations of success, coming not as a silent film diva but as "a scared young girl on her first journey from home" with an intention to humbly beg favor.[16] In Dorothy Manners's article, Bánky is referred to as "merely a girl who is forced into the show," unlike Pola Negri, "the show girl who craves attention."[17] Indeed, fan discourse at large emphasized the notion of passivity as inherent to her career trajectory. What transpires from *Photoplay*'s account of Bánky's childhood, for instance, is that she was raised in accordance with Victorian ethics, engaging in the traditionally feminine, artistic pursuits, and that she was never particularly passionate about either stage or screen acting. If one accepts the common lore, the poor economic standing of her family in the aftermath of the Great War forced Bánky into the movies:

> She grew up, as is the custom even in Hungary, and outside of a love of books and music she had no particular urge in life. The family was well fixed and Vilma was beautiful. So why worry? She would never have to do so except for the war. . . . When it was over Vilma was faced with the problem of working or not eating. And she liked to eat. But no girl with a face like Vilma's can really starve. She met Bella Balagh who is a Hungarian movie director. He put her before the camera. His productions called her to the attention of UFA who put her under contract to work for them in Berlin and Budapest. Enter now upon the scene Mr. Samuel Goldwyn of Hollywood U.S.A.[18]

Cinderella was born into higher class, only falling into deprivation because of the death of her caring parents. The notion of aristocratic heritage, defined as an internal quality that moves one beyond the realm of ordinary (rather than simply a matter of financial standing), can be understood as one of the most vital characteristics of the heroine. The vision of romanticized Old World royalty, and the parallel narrative of personal loss, was used within media coverage to create Bánky's star mythology. In other words, the sense that Bánky was somehow demoted to a lower status in Europe—as fan discourse would have it, her family lost all of their wealth during the Great War—only to be restored to her rightful position in Hollywood, constitutes another point of conflation between the imperialist narrative and the Cinderella story.[19] This dramatic formula, however, was easily applied to other star images, constituting a main avenue through which American audiences encountered the fantasy of nobility.[20]

According to the press coverage, Bánky's father was a high-ranking official working for Franz Joseph, the king of the Austro-Hungarian Empire. Her almost regal upbringing was an entirely fictitious tale endorsed by the studio that employed her. In fact, Rachel Schildgen points out that the details regarding Bánky's personal background were reshuffled and reinvented by the studio so many times that the facts still prove difficult to rediscover.[21] *Picture Play* worked to establish Goldwyn's new star as a "mass-marketed rendition"[22] of a fairy-tale princess by providing its readership with a biographical note on Bánky's childhood:

> As her father was a prominent politician, to their home came dignitaries of the government to discuss weighty problems, officials resplendent on state occasions with much gold braid. The social life that moved sedately about her would offer the charm of an old pride to is of the world born but yesterday [*sic*]. To the young dreamer Vilma, stirred by an impulse to get out and achieve, it seemed at times frightfully dull and stodgy. Grounded from her infancy in that old civilization, surrounded by still magnificent relics of its grandeur, palaces and museums full of antiquities, galleries with pieces centuries old, she absorbed art and culture un-consciously—and longed to get away from it all into a busier life where one did things instead of musing over the archives of the past.[23]

At first glance, the description resonates as particularly nostalgic, in a sense it both seeks and refutes what Michael Williams poignantly refers to as "the lost past [that] lies somewhere beyond reach."[24] What marks this melancholic vision of Bánky's past is its reliance on the idea of high society as refined but inherently old-fashioned and resistant to progress. *Picture Play* portrayed a florid world constructed in opposition to the dynamism of American culture, which compensates for its lack of sophistication by providing constant opportunities for personal growth. It paints Europe as a world that, to use Said's terminology, is "synonymous with stability and unchanging eternality"[25] while simultaneously foreshadowing the promise of the New World. Hence, in attributing young Bánky with longing for something other than "archives of the past," it gives her a sense of agency, usually absent from the majority of press accounts penetrating to her. Most importantly though, such scenarios served an ideological role supportive of imperialism by highlighting the potential offered by America, the beacon of modernity, for all driven individuals. Myrtle Gebhart painted a similar, albeit more idolizing, picture, explaining how Bánky could have dreamed "of gold-carpeted America as the place where all things were possible because people worked and made them so" all through her childhood years. "Glamorous stories had come across the ocean to set little melodies aquiver in her heart. Ach, if only she had wings to fly to that wonderful America!"[26] The Cinderella mythology gains particular currency when read in conjunction with nationalism, as it exposes practical conventions that represent Hollywood, and the United States on a broader scale, as a place where people from all over the world are given the opportunity to reach their full potential. Symbolically, foreign players provided a unique opportunity for appraisal of the absorptive capacities of America.

Another tenet of the extratextual narrative of Bánky as passive, or even helpless, came into being by drawing attention to the problems encountered by the actress in her new national setting. The alleged difficulties she experienced in learning English were a central focus of many columns related to her private antics, especially in press features written at the beginning of her career, in 1925 and 1926. An article on Valentino's new leading lady reported Bánky cannot say much more than "lamb shops" and "pineappfel" ("an essential part of the conversation of every lady movie star"), while also insisting she is capable of expressing herself perfectly well with "her violet eyes, innocent yet coquettish, and with her pretty slim hands, and eloquent shoulders."[27] *Photoplay*'s regular column "Studio News and Gossip" was particularly prolific in bringing its readers anecdotes relating to Bánky and her frequent but often failed efforts to learn American slang. One such story remarked: "No month is complete without a bright remark from Vilma Banky. She makes life in Hollywood worth living."[28] Another month within the lifespan of the gossip column delivered a similar verdict, concluding: "Half of Vilma Bánky's charm is in the quaint way she contorts our tongue into a language of delicious meaning."[29] A common strategy in capturing the spoken English of non-American players, the press tended to mark Bánky's speech with a phonetically described Hungarian accent, also quoting her odd syntax and incorrect use of prepositions (figure 11).[30]

The concept of cuteness, as exploited by these magazine accounts, unearths a new area of consideration. First of all, presenting Bánky as unaware of the linguistic convention—and, hence, resembling a young child—was crucial in the process of erasing the specter of foreign threat, however vague, from her public persona. Reoccurring descriptions of Bánky as a delightful individual who wants to "spik—speak Eengleesh [*sic*] like as an American"[31] can be associated with the progressive juvenilization of her figure, a certain type of patronization. Although not extended to her film portrayals, the off-screen image of the actress in the first two years of her career inscribed her, somehow ambiguously, with the characteristics of both a child and a grown-up woman.

The representative scheme that defined the star as a slightly misguided yet still charming foreigner generated emotional warmth while simultaneously equating her figure with a lack of agency, which effectively rendered Bánky a safe, trouble-free version of immigrant womanhood. In the words of one columnist, Bánky's accent was "captivating and her good-natured distress at being unable to say what she wants to say is quite enchanting."[32] This specific treatment stressing childlike innocence was, to an extent, paralleled in the publicity produced for one of the greatest stars to appear on the silent screen: Mary Pickford. Although Pickford's "on and off-screen masquerade of childishness"[33] was developed much

"Marry? I Zink Ya!"

"Maybe ze husband make Meestaire Goldwyn let me bob ze hair," says Vilma Banky

By Mildred Kenworthy

IT was about as peaceful as a pre-Volstead Tammany picnic when I dropped in at the Goldwyn studio to see Vilma Banky the other day. A highly dramatic scene was in progress. Vilma in real tears; Samuel Goldwyn pacing the floor in a rage, with renewed tearing of his hair at each glance at Miss Banky's smart new shingled bob.

"Ach, but Meestaire Goldwyn, it ees only a *wig* an' can you not to see? I mus' to cut my hair—so!" she sobbed. "You do to wish me to be a true Amereecan girl, but how I can to be with ze long hair?"

"No! Do you want to lose your charm, your crowning glory?" then, exasperatedly, "Ycu simply can't cut it."

She continued to beg, "I even can to work for lees one hundred dollars on a week if but you weel to allow—"

"No! Never, and that's final!"

Learning to be an American is Miss Banky's pet hobby. That is reason enough for the affray at the studio that particular day. Her explanation of the affair impressed me as being an appeal for her happiness.

"You weel to excuse me for my Engleesh—ze ees so veree bad yet. You know?"

She laughed over it as she greeted me, but I assured her that I could understand perfectly. In fact, to lose her adorable Hungarian accent, intermingled with French and English and foreign idioms, would be to forfeit some of her charm.

"Ach, how I do to envy you ze sheengle cut!" Then confidentially, "My long hair only ees ze zing which do not to make me completely happee. I want to wear short brunette wig in a picture once. You know? I like it so much, but Meestaire Goldwyn did not to like it an' said 'No!' I did to feel so sad. I zink maybe he zink black hair not to become me, so I have ze gorgeous blond wig made an' I wear it to see Meestaire Goldwyn. It fool him so much, he did to—what you say?—fly off handle. He thought sure I did to cut ze hair.

"So-o, you zink I look as Amereecan,—even with ze awful hair?" she beamed responsive to my compliment. "An' you ask, how can I to adapt me so weel?"

A GENTLE shrug, "I don't know. Maybe—for one year we are in Spain—we look as Spanish, for one year in France, zen we are French, in Amereeca, so—you know? Always we like to travel—to learn—maybe gypsies? Here, I wear, ooh color, like ze countree. You know, ze dress I like ze most ees ze Western like ze peoples wear for ze kosbul."

After that word, we both floundered. I was a total blank and Miss Banky, puzzled, trying in vain to find an explanation, made little circles with her forefinger on her forehead. Finally I guessed it—"Costume ball?" She nodded all smiles again and continued, "I like it—color here," pointing to an imaginary handkerchief tie at the throat, "Ze beeg hat so,—uh, zat ees for why I like so much ze part in ze 'Winning of Barbara Worth.'"

[CONTINUED ON PAGE 94]

84

Figure 11. In April 1927, *Photoplay* used misspellings to signal Bánky's strong foreign accent. Source: Mildred Kenworthy, "Marry? I Zink Ya!," *Photoplay*, April 1927, 84.

further than Bánky's, this facet of her persona functioned on similar terms: to downplay her independence as both a woman and a creative professional.

In discussing the cultural logic that underpins the phenomenon of cuteness in popular imagery, Gary Genosko explains that what one describes as cute often occupies a liminal position.[34] Small animals wearing human clothing are cute specifically because they are neither here nor there, behaving like animals but often appearing surprisingly and uncannily human-like. Without delving too much into the culturally rich notion of cuteness, I would like to signal that, ideologically, Bánky occupied a comparable position of an inbetweener: a woman aiming to be American but not fully Americanized yet, and someone whose relative verbal inarticulation is understood as charming and appealing. Fan magazines employed key attributes of cuteness to meet their own ends, to make Bánky more affectively involving, and consequently more profitable. Ultimately, what makes cuteness alarming for Genosko is its ability to disarm, since, as a characteristic, cuteness is not shared by those in control.[35] Being powerless is the antithesis of being threatening; thus, the Hungarian star is deemed adorable inasmuch as she is helpless.

White Femininity

Bánky's star coverage propagated the concept of perfect white womanhood by emphasizing tranquility, elegance, and grace as characteristics inherent to her persona. "Miss Banky's charm is a subtle, winsome appeal which one associates inevitably with the truly feminine," declared one journalist writing for *Picture Play*.[36] Correspondingly, Eugene V. Brewster spoke of Bánky as "a gentle type of femininity" who "has a soft, sweet voice, a pleasant smile and a winsome personality. She is distinctly feminine, rather quiet and vivacious, and subdued rather than demonstrative."[37] Such discursive remarks went hand in hand with descriptions of Bánky's physical, conspicuously white appearance. Although not doing so explicitly, all these accounts share a common denominator of lauding Bánky as representative of the highest, universally appealing standards of humanity.

Arguably, films shot in black and white cannot bring out the contrast between certain hair colors as distinctively as color photography, so the audiences had to gain their understanding of star features through other, noncinematic sources. Colorful covers of popular fan magazines were one such source (figures 12a and 12b). Articles did not fall short in reminding their target readers who is fair-haired and who is not in Hollywood: "It seems, too, to have been a season for blondes, when one considers a spotlight of interest that has been cast upon such golden-haired personalities as Vilma Banky, Norma Shearer, etc."[38] Bánky's blue eyes that "could melt a heart of steel"[39] were potent signifiers of radiant beauty

Figures 12a and 12b. The cover girl. Bánky, as imagined on the covers of popular fan magazines. Source: *Photoplay*, April 1926, and *Picture Play*, December 1926.

and spiritual virtue. In discussing on-screen blondness, Ellen Tremper views it as emblematic of a precapitalist, near-mythic past—a form of nostalgia for pastoral but inherently lost agrarian culture.[40] Particularly in the historical setting of the 1920s, the privileged characteristics of innocence and humility found their fullest realization in the blonde beauty type, a trope investigated, to some extent,

in the Pola Negri case study. Moreover, the notorious emphasis on physical attractiveness exacerbated passivity in Bánky's career, placing looks above acting craft.[41] Therefore, it is telling that the star is never referred to in relation to her talents, but in the context of her appearance and modest demeanor.

Richard Dyer has shown how, according to Western racial ideology, whiteness is not an ethnicity but, instead, a lack of it; it is a naught that has to be brought forward in juxtaposition to darkness because "being white is simply being human."[42] Dyer's work has also illuminated the ways in which lighter, paler skin is synonymous with beauty, especially in women; indeed, as he notes, the gallant term for women, "the fair sex," implies a distinct skin color.[43] The way in which fan discourse framed Bánky's beauty as a universal feminine ideal—rather than an example of a specific ethnic type—exposes the ideological imperatives of the West, with its pragmatic assumption that whiteness represents a superior way of being.

Star texts are based on the norms shared by Western society as a whole. They are a part of a cultural ethos that continues to conflate whiteness with normality and universality, which guarantees white people a position of privilege over people of color.[44] Overwhelmingly, the whiteness of white bodies functions as an invisible standard, constituting what Francesca T. Royster calls "the unraced center of a racialized word."[45] Thus, one of *Picture Play*'s features identified Bánky's physiognomy as "cosmopolitan" and not indicative of any particular nationality,[46] while *Photoplay* considered her to be "the almost perfect Anglo-Saxon type," whose beauty registers as English in front of the camera, despite her Hungarian heritage.[47] The latter mention capitalizes on the highly positive connotations of the English as residing at the top of the international hierarchy of whiteness, one of the "whitest" ethnic groups (superseded only, it can be argued, by the perfect whiteness of the Nordic races).

Seen through the racial myopia of the era, Bánky was presented as a delicate woman of grace, refinement, and last but not least, modesty. This narrative tendency comes as no surprise, given a long-standing iconographic tradition that associates female beauty with moral virtue. By inscribing Bánky's bodily capital with visible aspects of whiteness—such as blonde hair and blue eyes—the star system perpetuated a positive view of Bánky as a woman of "transparent and spiritual kind that should bring a new note of refinement" to the screen, someone "very gracious and composed."[48] Restraint, assigned so frequently to Bánky's off-screen demeanor, is—as Julian B. Carter asserts—a part of the normative web of ideas related to whiteness, which is both "natural" and a result of constant self-control.[49] The symbolic connotations of the color white, such as purity, spirituality, transcendence, and simplicity, constructed a frame that supported the construction of Bánky's persona.

The privileged place of whiteness in Western discourse comes at a price: to be truly white is to be clean both physically and metaphorically, to be pure and innocent; these qualities prove incredibly hard to sustain in the context of modernity and its constant liberalization of sexual norms. Again, Dyer details how the lure of the white ideal is haunted by anxiety linked to the contamination caused by the outside world.[50] The idea of Bánky as representative of racial and sexual wholeness is evident in the letter written by a fan to *Photoplay* at the dawn of her popularity. Noting what she perceived as the increasing presence of sex on American screens, the author expressed her worry over the future of one of her favorite screen players: "Vilma Bánky will rise to great heights if they do not spoil her. She has beauty and refinement, combined with perfect technique. It is extremely unpleasant to contemplate what they might make her into: an over-marvelled, over made-up unnatural puppet."[51]

Mobilizing the contrast between the idealized version of femininity and visibly constructed representations of womanhood, the letter presumed that Hollywood's commercial product is essentially based on a degree of artificiality that can somehow stain the perfect reputation of its leading stars. The fan goes on to suggest that the popular commercial tactic of using eroticism to sell films is as despicable as it is unnecessary, given the financial success achieved by *The Dark Angel*, an allegedly sexless film. "Those who claim the public demands sex plays are wrong," she concludes.[52] The fan press helped sketch the contours of Bánky's persona for moviegoers in aligning the actress with discourses of authenticity. Professing his admiration for an "almost extinct charm of the lady," another journalist successfully juxtaposed Bánky to "celluloid counterfeit so common to Hollywood,"[53] as he termed the majority of female film players. Again, the strategy that underpins these texts echoes the cultural understanding of whiteness where, to maintain its illusion of superiority, it has to be presented as natural and not performed.

The writers of *Photoplay* regularly compared Bánky with Pola Negri, either to dwell on the potential rivalry between the two—Bánky played Valentino's lover in *The Son of the Sheik* (1926) at the time when the actor was rumored to be engaged to Negri—or to explore their contrasting ethnic images. Cal York employed Bánky as the edifice of natural beauty, writing that she regularly attended dinner parties "without any vestige of lipstick, rouge, mascara, and only a light dusting powder to prevent shine."[54] In abstaining from artifice, she provided a visual alternative to the look favored by Pola Negri, with her penchant for heavy makeup. In fact, the connection between whiteness and naturalness is made explicit through the assertion that "no makeup off-stage" is a look that can be sported, to startling results, specifically by blonde women. The article elevates white female sexuality in relationship to non-white sexuality and assumes that Bánky represents inaccessible perfection, a "sublime object of desire," as opposed to the "accessible, material means of attaining carnal satisfaction" connoted by Negri's signature, highly sexualized look.[55] These dynamics were elucidated in the discourse of the late 1920s by referring to Negri as the former love interest of Bánky's then husband, Rod La Rocque:

> Before Rod La Rocque met and married Vilma Banky, the only other lady with whom his name had been linked seriously was Pola Negri. Now, I ask you! Outside of the fact that Rod seems to prefer foreign attraction, you couldn't say there was any point of similarity between these two. Where Pola is the vivid, scarlet flame, Vilma is the soft candle-light. One is dark. The other is

> light. One is the woman of the world. The other is a girl who might have been merely a wife if circumstances haven't [*sic*] made a movie star out of her. Pola's face is chalky-white and her eyes are black pools of both expression and make-up. Vilma seldom bothers to dust her lovely nose with powder. Pola can't play unless she can hold the center of the stage. Vilma timidly seeks quiet corners.[56]

Here, the juxtaposition between Bánky and Negri extends beyond the visual terms, incorporating everything they stand for, their temperaments, different outlooks, and even the sense of agency they exerted over their consecutive rises to the Hollywood pantheon. Other gossip surrounding Bánky described her as a reason for jealousy on the part of Negri. In August 1926 *Motion Picture Classic* claimed that the Polish star did not feel confident knowing Valentino had to hold Bánky in his arms, even if it was only a part of his professional endeavor. Regardless of rumors, moviegoers could safely assume that "there is not and never has been any romance between Vilma Banky and Rudolph Valentino. . . . Vilma dines all alone in her dressing room."[57]

Yet, even within those narratives, Bánky is constructed as an antithesis of the seductive. In fact, contemporaneous fan magazines contain no suggestion of anything other than friendship between the leading stars of *The Son of the Sheik*. In keeping with the image of innocence ascribed to her persona, there is an aura of otherworldliness, an escalation beyond matters of sex in her conduct. The lack of interest in romance fed into the image of Bánky as representative of perfect womanhood; the purity she connoted was incompatible with the highly sexualized image of Valentino, the famous Latin lover.

Extratextual strategies built around Bánky's early life in America contained references to her struggle in adapting to new surroundings, namely in mastering the language and becoming part of the Hollywood circle. *Motion Picture Classic* described difficulties she had in expressing herself in her new tongue, attributing her perceived aloofness—and the resulting loneliness—to her heavy foreign accent. "Yes, she is lonesome at times," explained the article, "and then she reads."[58] In February 1926, *Picture Play* quoted the star: "I ant lonesome at first, mooch homesick. I know so few peoples, and I never go out. Home to my bong-mow from the studio, my dinner, an hour to read, then bed. My rest I must have or I cannot work. After a while I meet peoples. Inn it is hard to make friends. One, two, tree, enough."[59]

To an extent, these accounts used the star as a means of articulating broader cultural shifts of the time, particularly those related to personal isolation caused by the increase in social mobility and weakening of familial ties. They evoked a certain construction of the 1920s émigré, introspective and alone, applicable to Jetta Goudal and Greta Garbo, as the next case study will outline. Most importantly, though, they cultivate the notion of Bánky as a "lonely stranger"[60] located "three thousand miles away from home"[61] and someone who needs guidance in navigating the buzzing world of the capital of movies. According to the fan lore, she treasured the kindness extended to her by Goldwyn, her producer, and by fellow actress Norma Talmadge. One cannot help but notice the striking contrast between the terms that described Pola Negri's arrival to America—where, to quote William McKegg, she was about to "dazzle the film colony"[62]—and the descriptions of Bánky and her first quiet months in adjusting to the industry. "The Discovery of Vilma Banky"[63] centers on such contrasts. Here Bánky comes forth as first and foremost an outsider, a misplaced and despondent little girl, which naturally located her in direct opposition to the persona of a foreign diva. Where Negri was disrupting the status quo and abusing the system in full awareness of her power, Bánky kept to herself, appearing confused or even unable to cope in the new cultural environment.

Class

Many critical examinations of whiteness point to the intersectionality between race and class. In his analysis of whiteness in film, Sean Redmond has demonstrated how star images were underpinned by racial cartography, where "spirit, purity and power became the markers of the refined upper class or nobility, while nature, earth/dirt and primitive urges became the ideological indicator of the working class."[64] Alistair Bonnet theorized how ethnic identities were historically class inflicted, indicating that the highest echelons of Western society were traditionally occupied by people whose skin tone seemed "hyper white" in comparison with the darker complexion of the working classes.[65] Furthermore, the promise of upward mobility—the structuring principle of the American Dream—was not extended to nonwhites, suggesting a social pattern where skin color is the determining factor of class, and "no amount of beauty, money, aristocratic trappings or movie fame" could change one's ethnic character.[66] Applying this paradigm to Bánky's figure, one can see that discourses of class and race are inescapably bound to one another. Writing in *Motion Picture Classic*, Brewster deployed the idea of high social standing in the description of Bánky's immaculate demeanor: "She was dressed very simply, almost plainly, and her manner and appearance were that of a lady high-born—a typical princess."[67] Thus, Brewster's account mitigated the symbolic positioning of Bánky within the realm of the upper class, advocating she possesses a special quality that eludes clear-cut definitions. The modest dress she wears remains at odds with the cultural notion of fashion that would be favored by "a princess," usually associated with expensive clothing, wealth of detail, and ornament.

In juxtaposing plain attire to the privileged background of his subject, the journalist creates a paradoxical image that articulates uniqueness of the star, where Bánky appears at once ordinary and superior to the members of the public.[68] In cultural terms, her identity as a princess is represented as hardwired in her biology; she is imbued with a distinct "aura" that cannot be disguised by the simplicity of her outfit. The rhetoric that described Bánky in the context of high class positioning remained its potency even decades after her retirement from the screen. In 1959, Joe Franklin wrote: "[Bánky] was a graceful, beautiful creature, a lady in the fullest sense of the word, with a regal bearing in every moment and gesture she made. She should never have played anything but princesses and aristocrats—and for the most part she never did. . . . And Vilma's beauty—a timeless beauty that doesn't change with the passing years—is still available on celluloid to those who have never forgotten."[69] In June 1929, William McKegg described his meeting with Goldwyn's chief star in the following words: "[Bánky] was dressed in white, which made her look wraithlike. The sun lit up her golden hair, and the whole effect caused my poor senses to swim and swim. Vilma was quiet at first. . . . It was obvious that this shyness was natural with her. I was quiet, too. But I had been stricken dumb by her ethereal loveliness."[70]

Here the star is narrativized in reference to the fruitful iconography of the color white—the symbol of purity—and to sunshine and light, which connote translucence and ephemerality. Accounts of this nature became a staple offering in the repertoire of articles on Bánky. For Redmond, whiteness manifests its extraordinary position especially in relation to light, which makes white women "glow, appear angelic, heavenly, and, ultimately, to be not-of-this-world, heavenly absences rather than fleshed beings."[71] By focusing on her white dress, the account not only highlights the radiant, ethnic characteristics of the blonde star but also suggests a sense of moral superiority. As proposed in Alison Lurie's discussion of the importance of color in fashion, "white has always been popular with those who wish to demonstrate wealth and status through the conspicuous consumption of laundry soap or conspicuous freedom from manual labour."[72] When employed in a context of luxury, white clothing functioned to convey the same ideological meanings to that of white people themselves—that is, the sense of superiority paired with restraint.[73]

"Vilma, with a bright aureole of love shining about her, wore a gown of chartreuse green and silver,"[74] wrote *Photoplay* about Bánky's look at the opening of a new picture palace. The popularity of silver in dress is linked, as Stephen Gundle and Clino Castelli contend, to the measure of restraint and "a sense of [the] plurality of treasures" it conveys, because its aesthetic effect is comparable to that of white and gold.[75] Clothes and aspects of costume are implicit in cultural connotations, but are also assumed to indicate the personality and temperament of the wearer. The process of pointing out both wider social differentiations and one's personal taste is what Dyer calls a dual articulation of dress.[76] In arguing that "silver and gold could equally be represented by white and gold or by white garments and blonde hair,"[77] Gundle and Castelli make an explicit connection between these colors, ethnic whiteness, and the notion of good taste.

Thus, the popular discourse evidences how the diligently regulated racial body of the star was utilized as a class marker, effectively situating Bánky within a fantasy of nobility and status.

Advertising constituted another avenue that succinctly outlined the appeal of Bánky's star image by attesting to her conspicuous whiteness. Within the confines of commodity culture, stars are both subjects and objects of advertising, because their endorsements capitalize on their image while concurrently working to increase their star value. In sponsoring luxurious goods such as perfumes, soap, or cigarettes, movie players multiplied their commercial potential.[78] In 1927 fan magazines ran a series of promotional articles that used Bánky's image to endorse Palmolive soap, a product that, as Dyer argues, has a particularly troubled history of generating racist images.[79] Soap advertisements tend to implicitly refer to the idea of racial purity, promulgating the message that the cleaner one is, the whiter one's skin.[80] Fox suggests that the obsession with cleanliness and personal hygiene is in fact just a visual extension of the fascination with whiteness, as it promotes "a white, Anglo-Saxon protestant vision of a tasteless, colourless, odourless, sweatless world."[81] Thus, cultural fantasies of whiteness tied physical cleanness to spiritual purity.

The racial dimensions of the image are brought home by the association between white skin and the manufacture of the body that requires minimal intervention—or, in fact, just maintenance—so it can be kept "natural, unpolluted and pure."[82] This piece of promotional material equates American women with the perfect evocation of beauty, claiming that "America's complexions are the envy of the world."[83] As such, the article is careful not to mark Bánky as non-American. What is aesthetically intriguing here is the image of Bánky with a peculiar figure of a man, lit so purely as if to resemble a silhouette. By deploying this contrasting imagery, the visual composition allows the whiteness of the star to come to the forefront.

The way in which Hollywood managed Bánky's ethnic identity, clearly evidenced by the codified attributes of Palmolive advertising, remained intact even when her career was on the wane. For example, the lexicon employed by a letter published by *Picture Play*—written by an overzealous fan who saw Bánky perform live in Pittsburgh—encapsulates a broader ideological vision of whiteness and its compliant notions, such as immaculateness, naturalness, and extreme beauty. On stage, the star appeared a "thousand times more beautiful" than on celluloid; her skin was smooth and white.[84]

Conclusion

The fetishization of Bánky in the context of the Cinderella myth is significant not only for its construction of European heritage as a commercial selling point but also for its "rags to riches" and gender connotations. To the moviegoing public, the actress achieved stardom through a fortunate wrench of fate rather than through her conscious efforts; thus, her rise to movie fame was encoded as a patriarchal text that denied her any form of agency. Her star narrative shares a conceptual alliance with the figure of Cinderella, because she was positioned in terms of who she was not—that is, not influential, not active, and not male. In orchestrating a publicity campaign that marked Bánky as a delicate woman of noble blood—and someone who was, to paraphrase one of the fan magazines, pushed into the show—Goldwyn made sure that she was constructed as both normal and extraordinary.

In enclosing Bánky within the narrative of émigré solitude, the studio managed to legitimize her as inadvertently more authentic than the majority of Hollywood's star product, precisely because she was preoccupied with ordinary actions most, if not all, film fans could identify with, such as cooking and reading. The publicity surrounding Bánky's personal life shortly after she commenced working for Goldwyn's production company would continue to employ the notion of misplacement and loneliness, partially to accommodate for her image as a shy bookworm, and partially to frame her as nonthreatening. Similarly, the proliferation of sources accentuating her cuteness served an ideological function in cultivating her submissiveness. It also showed Bánky as an eager subject of Americanization, not only as an actress who owed her "lucky break" to her producer but also an individual in debt to the transformative power of America at large.

Some scholarly evaluations of whiteness have followed Dyer in suggesting that Western culture frames it not in terms of ethnic belonging but as a universal human ideal.[85] Mainly in the mode of behavior ascribed to women, being white is highly reliant on restraint and modesty, ideas that were repeatedly echoed in magazine mentions of Bánky. Details developed in these articles suggested that Bánky was, to use William K. Everson's words, "solidly locked into the innocent, almost Victorian simplicities."[86] To put it simply, she incarnated the highest ideals of whiteness; her gentle way of being and feminine charm were a natural extension of her (conspicuously white) physical attributes. In juxtaposition to the sultry presence of Pola Negri, Bánky's stardom connoted the ideas of naturalness and bespoke a sense of white superiority, which, in turn, helped her lodge herself into the dominant discourse of interwar America.

CHAPTER 4

Vilma Bánky as the Leading Lady

"BEDECKED IN FLOWING GOWNS . . . AND LAYERS OF PEARLS AND JEWELS"

Summarized by *Picture Play* as an "old story of a blinded soldier,"[1] Bánky's American screen debut, *The Dark Angel* (1925), was a romantic drama set against the backdrop of the Great War. Receiving wide critical acclaim for its realism, magnificent settings, superb photography, and the beauty and acting skill of its leading lady, the film propelled Bánky to the spotlight virtually overnight.[2] Based on a scenario written by Frances Marion, it provided a blueprint for the future celluloid characterizations of the Hungarian star, as well as establishing Ronald Colman, an English actor, as her most frequent co-star. Buoyed by the public's reception of their on-screen chemistry, Goldwyn made plans to team them up in his upcoming film ventures.

I have already explored the ways in which Bánky was promoted as a modern incarnation of Cinderella across such sites as magazine articles, interviews, and fan letters. In this chapter, I draw on the totality of Bánky's star vehicles—some of which are no longer extant—to inspect how cinematic sources of her stardom both informed and validated her off-screen persona. Hollywood's history is notorious, as Virginia Wright Wexman argues, for investing the fictional roles of matinee idols "with a degree of verisimilitude that allows not only the actors themselves to be positioned as social models but also the characters they play."[3] In accordance with venerable convention, the characteristic features of an actress's on-screen performance could serve to inform her public persona, and vice versa. Such claims resonate with the notion that audiences manufacture star identities by looking for traces of the authentic self of the actor in their performance, even though the role itself is understood to have little to do with the realities of the actor's livelihood. These ideas have been touched on in the Pola Negri case study.

My main interest lies in the recurring elements of the various romantic heroines Bánky came to portray throughout her Hollywood career. Concentrating on the silent features that are still extant, such as *The Eagle* (1925), *The Son of the Sheik* (1926), and *The Winning of Barbara Worth* (1926), this part of the study provides an overview of films that were met with commercial success, and thus proved crucial in sketching the outline of Bánky's persona, particularly in the context of her safe sexuality. In the case of the movies that are not extant, I rely largely on reviews and plot outlines provided by the contemporaneous press.

Debut and *The Eagle*

Goldwyn's studio was heavily invested in the promotion of its newest contract player, lauding Bánky nationwide "as the greatest star ever to arrive on American shores."[4] The fierce publicity process surrounding the release of *The Dark Angel* attracted criticism from some quarters, including moviegoers who thought it unfair to pay so much attention to someone who was merely an inexperienced newcomer to the national film industry. In the words of one skeptical reader of *Picture Play*, "Miss Banky was billed as 'the most beautiful actress on the screen,' 'the actress with the most beautiful form,' 'the leading emotional actress of the screen,' and various other extreme though ambiguous statements. With a sensational fanfare such as this, most [*sic*] everybody went to see Miss Banky with that *you-gotta-show-me* attitude, and many felt that they had been *fooled again*."[5] The letter noted, however, that leaving aside all studio-generated praise, Bánky was undoubtedly a very skilled actress. Certainly, the popular press was unanimous in describing her debut in *The Dark Angel* in highly positive terms. "Vilma Bánky is not only a radiant beauty, but also an actress who performs with ease and charm," suggested the *New York Times*, adding that "her loveliness will be a feature in any screen story in which she appears, as nobody will be surprised at a hero falling victim to her soft pleading eyes."[6]

In her evaluation of Bánky's career, Rachel Schildgen has suggested that Bánky's oeuvre was replete "with dramatic retellings of the glorious past."[7] Indeed, four of the eight American silent features Bánky starred in were broadly understood as period dramas, which made the actress something of an expert in portraying "women bedecked in flowing gowns and festooned with layers of pearls and jewels."[8] Lea Jacobs also makes an explicit link between romantic dramas—one of the most financially successful genres of the decade, in which stories were "set in the exotic locales or in the distant past"—and Bánky, as she lists her as one of the major stars associated with the genre, alongside Rudolph Valentino, John Gilbert, and Ronald Colman.[9] Of course, it has to be noted that moving pictures of the era were produced as so-called star vehicles, showcasing the star's public persona by providing some aspect of consistency with her previous work, either in teaming up with the same male lead or in casting as a similar type or within comparable historical settings.[10]

Big-budget costume dramas were a prominent fixture in the changing landscape of early and mid-1920s Hollywood. On one level, the growing production of films set in the historical past was dictated by pragmatic financial choices faced by the studio executives. "Bookkeepers wrote the costs of all sets and costumes against the film for which they were made; as a result, any subsequent uses were free. This encouraged the reuse of sets and a return to the same genres," explains David Bordwell in his seminal work on the American film industry.[11] On another level, and beyond economic considerations, costume dramas were instructive in responding to "a specific spectatorial desire for escapism into an ahistorical time of myth and magic, inured to the ravages of urbanization [and] industrialization."[12] In other words, silent historical epics were tailored to cater to audiences' desire for spectacle while also providing a conceptualization of chivalry and romance untarnished by the shifting gender discourse of the time of their production.

Jeffrey Richards describes the manner in which, as a genre, these films were characterized by prioritizing aesthetic stylization over realism, and emphasizing the sense of adventure and daring rather than historical fidelity.[13] He defines them as "swashbuckler films"—a subcategory of costume drama where romance and swordplay are mainstays—as a prevalent form taken by the genre during the 1920s. Bánky's stardom was constructed around the notions of respectable (and largely passive) femininity, concepts that were easily accommodated by this type of drama. Because it was one of the most conservative genres, at least as far as gender portrayal is concerned, it positioned its female protagonist as a damsel awaiting a savior.

In her second vehicle, *The Eagle* (1925), Bánky was cast as the daughter of a wealthy Russian landowner during the reign of Catherine the Great. As stated by Goldwyn's biographer, Rudolph Valentino insisted on employing Bánky as his co-star for the film, being enamored with her after watching *The Dark Angel*.[14] This time, the production was made under the banner of United Artists, which allowed Goldwyn to cash in by renting out Bánky's services as a performer.

The opening sequence of this epic depicts the first encounter between Lieutenant Dubrovsky (Valentino) and Masha (Bánky), as the handsome man saves her from being kidnapped. One might extrapolate the significance of their meeting for the further development of the plot, given that the motion picture builds on the trope of the damsel in distress, a patriarchal fantasy that has long foregrounded the depictions of love in mainstream art. In accordance with this representational pattern, the act of rescue perpetuated by the hero equates Bánky's character with the trophy awarded for his exceptional bravery. At that point, Dubrovsky is unaware of Masha's precarious status as the daughter of the man who had seized his father's familial estate. In a plot description by Miriam

Figure 13. Valentino as Dubrovsky with the czarina (Louise Dresser). Source: German postcard by Ross Verlag, no. 3677/1, 1928–1929. Photo: United Artists.

Hansen, "as the young woman returns the glance, she enters the romantic pact, acknowledging the power of his look(s)."[15] While Bánky exchanges the look from the film's protagonist, her "to-be-looked-at-ness"[16] within the scene is counterbalanced by the negative position appointed to Catherine the Great (Louise Dresser), who observes the rescue action unacknowledged by Valentino's gaze, with her face "momentarily transfigured in desire."[17]

Portraying Catherine the Great in terms of sexual insatiability was by no means a development pioneered by *The Eagle*, but a long-standing tactic that has persisted across a plethora of other cultural texts.[18] One noteworthy source that defined the empress in such terms was, in fact, *Forbidden Paradise* (1924), analyzed in the previous case study.[19] Suggesting debauchery in relation to the monarch operated to highlight the notion that female political power constitutes an ultimate reversal of the ascribed gender positions. Much of the film's comedic potential is built around the juxtaposition between the young, seemingly inaccessible Masha and the czarina, an older and sexually aggressive woman who pursues soldiers in her own guard in exchange for military status. Masha's standing as a representational antithesis to the czarina is inadvertently highlighted through visual means, particularly by costume: while the former wears delicate gowns and elaborate Russian dress, the latter is seen mostly in military uniform (figure 13).

Moreover, Bánky's heroine gains in moral stature because she is constructed in opposition to the corporeal aspects emblematized by the czarina and, by extension, in referencing the idealistic notions of the spirit rather than the body. This binary equation harks back to the ideological schemata of whiteness as transcendent, inasmuch as a physical quality. Confronted with this notorious man-eater, Dubrovsky chooses to desert the army rather than to conform to the czarina's advances, eventually assuming a new identity as a Robin Hood–esque hero, the defender of the downtrodden, by the name of Black Eagle. "I enlisted for war service only" proclaims the proud lieutenant as he leaves the czarina's chamber in haste. To paraphrase Wood, *The Eagle* testifies to the universality of Western fantasy because it reduces two major female characters to archetypes of the Mother and the Whore, two fundamental myths reinforced within patriarchal society.[20] In the initial scenes of *The Eagle*, Valentino is defined as a target of seduction, a "reluctant male trapped by the lustful designs of a female seductress," which constitutes an ultimate reversion of his most famous role of predatory lover in *The Sheik*.[21]

The main challenge encountered by Dubrovsky in his quest to challenge Kirilla—the corrupt man who robbed him of his inheritance—is that the villain has a familial relationship with his love interest. One might argue that this obstacle naturally falls into the remit of "courtly love,"[22] in the sense that Masha's inaccessibility not only elevates her status as an object of desire but also creates the chief force driving the narrative forward. For Lacanian theorists, this is a culturally persistent trope structured around "libidinal intensification" where hindrances and complications function to strengthen the desire to attain one's goal. "Obstacles," writes John Richardson, "are necessary in this understanding to preserve the illusion that without them the object would be *instantly accessible*."[23]

Masha's initial rejection of Black Eagle's advances ("I don't associate with masked men as a rule") is hardly surprising, given the representation of romantic courtship in the bulk of popular Hollywood productions, as well as within Western cultural texts more broadly. Popular fictions on page and screen have long favored a contrivance in which heteronormative unity is achieved through the process of deferred courtship—that is, where the heroine is initially reluctant to fall under the hero's spell but does so eventually after he proves himself worthy of her affection. The "seduction plot," as Jacobs terms it, was one of the central motifs of eighteenth-century sentimental literature that has been successfully disseminated across a great number of films, albeit in varying forms.[24]

As the action moves on, Dubrovsky gets closer to his arch nemesis—and, most significantly, to his daughter—by applying for the position of a French teacher in Kirilla's household. Bánky's character resents Black Eagle at first, thinking very little of his chivalry and compliments. After she discovers the real identity of her French teacher, the narrative trajectory moves to emphasize Masha's internal conflict: "I hate you!" she screams. Eventually, she can no longer maintain the distance between herself and Dubrovsky, admitting, "Day and night I have fought against loving you—fought and lost!"

Of course, Masha wields little power on her own, being defined primarily through her relationship with the film's chief antagonist. In the end, the masked hero forsakes the oath of vengeance he has taken, concluding that "revenge is sweet, but sometimes a girl is sweeter." In its critical appraisal of the film, the *New York Times* deliberated that this dramatic shift is understandable, given the astonishingly good looks of Bánky's character; "her beauty makes the hero's gallantry all the more convincing."[25] *The Eagle* culminates with the assumption that romantic fulfillment is a panacea for virtually all societal problems, including class struggle. The fight between the underprivileged citizens of the Russian state and the landowning class, epitomized here by Kirilla, is effectively eclipsed by the nuances of heteronormative romance.

The film's release was followed by a campaign that, in many respects, transplanted the qualities of Masha-the-heroine—her desirability, but also lack of agency—to Bánky-the-star. Strategically placed press reports spread the news that the man claiming to be Bánky's Hungarian fiancé came to Paris to confront her co-star Valentino, whom he perceived as a love rival. Schildgen points out that the accounts reporting on a transatlantic love affair between Bánky and her suitor first entered the magazine discourse in early September 1925; by mid-October the narrative was, to use the author's phrasing, "a full-blown tale of love, longing, and lust separated by the Atlantic Ocean."[26] It continued to appear in the press until February of the following year.

According to Goldwyn's biographer, the story and its main protagonist, the ersatz baron (also referred to as a count) Imre Lukatz, were fabricated for promotional gain by the said producer and his publicity director, Roy Coffin.[27] As professionals in charge of public relations, they knew that many film vehicles would attract little notice if it were not for the public "frenzied with curiosity" about the previously unknown female lead.[28]

In many instances, the gossip columns relating to the event took the exact same shape—this is specifically true of newspapers, less so of film publications, which tended to be more creative with the guidelines and material supplied to them by the studios—including the featured text, headline ("Just Like the Movies"), and accompanying photos.[29] Such uniformity confirms the status of the Valentino/Lukatz affair as a promotional endeavor arranged and circulated by the studio officials.

The *Pittsburgh Press* reported that the crazed baron waited for Valentino in the lobby of the Mogador Theatre to challenge him to a duel: "The love-sick Baron Imre Lukatz, who still imagines himself the fiancé of the pretty screen star, picks a fight with Rudolph Valentino and they stage one of those nobody-gets-hurt French duels."[30] The following dawn, Valentino was said to take a pair of swords to their meeting spot. No clash of steel transpired, though, since the baron realized the inappropriateness of his behavior. The duel did not miss the attention of the editors of *Photoplay*, who described Imre Lukatz as a man driven by lovesickness, so exasperated by Valentino's cinematic lovemaking to Bánky that he has lost the ability to distinguish between reality and fiction.[31]

It is important to note that dueling in the United States had fallen out of favor by the outbreak of the Civil War. The practice survived longer on the Continent, although it commenced to be seen as an anachronism by the turn of the century. The outdated nature of Lukatz's challenge gave him an aura of a relic and an outsider immersed in the past so deeply that he became unable to navigate the dynamics of the modern world, incarnated by the cinematic medium and, by extension, the American ways of living. He personified Europe not only at its most highbrow, but also at its most redundant.[32]

Intrinsically, Bánky's position as a passive observer within this publicity-driven ploy replicated the narrative formula of *The Eagle*, where she is assigned a position of an object of admiration. She has very little, if nothing, to say about her own fate. Her reaction to the incident is consciously absent from the fan magazines, as she is not marked as a participant of this manly pursuit, functioning purely as an ideological means to elevate the position of the winner, merely a prospective trophy. The story of Lukatz's jealousy is reminiscent of the patriarchal logic framing the tales of romance within the parameters of "courtly love" and love triangles, both ideas that I have outlined in the context of *The Eagle*.

The Son of the Sheik

The Eagle was not the only professional obligation for Bánky working on loan to United Artists. A few months after the release of the film, the star was signed to perform alongside the famous Latin lover in yet another picture, a sequel to the critically acclaimed *The Sheik*. In respect to its mixture of lavish mise-en-scéne and a storyline that combined action and farcical elements, *The Son of the Sheik* drew heavily on what could be considered a model for commercial success formulated in the vehicles that preceded it, *The Sheik* and *The Eagle*. Released in September 1926, *The Son of the Sheik* capitalized on the popularity of Orientalist tropes in filmmaking at the peak of the silent era. Set amid epic chases on African plains (in a semi-fantastic realm far removed from the mundane world of ordinary Western existence), the film included, in Gaylyn Studlar's words, "allusions to the Orient through prologues, flashbacks, and dance interludes, through set and costume design."[33]

The plot revolves around the daring exploits of Ahmed, a youth of the Sahara Desert, who falls in love with Yasmin, an Arabian dancer, played by Bánky. Yasmin is promised to a horrifying cutthroat, Gahbah, "whose crimes outnumber the desert sand." Yet these plans are thwarted by her growing affection for Ahmed. Overcome with jealousy, Gahbah captures and tortures the titular protagonist, making him believe Yasmin is responsible for the abduction. In turn, convinced that the dancer has betrayed him, Ahmed escapes his captors, deciding to seek his revenge. What follows is a quick succession of rip-roaring fights, kidnappings, and reconciliations, all completed in the name of heterosexual desire.

In arguably one of the most problematic encounters in the history of silent film, Ahmed abducts Yasmin and brings her to his tent. Jeanine Basinger describes the scene as Valentino "tosses [Bánky] around" to display his anger; he is finally seen herding her ruthlessly toward his bed as he slowly raises his arms up to both push her down and embrace her ("Rape as romance!"[34]). Although not presented in graphic terms, the skirmish does indeed heavily suggest rape. In sexually assaulting Bánky's heroine, Valentino traded on his physiognomic ability to be the racial Other, both incapable of controlling his animal urges and using sexual violence as a form of vengeance. By this measure, the desert chieftain deploys the dark force of sexuality to humiliate his victim and contaminate her purity. "So, my young charmer, your mission in life is to lure men into lonely ruins—to be robbed and tortured!" he exclaims in anger, with the intertitle being followed by a close-up of a fearful Yasmin. Throughout the scene, Valentino assumes a position of superiority, his hands crossed on his chest in a manner that speaks of aggression and power. Bánky is repeatedly pushed to the floor. She looks up to Ahmed in an attempt to explain herself, but seemingly to no avail. In the midst of the fight the man moves his hand up in dramatic gesture, to proclaim "an eye for an eye—a hate for a hate—this is the law of my father!" a direct rephrasing of the infamously cruel ancient code of Hammurabi. The reference functions as a means of reaffirming the position of the Orient not only as a brutal place beyond the rules of civilization but also as one that is deeply immersed in its semi-mythical past. This is a prime example of Edward Said's argument about how the representation of exotic Arabian worlds as never-changing realms that contradict principles of modernity has gained wide currency in the cultural traditions of the West.[35]

In the film's rape-seduction scene, Ahmed moves toward his victim, emerging from the shadows, as she moves back in fear. The arrangement of light and dark, transparency and substance, full-blown sexuality and sexual indifference,[36] is used to bring Yasmin's delicate white femininity to the forefront (figure 14). Her facial features are framed here by the soft diffused lighting that minimizes the irregularities of surfaces, making her skin appear naturally smooth and radiant. As theorized by Kobal, "the balance of light and shade is crucial in dramatizing and conferring an atmosphere of sexual allure on the [film's] subjects."[37]

The dancer's body is covered in a white gown that glistens with jewels, whereas Ahmed's face, by contrast, is given a crisp, sharply defined outline through the use of low-key lighting. Traditionally, technological developments embraced by Hollywood filmmakers drew on this aesthetic apparatus to render white women as idealized beings, permeated by an otherworldly glow.[38] Additionally, Dyer

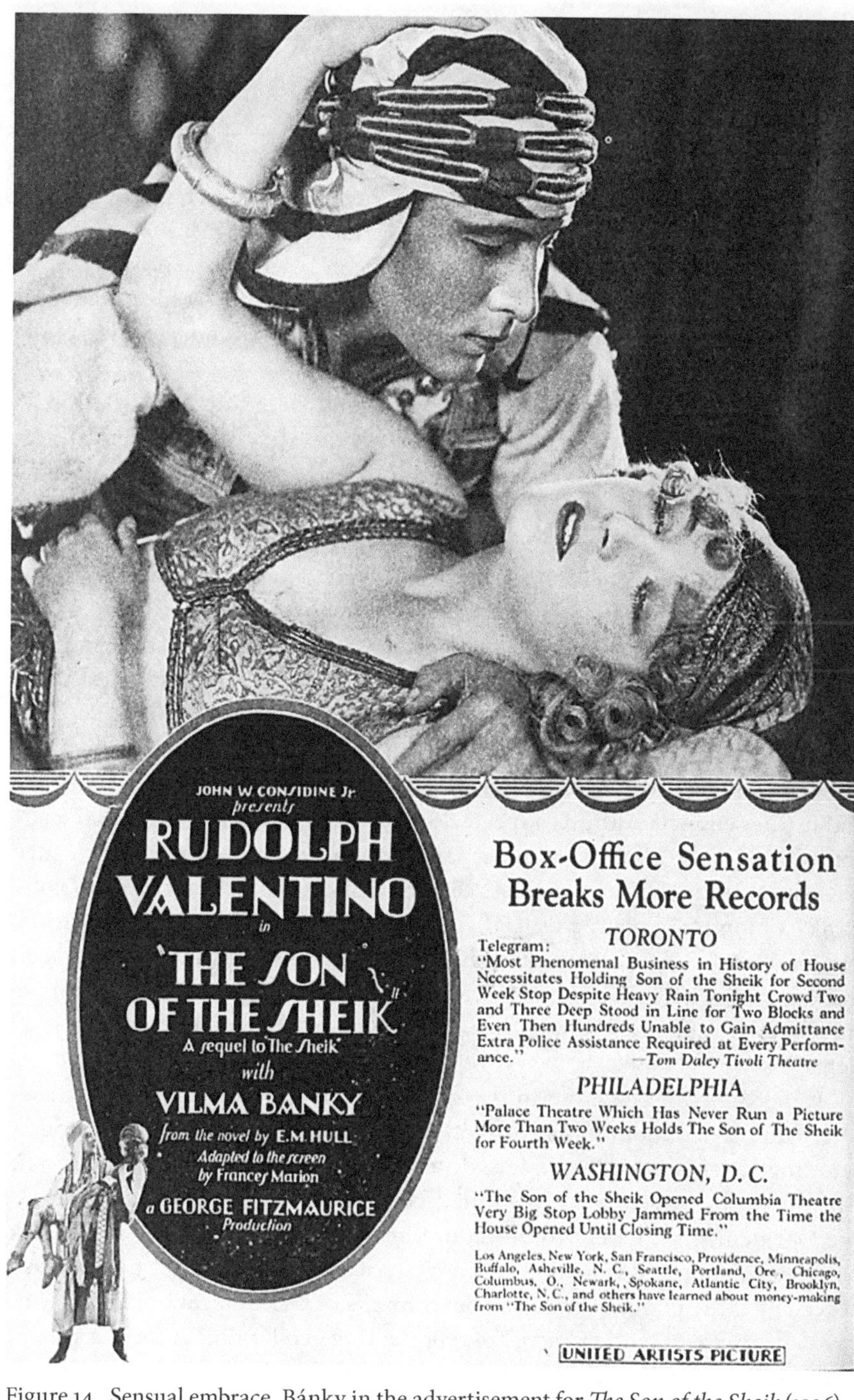

Figure 14. Sensual embrace. Bánky in the advertisement for *The Son of the Sheik* (1926). Source: *Motion Picture News*, September 25, 1926, 15.

notes how the technique of backlighting ensures that blonde hair looked blonde on celluloid, producing the image of "effulgent dazzle."[39]

Studlar argues that sexual violation and a transgression of sexual boundaries form one of the most important parts of the Orientalist narratives that promulgated in the 1920s.[40] The act of violence perpetuated by Valentino's character results in Yasmin becoming even more attached to her abuser, although even she finds her never-ceasing adoration problematic, "going as far as to pray to Allah to get rid of her feelings."[41] When Gahbah meets the dancer again, he confesses to his wicked intrigue—it was he "who sowed the seeds of doubt in Ahmed's mind"—so Yasmin's love for the protagonist is validated, even if the way Ahmed treated her defies justification.

Consequently, the plot of the film portrays their mutual relationship as marked by initial misunderstanding, followed by the big reveal and eventual reconciliation. Within that contextualization, what Ahmed's revenge scheme amounts to is not rape but a (successful) attempt at seduction. Taking this on board, Dyer's analysis of this section of the film differs from the one offered by Basinger, in the sense that he does not see the confrontation as vital in seducing Yasmin. Rather, the belly dancer continues to love the son of the sheik *despite* the act of sexual violence, not *because* of it.[42]

Paradoxically, the film constructs Yasmin's ethnic position as white, completely disregarding her alleged ethnicity as an Arabian woman. At first glance—with her delicate physique and blonde locks—she emerges from the story as a vision of whiteness deployed to underline Valentino's status as the ethnic Other and further enunciate him as a spectacle of exotic masculinity. The titular character starts off as a savage, a mercenary figure of dark desire, which in turn illuminates the racial difference between him and the woman he is involved with. Bánky's blondness plays a crucial role in aggrandizing her ethnic position. Marina Warner theorizes images of blonde women as compliant with Christian iconography, where their hair signifies a "heavenly effulgence" that appears to "reflect solar radiance, the totality of the spectrum, the flooding wholeness of light."[43]

At the same time, it is noteworthy that Bánky portrays an Arab dancer, therefore naturally connoting the carnality of the East. This unsettles any understanding of her image as a simple reformulation of the rhetoric of revered female whiteness. Thus, the rich and seemingly contradictory concept of Orient versus the Occident, so inherent to her figure, merits a brief exploration. The link between dancing and seduction in the Western imaginary cannot go unnoticed, especially if the performance itself bears marks of Orientalization. Laura Mulvey ties this down to the strategy of representing gender difference as a spectacle,[44] while Lucy Fisher discusses the status of the female performer in reference to her sexual relations with men. In the dominant regime of truth, a dancer or an actress epitomizes the peculiar position of women at large, all inevitably forced to perform on the stage set by patriarchal expectations.[45] Mulvey's discussion of fetishism and the on-screen image also references the importance of orchestrated movement, particularly in relationship to charismatic female stars.[46]

"Like all youths, he loved a dancing girl. Like all dancing girls, she tricked him!" says one of the Arabs about the son of the sheik, playing out the cultural assumption that female dancers use their craft to seduce men. At that point in the film, the audience knows Bánky's heroine has no intentions of doing any harm to Ahmed, and that she is used as bait in a ploy devised by others. This strategy also points to the notion of absence in terms of agency, whereby she is effectively denied any identity that goes beyond her association with men, with her father and her lover consecutively. Therefore, the difference between Yasmin and the likes of Carmen—as discussed in the Negri case study—depends on the fact that the former does not choose her profession consciously but is merely a tool to make money for her ungrateful troupe and irresponsible father. Consequently she cannot fully conform to the archetype of an Oriental dancer. Yasmin is a victim of her circumstances, which comes to the fore in a scene where she laments the fact that her father gambled away her daily earnings in a single hour.

Arguably, Bánky's physical appearance is a crucial dimension of performance that constructs her as "good" (i.e., not promiscuous), especially given that all Arabian women apart from her are presented as wanton within this diegetic universe. She has fair locks and light eyes. This denotes the spiritual qualities of her character but cannot possibly convey Arabian origin. Despite the peculiarities of this casting, Bánky signified everything that an Oriental woman could not stand for, at least not according to the principles of Western iconography. Far from being deceitful or oversexualized, she symbolizes cleanliness, devotion, and a certain kind of girlish naïveté.

Many aspects of the plot presented in *The Son of the Sheik* replicate the narrative devices in place in *The Eagle*. Unquestionably, both films reflect the paradigms of Western courtship where a woman yields to the seduction attempt of the hero, as the pair must overcome significant obstacles to earn their happy ending. Another common denominator between this motion picture and Bánky's previous endeavor with Valentino relates to the dynamic in which her heroine is situated amid two conflicting forces, encapsulated by her relationship with her cruel father and her burgeoning love of the titular son of the sheik. Again, Bánky is the daughter of the hero's arch nemesis and, once more, he manages to win her affection regardless of these setbacks.

The Night of Love and *The Winning of Barbara Worth*

A similar scenario of external and internal conflict is played out in another Bánky film, *The Night of Love* (1927). Here, Colman plays Montero, a Spanish gypsy in conflict with a despotic feudal lord who kidnaps his fiancée on their wedding night. The young woman chooses suicide over submitting to the lecherous duke. Years after the incident, Montero decides to exact vengeance by abducting Bánky's character, the wife-to-be of his archrival, and ends up winning her love. *The Night of Love* provides a long list of recurrent elements of the swashbuckler genre that are superimposed on devices familiar from Bánky's earlier films. These include a Robin Hood–esque protagonist in pursuit of vengeance and a damsel in distress positioned between the desires of two men.

The year that witnessed the release of *The Son of the Sheik* also saw the release of Goldwyn's epic modern drama, *The Winning of Barbara Worth*, set in the Nevada desert. This was a financial undertaking of unprecedented proportions for both the producing company and Bánky herself, who was to star in the eponymous role of Barbara, a daughter of the mayor of the local rancher community. Ideologically, the setting of the film authenticated the link between Bánky and the issues of American nationhood. As historians and cultural theorists have shown, the myth of the frontier, with its unforgiving environment, harsh realities, and opposition between wilderness and civilization, formed a cornerstone of the American national identity long before the emergence of cinema.[47] Moving pictures naturally reflected and elaborated on the polemic incorporated in earlier works of fiction. Recognizing the cultural importance of the American West as a theme, Goldwyn decided to pay a record-breaking $125,000 for the rights to the best-selling novel for this screen adaptation, arguing that its histrionic appeal was "as vast as the earth—this story of converting a hell of parched lands into a paradise. This mighty struggle of man against nature. It's drama in itself."[48] The film was a critical (if not an economic) success, with reviewers praising its cinematographic ability to capture the sprawling vistas of the Nevada desert.[49]

As in her previous vehicles at large, Bánky's on-screen incarnation here shares a similar fate in being portrayed as the love interest of two men. Willard Holmes (Ronald Colman), an engineer sent to the desert town of Barbara to improve its irrigation system, is immediately impressed by the heroine and her excellent horsemanship. In trying to gain her affection, Holmes has to compete with one of Barbara's old friends, a local cowboy by the name of Abe Lee (Gary Cooper in his first major role). *The Winning of Barbara Worth* intercuts the misadventures of Holmes and Lee with sequences that show the leading lady waiting for their triumphant return; thus, throughout the film, Bánky's character is painted as peripheral to the progress of narrative action. Such a structure also draws a sharp line between traditional gender roles where women are identified with the domestic sphere and full integration into the local community. Men, on the other hand, stand for independence, dynamism, and daring. Within the symbolism of the American frontier, women exist primarily, as Winona Howe notes, in the form of a context or object. They are marginalized and significant only insofar as they provide moral support to male characters in the roles of either dutiful daughters or obedient wives.[50]

Again, the heroine enjoys a higher societal status as the daughter of an important male character, yet is simultaneously stripped of autonomy outside of the patriarchal structures. As the plot progresses, Barbara is faced with the dilemma of choosing between Abe Lee, her childhood friend, and the engineer, of whom she has grown increasingly fond. She makes up her mind after becoming convinced that Holmes is working against the interest of her father and his people. She turns her back on him. As is the case in many other motion pictures in Bánky's body of work—*The Dark Angel*, *The Son of the Sheik*, and *The Magic Flame*—a quick succession of incidents proves Barbara's convictions to be wrong, so, after the whirling action sequence of the finale, the couple is reconciled by means of marriage.

A ballroom scene in which Bánky enjoys small talk with Holmes, at that point a new acquaintance, offers a poignant example of the paradigms of courtly love interrogated previously. The costume she wears can also be read as symbolically loaded in racial implications. Adorned with a simple, long white dress accentuating the whiteness of her skin, she connotes innocence, purity, and radiance.[51] In combination with the blue tinting of the celluloid, her character appears to glimmer. Taken by surprise by Holmes's sudden confession of love—the engineer asks the young woman how to say "I love you" in Spanish, a language she is fluent in—Barbara moves away but continues the conversation from the safe distance of her room's balcony.

In a rather straightforward manner, the mise-en-scéne references visual imagery well known from theatrical interpretations of Shakespeare's *Romeo and Juliet*. In compliance with the patriarchal ideals of romantic love, the staging of Bánky-the-actress elevates her to the position of a venerated love object. It is a visual strategy that accentuates the fact that she is an idolized "courtly mistress" beyond one's reach. Physically placed above her suitor, Barbara issues an ultimatum: "Out here, Mr. Holmes, one doesn't learn how to say *I love you*—one learns how to prove it." Her love is not unconditional but part of the act structured along the lines of Hollywood's staple "boy meets girl—boy loses girl—boy gets girl" scenario.[52] In order to win the heart of this wholesome leading lady, Holmes has to demonstrate his willpower and, by extension, his masculine value. Eventually, of course, he achieves that feat by building an irrigation system that turns the small desert town into a blooming suburban paradise. The complexity of engineering conquers the wilderness. Worth, on the other hand, is endowed with the visual and symbolic significations of whiteness from the outset, although her purity is given by nature, not something achieved.[53]

Holmes's heroism, moreover, extends beyond his technological victories, resting mainly in his imperviousness to corruption in a world full of soulless executive greed. In her book *Shifting Gears: Technology, Literature, Culture in Modernist America*, Cecelia Tichi interrogates the frequency with which early twentieth-century American literature has taken the engineer as its chief figure, representative of technological advancement as well as the purity of the American vision: "Inherently ethical, he resists every effort at political or financial influence liable to compromise his work or liable to endanger those whose safety depends upon it."[54] It is through the engineer-hero, Tichi argues, that the myth of the American spirit prevails. Indeed, Holmes transcends the corruption of the corporate conglomerate by resigning from it the second he learns that the proposed water-intake designed by his uncle would put the small populace of Barbara in jeopardy. He then proceeds to build a water dam to save the settlements from a potentially catastrophic flood. It is interesting to note how the greatest danger to the protagonist's happiness in *The Winning of Barbara Worth* comes not from the nonwhite Others, such as Mexicans or Native Americans, but from a more powerful force, from "bad whites." This is because, as Dyer contextualized in reference to the western genre, "to make the non-whites the greatest threat would accord them qualities of will and skill, of exercising spirit, which would make them the equivalent of white people."[55] Black or brown people might be dangerous, but they can never be equally intelligent, scheming, or devoted as the all-American antagonists.

Significantly (and true of many other motion pictures of the silent era), *The Winning of Barbara Worth* displaces wider issues—the conflict between industrialization and the vanishing of the natural landscape—with the framework of courtly love and romance. For Tichi, the ideas relating to nature are incorporated here in the figure of Barbara, a woman who embodies a primitive America unmarked by industrial changes.[56] Through having woman-as-nature symbolically give her blessing to the vision of Holmes's culturally sanctioned transformation, and through the subsequent reunion of the pair in marriage, the narrative trajectory manages to evade political conflicts. In consequence, the film climaxes by refusing to acknowledge any ambiguities inherent to its central theme. Yes, pristine nature might be disappearing, but it is a matter of little significance.

The filming of *The Winning of Barbara Worth* took place in the middle of the Nevada desert, thirty hours from Los Angeles. Starting on June 21, 1926, it took approximately three months to complete.[57] With sandstorms and temperatures rising to over 104 degrees during the day—which dictated the directorial decision to start work at 5 a.m. each morning—an impressive 2,000 members of the cast and crew experienced a number of setbacks, widely reported by the popular press.[58] *Photoplay* was particularly prolific in describing the sheer ambition of the undertaking, focusing its attention on the hardships endured by the main picture players on the set:

> The West—particularly the desert—is interesting to our Hungarian beauty. But the names they give their inhabitants! "Cowboys", for instance, who hold no resemblance to the long-horned steers. And the women . . . what to call them? . . . it is all so puzzling? . . . Someone asked Vilma Banky about the bathing facilities at camp Barbara Worth. Her wide eyes open and her hands move expressively. Roundly her mouth forms soft syllables: "There is a big box overhead and two handles on the wall. Turn the one that says "Hot" and cold water comes. Turn the one that says "Cold" and hot water comes![59]

One can see the mutual imbrication of Bánky's on-screen characterization as a "one hundred percent American girl,"[60] well used to the struggle of living in a front-parlor civilization, with her private narrative of endurance and cheerfulness eagerly promoted by the trade press. Bánky's place in the discourse of a good work ethic is notable, given that the identity of most European stars at the time focused on the notions of temperamental tantrums and displays of highly demanding behavior on set. While a number of stylistic and textual codes transformed Negri into a figure of foreign exaggeration, as I demonstrated, such themes of irrationality and passion are nowhere to be found in discussions of Bánky's approach toward her profession. Unlike the personae of Negri, Goudal, or other stars hailing from the Old World, the identity of "The Hungarian Rhapsody" (as Bánky was referred to at times) did not incorporate a sense of diva-like antics, instead stressing discipline and self-control.

Norbert Lusk of *Picture Play* criticized *The Winning of Barbara Worth* for the unrealistic costumes worn with panache by the titular protagonist. Lusk gives Worth the doubtful distinction of being "the dressiest Western heroine ever seen on the screen," deeming her daintiness—"with not a particle of sand in her hair"—ridiculous.[61] Lusk's critique can be viewed as a lack of endorsement for the type of immaculate femininity emblematized by Bánky. Taken together, though, such rhetorical questioning of the film's artistic choices was not common, as the reviewers remained fascinated by its realism and high production values.

The Magic Flame and *Two Lovers*

Bánky's next release with Colman, *The Magic Flame* (1927), was advertised as a powerful romance, a story of a clown "who became a king . . . and his sweetheart, a beautiful trapeze artist, who ruled him."[62] Not unexpectedly (given Bánky's filmography to date), her aerial artist Bianca is desired by two men: Tito the clown and his evil twin brother, the count. Even the name of the female lead foregrounds her in relation to ethnic identity and suggests personal traits, as the word translates to "white" in Italian.[63] In love with the honorable clown, Bianca at one point presumes him murdered by his jealous rival. As the despairing woman plans to avenge her beloved, an ironic twist of fate is revealed: we learn that Tito used his startling resemblance to the count to assume his identity. This dramatic conflict is resolved before the eventual redemption at the fadeout, as the lovers are reunited in their happily-ever-after.

The cover of the sheet music for *The Magic Flame* offers a symbolically potent representation, particularly in the light of the preceding discussion of the physical staging between Bánky and Colman in *The Winning of Barbara Worth*. The bottom half of the composition is occupied by a man playing a banjo; a blonde woman in a tutu is seated on a swing above him. Certain elements of this black-and-white photograph are tinted. Bánky's hair, significantly, is colored gold, and so are her pointed shoes. Visually, this image delves into the iconography of whiteness through the potent stereotype of the ballerina as a translucent, incorporeal being[64] who, in existing beyond corporeality, constitutes the very apex of whiteness.

To truly emblematize the essence of whiteness, as Sean Redmond maintained, is to "literally disappear into the ether," to be dead;[65] out of all the racially saturated archetypes available, the ballerina is the one that comes the closest to achieving that contradictory ideal. Despite her profession as a dancer, the stereotype entails a negation of natural constraints relating to the body, such as body weight or perspiration.[66] To use Stéphane Mallarmé's explanation of the ballerina as a model of human potential, she "is not a girl dancing . . . she is not a girl, but rather a metaphor which symbolizes some elemental aspect of earthly form."[67]

Widely announced to be the last in a series of creative collaborations between Colman and Bánky, *Two Lovers*, released in March 1928, generated a wealth of positive critical responses. Although the leading stars received accolades for their splendid performances, the film attracted some minor criticism for its repetitive storytelling, meaning that it replicated the same narrative features as existing films of the Colman/Bánky duo. *Photoplay*'s reviewer commented that, as the last picture co-starring the two actors, it is still worth seeing, even despite its shortcomings.[68] What emerges from the coverage given to *Two Lovers* in the press is its alliance with the principles of the swashbuckler genre. According to Laurence Reid, a contemporaneous journalist, it was a romance that "takes the spectator back to a bygone era, one which depended on chivalry and intrigue. . . . And into this picturesque background is brought a story that moves at a smart pace and offers up plenty of love interest and adventurous thrills. It is told with fine simplicity and with color and dash."[69]

One regional newspaper defined the film as a tale of daring escapades, containing "all the elements which make medieval adventure so attractive."[70] The usage of the term "medieval" is noteworthy, given that the plot is in fact set during the sixteenth-century occupation of Flanders by the Spanish. In being incorrect in positioning the action in terms of its supposed time frame, the review illuminated one of the most distinctive characteristics of the costume drama of the silent period: its dependency on historicity as a widely understood "inspiration" rather than a direct source.

Similarly to *The Eagle*, the story of *Two Lovers* focuses on the daring feats of Mark Van Ryke, a Flemish patriot who adopts the guise of "Leatherface" to avenge his enemies. In reworking a ritualized narrative template, the story can be seen as exemplary of the swashbuckler genre more generally; that is, it offers an endorsement of the dominant authoritarian structures of power, such as the monarchy. "The swashbuckling hero may act to protect the throne of the absent king . . . a saviour of the aristocracy or a protector of the rights of the landed classes," writes James Chapman about the politics of those films.[71] Van Ryke's plans are halted after he develops an infatuation with Donna Leonora de Vargas, a Spanish aristocrat portrayed by Bánky, to whom he is betrothed in an arranged marriage of political significance. Donna Leonora starts to gradually reciprocate his affection, and, to paraphrase *Picture Play*, she learns how to make his cause her own.[72]

From this brief synopsis, we might extrapolate two narrative themes also at work in *The Eagle* and *The Son of the Sheik*. First, the plot establishes the lovers-to-be as representatives of two conflicting forces in a particularly clarified political form. Second, in allowing them to fall in love, it promulgates the belief that no national allegiance matters in the face of passionate, heterosexual romance. Hence, the overriding ideological project of *Two Lovers*—the triumphant assertion of dominant ideology—is achieved by eliminating political conflict through the imposition of passionate love. As a moral lesson, it partially mirrors the narrative closure promulgated by *The Winning of Barbara Worth*, in the sense that it also shows the leading lady as willing to forsake her way of living in order to adapt to the desires of the male protagonist. Thus, the film takes the cornerstone of traditional gender ideology to its logical conclusion: Donna Leonora, to paraphrase Adrienne McLean, essentially starts to lead her life in servitude to her husband.[73]

The majority of columnists mourned the upcoming screen separation of the Bánky/Colman duo, arguing that together they constituted more than the sum of their parts, combining "the *ninth* degree of beauty and finesse."[74] Schildgen comments that audiences flocked to see the two on-screen because they personified the ideals of patriarchal coupling: "Women loved Colman's passionate embraces and machismo, while men clamoured to see ethereal beauty that was so lovingly photographed."[75] Undeniably, popular discourse contextualized Colman as an example of a quintessentially English gentleman, whose stern and quixotic manners complemented Bánky's gentle femininity and impeccable looks.[76] The press went on to explain their professional parting as a mutual decision dictated by the growing level of familiarity between the actors, who both saw it as compromising to their art. In other words, Colman had reached a level of understanding with Bánky where dramatic turns and unknowns are absent;

yet, aspects of novelty can be extremely rewarding when it comes to screen acting. "The intimacy engendered by working together in a number of pictures makes for smoother and better performances each time—up to a certain point," Colman allegedly revealed. "Then you begin to know each other too well. You work so smoothly that it begins, almost, to be uninteresting."[77] The actual reason might have been much more pragmatic: after earning over $1 million from four Bánky/Colman pictures he produced, Goldwyn was hoping to make twice as much profit by establishing them as independent stars.[78]

While it is hard to argue with the commercial potential held by the romance drama of the 1920s, many reviewers had reservations about the artistic value represented by such productions, criticizing them mainly, as Jacobs notes, for overblown love scenes and weak plots.[79] Other scholars such as Richards agree that these films reveled in depicting one-dimensional characters showing "stereotyped emotions."[80] The relatively lowbrow connotations of the genre can at least partially account for the fact that Bánky's reviews hardly ever complimented the virtuosity of her performance. I would be inclined to suggest, however, that the conscious displacement of the discourse of acting-as-a-skill in favor of acting-as-a-possession-of-charm had something to do with Bánky's gendered image. The idea that she had a naturally graceful presence that registered well on screen further asserts her position of passivity, already integral to the way the trade press portrayed her. For *Picture Play*, little is required of Vilma Bánky, "always lovely to look at," apart from simply "being on the screen."[81] Arguably, this manner of contextualizing performance stood in stark opposition to the discourse on Negri's conscious efforts to excel in the acting profession, and by extension, worked to diminish the importance of Bánky in the creative process.

This Is Heaven

One can argue that *This Is Heaven* (1929), one of Bánky's next ventures, offered a conscious although highly unexpected subversion of thematic tropes familiar from earlier cinematic portrayals in her career. Bánky enters this modern romantic comedy as Eva, a sweet but penniless immigrant who comes to live with her uncle in the Bronx, earning her living as a waitress. In the words of *Motion Picture Classic*, "she must serve, cook pancakes and sweep tips from the table in a single motion,"[82] a feat never attempted by any of Bánky's heroines to date.

The executive decision to cast the star in a role so far removed from her usual repertoire can be understood as Goldwyn's attempt to keep up with the technological changes within the industry. These shifts were feared by many foreign-born stars. *This Is Heaven* included three sequences of dialogue with synchronized sound. Bánky's speaking voice—an important criterion for further development of her stardom—did not provide a seamless match with her persona.[83] With the advent of the talkies, she could hardly pass for the hard-boiled

American heroine of *Dark Angel*, so using her to portray a Hungarian woman might have appeared to be a logical step for the producer. The dilemma of keeping a level of coherency between the actors' *actual* and *imagined* voices was emblematic of the transitional period; faced by many studio executives, even fanzines feared that real sound would not live up to the high level of expectation held by the audience.[84] In reality, viewers' responses varied from admiration for Greta Garbo's low-pitched timbre[85] to shock that William Powell's speech, so easily understandable and soothing, does not fit a villainous representation he has been accustomed with.[86] Initially, Bánky's voice was met with positive treatment in critical circles, with *Variety* proclaiming her radiant, irrespective of whether she was silent or talking.[87] "Miss Banky need have no fear of the talkie bugaboo. She reveals a rich, natural, dramatic voice," predicted the *Telegraph*.[88]

Yet, the inconsistency between Eva and the image of Bánky put forward in both promotional publicity and constructed private antics to date becomes apparent when looking at the way *This Is Heaven* fared at the box office.[89] A big financial failure, the film lost Goldwyn a staggering $200,000, which constituted one-third of its total production costs.[90] Of course, the issue of low class positioning is of vital relevance here, specifically regarding the characterizations Bánky's fans came to expect from her, with her stardom functioning as synonymous with on-screen gentility rather than working classness. In denying Eva the semi-mythic quality of Bánky's previous heroines, the feature offered a type of representation too distant from her established persona to be commercially successful. After all, the star system was built in part to bridge the gap between the performer and their role, in creating the illusion of stars "as people who are simply *being themselves* on screen."[91] This is what Stanley Cavell refers to when he states that "for the stage, an actor works himself into the role; for the screen, a performer takes the role onto himself."[92]

Furthermore, the way the motion picture commented on Bánky's own national identity as a Hungarian citizen seemed to be at odds with her star persona in 1929, at a time when she was no longer framed in reference to her immigrant status but, more often than not, praised as an example of successful integration into the fabric of American society. Essentially, the conflating form of class/national embodiment that lay at the core of Eva as a character stood in stark opposition to Bánky's own star persona. This found its reflection in the critical debates surrounding the film. *Photoplay*'s piece criticized the plot of *This Is Heaven* for being "another trite Cinderella yarn," while simultaneously complementing Bánky's speaking voice as not devoid of charm.[93] *Picture Play* took a similar stance in deeming the film's "commonplace" story as not suited for the talents of a star as exquisite as Bánky: "Obviously an attempt is being made to Americanize Miss Banky, to divest her of the gorgeous costumes she wore in period pictures and to reduce her to the understanding of the herd," lamented the columnist.[94]

Viewed from a different perspective, the story presented in *This Is Heaven* can be analyzed as a testament to the absorptive potential of American society, where everyone is offered the opportunity to ascend the class ladder. Even so, in this highly gendered version of the rags-to-riches story, Eva rises to the most desirable social caste not through hard and honest labor but through her compliance with the ideals of Western beauty, and through the resulting ease with which she finds a suitably wealthy husband. This points to the existence of two gender variants of the American myth of social mobility, where men occupy a self-made position of hardworking entrepreneurs and architects of their fortune, and women leap out of poverty in Cinderella-like fashion, straight into the heart of a conveniently rich leading man. In his in-depth discussion of cross-class romance in American film, Stephen Sharot identified ninety-nine films produced between 1920 and 1928 that deal with the issue, with eighty-three stories constructing the male as the upper-class protagonist.[95] Lois Banner summarizes that "young men in business dreamed of rising to the top through entrepreneurial skill. Young working women dreamed of marrying the boss's son."[96]

Sumiko Higashi demonstrates that silent films were articulated with respect to the existing conventions of genteel culture and its mixture of realist and sentimental motifs—traditions that, in resolution, privileged romantic reconciliations over "diluted grim expressions of urban realism."[97] What makes these fantasies problematic is their cult of individuality that moves attention away from larger social issues, and the subsequent repression of any form of political awareness. Within this monolithic view, no collective action is needed to change the dynamics of the current system, as women can overcome the boundaries of their class if they hold enough value in being beautiful and kind.[98] Corresponding to such modes of representation, *This Is Heaven* additionally stressed the weight of Americanization over cultural diversity.

Conclusion

The influence of Bánky's passive on-screen roles in the process of establishing her private star persona cannot be undervalued. Certain narrative conventions I have outlined in this chapter span all films she was cast in. For example, in virtually all her roles—with the notable exception of *This Is Heaven*—the star's heroine occupies a position within a classical heteronormative love triangle. In *The Eagle* and *Two Lovers* the figure of a jealous, competing suitor is transformed into a metaphor for antagonistic ideological force. The plot of *The Eagle* personifies this contradictory influence through an evil father, a feudal lord whom Masha eventually abandons so she can marry the handsome leading man. What is more, the worldview presented in Bánky's vehicles is founded on the assumption that political conflict and romance can not only co-exist, but that the former can be subdued with the aid of the latter; this is a dynamic that in many respects denied the importance, even the very existence, of the collective class struggle.

The strong association between Bánky and period drama works in conjunction with archetypal patterns, feeding into the construction of her whiteness. What were revered as the highest ideals of womanhood were constantly underscored by ethnic concerns in the popular discourse. "Appearance, performance and nationality are . . . inseparably linked," writes Lisa Rose Stead, and it rings true especially in the context of the formation of one's star quality.[99] In instances where Bánky portrays characters easily described as exotic (in Said's understanding of the term), her conversion into an Arabian dancer—or a Spanish aristocrat, for that matter—is never fully complete. Yasmin in *The Son of the Sheik* displays a set of physical and mental characteristics that move her away from the image of exotic seductress, and instead place her firmly within the representational scheme of female purity and sacrifice. In being an honest woman, whose honor is defended in the final scene of the film, she does not act as a stock Arab character. In practice, this type of idealized portrayal of white femininity was both a reflection and a consolidation of Bánky's off-screen existence, as promotional materials praising her for hard work, perseverance, and youthful cheerfulness.

The majority of Bánky's films are set in the historical past, where adventure and swordplay abound; hence, they can be categorized as exemplary of the swashbuckler genre. Her filmic romances unravel according to the contrivances of the seduction plot, identified by one contemporary columnist as a narrative that includes "the opening advances, later love-making, misunderstanding, and inevitably the complete understanding."[100] Throughout her career, the star was repeatedly given the parts of righteous yet inherently passive women whose decency eventually grants them a happy ending alongside the male protagonist. Bánky inhabited celluloid realms that reaffirmed conservative gender values, promoting a seamless match between her on- and off-screen self.

CHAPTER 5

Vilma Bánky and Marriage

"MY MOTHER BROUGHT ME UP TO BE A WIFE"

At the beginning of June 1927, a number of movie actors, the crème de la crème of Hollywood royalty, received a unique letter. The stylish envelope contained a wedding invitation that read as follows: "Mr. and Mrs. Samuel Goldwyn announce the marriage of Miss Vilma Bánky to Mr. Roderick La Rocque on Sunday, the twenty sixth of June One thousand, nine hundred and twenty-seven at the Church of the Good Shepherd, Beverly Hills, California."[1] It was the customary practice for wedding invitations to include the names of the bride's parents; the fact that the producer's name featured on the invitation spoke volumes about the alleged nature of the relationship between him and his employee. As the making of a sacred union between two of the biggest stars of the time, the nuptials were no ordinary affair. Planned meticulously by Goldwyn's staff and reported widely across the pages of fan and national press alike, the celebration formed a precedent to the phenomenon of the so-called celebrity wedding. According to Goldwyn's biography by A. Scott Berg, the producer spent approximately $25,000 on the celebrations (the equivalent of an impressive $330,000 today)[2] to take full advantage of the promotional opportunities it offered. The studio's publicity department sent out a press release to hundreds of newspapers and magazines a week in advance, encouraging publishers to circulate a series of fabricated wedding anecdotes.[3]

In the previous sections of this case study, I examined how the politics of white representation encompassed Bánky's narrative, in terms of both her on-screen characters and her private life. This chapter examines how the wedding ceremony and ensuing marriage successfully integrated Bánky's personal affairs into her filmic narrative by validating her alignment with the Cinderella myth, furthering her ongoing Americanization. From the moment she first appeared on American screens as Kitty Vane in *The Dark Angel* (1925), her star attributes connoted the most revered ideas of gentle womanhood, traditionally embedded in patriarchal discourses of white femininity. As an institution, marriage emphasized the pre-established, idealized components of Bánky's star text. It also cemented her image as an aspiring American subject. In other words, matrimony provided a traditional frame of heteronormativity that legitimized her assimilation into the society of the United States.

The carefully mediated image of Bánky-the-wife provides a focal point for the exploration of themes of nationality and gender. Estelle B. Freedman notes that, contrary to popular belief, the dominant discourse of the 1920s did not undermine the centrality of marriage but continued to emphasize the dualism of career and domestic female roles.[4] The promotional tactics ushered in by the studio system counteracted the potentially problematic facet of Bánky's persona as a married woman in full-time employment through emphasizing her extreme dedication to domesticity. Supposedly, she was ready to retire from Hollywood. For instance, *Picture Play* revealed that the star shared a conviction that no household could function properly without a fully dedicated mistress: "Shortly before her wedding she rashly stated the possibility of her retirement into domesticity. Quite sincere in her belief that marriage and the movies were two separate careers and could not be combined, she was convinced that a household over which its mistress did not preside vigilantly, would speedily go to pieces."[5]

Vilma Bánky and Rod La Rocque

According to the account given by Rachel Schildgen, Bánky made her intentions of getting married known to Goldwyn in early April 1927. At the time, she was involved in a production of *The Night of Love*, her third vehicle with Ronald Colman, her frequent lead. Initially, the imperious producer did not approve of her plans and seemed concerned that the marriage would sabotage his plan of promoting the on-screen partnership between Bánky and Colman as a romantic involvement off-screen.[6] His reservations were dictated by the fact that Bánky had the most potent star appeal among all of his stars, generating the highest box office revenue for the company.[7] Goldwyn knew that an ill-fated promotional campaign could cost him dearly. Yet, he soon decided to make a shift in publicity surrounding his chief star. In place of advertising the Bánky/Colman duo as real-life lovers, Goldwyn took advantage of the promotional opportunities held by the wedding, strongly opposing Bánky's suggestion to keep the ceremony off the radar: "How could you do this to me? I brought you to this country. I acted like a father. I protected you. What are you, ashamed? You want to go some place [*sic*] and hide, disappear?" A private ceremony, limited to a few guests, was out of question.[8] By this point, Goldwyn had become determined to use the wedding as a tool to boost Bánky's star value.

One of the challenges faced by fan discourse in the promotion of Bánky's relationship was the question of how to reshape the pre-established star image of

Rod La Rocque. In Schildgen's words, before meeting Bánky, the actor was considered to be something of an eternal bachelor who "had the unfortunate reputation of being a ladies' man around town, courting, among others, Pola Negri,"[9] while Kristin Thompson notes that between 1923 and 1927 his star persona relied on his association with the "Latin lover" type popularized by Rudolph Valentino. Like Valentino, La Rocque "had a general image of glamour, with a slightly foppish or flighty quality."[10] An interview published by *Picture Play* in June 1927—merely one month before his engagement to Bánky was announced—bears witness to attempts made by the studio system to uphold his image as a free spirit. It presented La Rocque as a man who, by his own admission, was "immune to matrimony."[11]

Interestingly, the same month saw an attempt to re-evaluate the narrative of La Rocque's off-screen life. The first mentions of the Bánky/La Rocque relationship started to circulate around the same time *Picture Play* attributed him with a strong stance against marriage, which provides an interesting, albeit temporary, inconsistency in the regulation of his persona. "Rod La Rocque is in the midst of a spring love affair," informed *Motion Picture Classic*, adding that Vilma Bánky, the object of his adoration, is "the marrying type of girl, it seems, and pessimists predict that Rod's spring romance will end in a wedding."[12]

The tone of such commentary is revealing in itself, as it demonstrates the gravity of Bánky's intentions; unlike Pola Negri or other extravagant female players, she is not "fooling around." An article authored by Dorothy Manners tried to close the gap between the romance and La Rocque's image by suggesting that the engagement came as a surprise even to their closest friends and "an awful shock to the rest of us who weren't even aware that they were acquainted. The engagement was announced before there was even a hint of rumor started," Manners continued. "Vilma and Rod are seldom seen at any of the haunts of the movie select and that probably accounts for their success in keeping their romance a secret until they were willing to let the world congratulate them."[13] *Picture Play*'s report on the engagement is similar, again noting that no one within the Hollywood elite knew about the blossoming romance. The announcement "came only a few weeks after they had begun showing marked interest in each other."[14] Another press account labeled it as "the shortest cinema romance in Hollywood history," which might indeed be true if the claim that La Rocque was introduced to Bánky three weeks prior is to be believed.[15] The short-lived period of courtship culminated in the engagement, which was made public at the residence of Samuel Goldwyn and his wife.

Some magazine features attempted to resolve the discrepancy between La Rocque's persona and his impending marriage by painting a picture of Bánky as an extremely desirable wife, implying that her outstanding beauty and kindness would force any die-hard bachelor to change his ways. Writing for *Picture Play* nearly a year after the wedding, Grace Kingsley dismissed La Rocque's single life as an insignificant period devoted primarily to the search for his one, true soulmate. This was achieved, at least in part, through a juxtaposition between Mrs. La Rocque and one of Rod's former lovers, Pola Negri. While Bánky had a long-lasting positive impact on La Rocque, the Polish star was a very fleeting presence in his personal life, "just another tempestuous affair which came to nothing. . . . What a rest to his soul must have been the gentle and trustful love of Vilma, the serene-eyed, gifted with sweetness, illusive charm, and the power to heal," concluded the article.[16]

Bánky's star persona, on the other hand, did not require significant adjustments, as fan discourses regularly implied her suitability for marriage; she had already expressed a desire to settle down. In March 1927, *Motion Picture Magazine* published an article in which it asked several unmarried female stars about what they look for in their future spouses. Bánky was quoted as saying that she would need to deeply love her husband and that she would marry as soon as she found an appropriate candidate. "I marry heem soon as I find heem! . . . I doo tun like to leeve alone [*sic*]. It is not happiness to me."[17] Being married would put an end to her lonely evenings, it was claimed. Another aptly titled feature, "Marry? I Zink Ya!," constructed Bánky as a young woman looking forward to matrimony, reinforcing the vision of a romantic attachment that, to quote Lois Banner, "predicated every relationship on physical longing and saw woman's life as incomplete without a man's love."[18] Jane Gaines described the logic emerging from such magazine articles as tautological: all women share the desire to be married, so the columns focused "on how to get a man rather than offering even a tentative suggestion for negotiating the world without one."[19]

The Wedding

Vilma Bánky and Rod La Rocque were married in the Church of the Good Shepherd in Beverly Hills—the same building in which Rudolph Valentino's second funeral ceremony was held only a year earlier (figure 15). According to *Motion Picture Classic*, the mass of people that flocked to see the bride was so dense it jammed the boulevard for a block on either side of the church. "Not since the church wedding of Laura La Plante and William Seiter has there been such a crowd of sightseers,"[20] observed the column. Indeed, over one hundred police officers were on duty to secure the grounds, closing several streets between the church and the reception venue to avoid traffic.[21] Given that the guest list comprised 600 people from the motion picture world, including Harold Lloyd, Ronald Colman, Bebe Daniels, Diana Kane, and Norma Tallmadge, it is no wonder it caused a sensation. Louella Parsons, one of the first and most esteemed journalists with a sustained interest in the film personalities (and one who criticized Negri's demeanor at Valentino's funeral), was the matron of honor.[22]

© Rayhuff-Richter

NO international society wedding received more public attention than the marriage of Vilma Banky and Rod La Rocque. And no young couple ever started in married life with more sincere good wishes for their future happiness.

Figure 15. Photograph of the newlyweds from the September 1927 issue of *Photoplay*.

The leading functions were undertaken by arguably the most influential figures who graced the affair, with Cecil B. DeMille, to whom La Rocque was under contract at the time, serving as the best man. Goldwyn acted as a surrogate father to Bánky by giving her away.[23] Instead of trying to shield his promotional efforts, the producer organized the wedding in full view of the public, which generated comments within and outside the industry. His financial involvement became a subject of commentary. For instance, in a letter written to her friend Sallie, Hedda Hopper recalled the impressive arrangement of flowers that adorned the church on the day, noting Goldwyn's financial input behind the decoration.[24]

The act of giving Bánky away in marriage provided a visual symbol of the financial obligations that Goldwyn decided to take on himself. Most importantly, though, it acted as a reflection on the romanticized story of Bánky's rise to fame, investigated in chapter 3. As a successful film mogul, he recognized Bánky's potential and brought her to America, effectively molding her into the star she was at the time of meeting her future husband. The paternal role assumed by Goldwyn on the occasion—however indicative of the position he occupied in relation to her stardom—brought him to the attention of the press, where his gesture elicited a number of varying responses, ranging from outright admiration to gentle mockery. Goldwyn's influence was articulated through the choice of bridal gown, a garment that served to further bridge the gap between Bánky's personal and public lives. It was the same dress that Kitty Vane (Bánky's character from her first American moving picture, *The Dark Angel*) wore for her wedding, thus making the distinction between Bánky's private life and her cinematic life increasingly nonexistent. Goldwyn's loans stretched beyond the studio's wardrobe department, as he decorated the tables at the wedding reception with viands made of plaster. As Stephen Birmingham noted, "Not a morsel of the nuptial repast was edible."[25]

Writing for *Picture Play*, Elza Schallert found it fitting that the producer who brought Bánky to America and elevated her to stardom would act as a surrogate father, especially in light of the fact that the bride was not getting married in her native Hungary.[26] With Bánky's parents absent, she reasoned, Goldwyn had every right to fill in.[27] For Schallert, the gesture was beautiful and moving: "I am very sure that more than one person in that congregation was deeply touched by the picture of Vilma on the arm of Mr. Goldwyn when she slowly walked to the altar. Her mother and all her relatives were so far, far away in Hungary on this important day of her life."[28]

Several contemporary commentators recognized Goldwyn's endorsement, and even orchestration, of the wedding ceremony. Indeed, to Malcolm H. Oettinger, also writing for *Picture Play*, Goldwyn assumed the role of a wedding planner specializing in staging lavish, impressive parties "guaranteed to hit the front page. His Banky-La Roque production was nothing short of a nuptial classic. Thousands attended."[29] The journalist suggested that Goldwyn's preoccupation with the ceremony stretched way beyond his obligations as a producer and, therefore, ostensibly marked the event as an excessive promotional undertaking, even by Hollywood standards. The conspicuous subjugation of Bánky's private affairs to her professional life turned into something of a running joke in the discourse that surrounded her. "A girlfriend asked Vilma what she was going to name her first child," reported *Photoplay* two months after Bánky became Mrs. La Rocque. "*I don't know*, Vilma answered. *You would have to ask Sam Goldwyn*."[30] This ironic reflectivity reveals the degree to which fan publications were allowed to disclose the inner workings of the studio system, or even criticize profile-raising efforts as explicitly fabricated practices. The same meditative approach toward practices of the film industry was rarely found in the discursive patterns of unspecialized newspapers.

Married Life

In the three years that passed between the wedding and the decline of Bánky's career as talkies took hold in the early 1930s,[31] the perfect life of the star as a married woman became one of the most regularly discussed facets of her image. As anticipated by Goldwyn's publicity, together Mr. and Mrs. La Rocque were more than the sum of their parts. Theirs was a perfect match between the all-American hero and a young actress of spotless reputation. The fan press located Bánky within the evolving understanding of marriage as a union dictated by love and mutual respect rather than based solely on social relations; this ties in with the historical argument that the 1920s saw a heightened interest in the idea of romantic love and the emergence of what social commentators labeled as a companionate marriage. In the broader sense, the term designated a spousal partnership that promoted mental and sexual intimacy over procreation, and accepted the possibility of divorce if such emotional ties deteriorated beyond repair.[32] Within this model, as Christina Simmons summarizes, women's paid work roles were acknowledged, at least in the earlier, pre-childbearing phase of the relationship.[33] We will see that Bánky's marriage, with its focus on individuality and consciousness, fit neatly within those parameters.

Motion Picture Classic repeatedly aimed to discover Bánky's secret to a joyful life together, as to supposedly share it with married women in its readership. "You cannot make a formula for love," she claimed. "But where two people want the same thing, there is no need for rules. And Rod and I each want happiness—for each other, first; and for ourselves, second."[34] *Photoplay* was more specific with its guidance, publishing the key principles that Mr. and Mrs. La Rocque "apply to keep peace in the family": "They eat dinner together. They go to parties together. They aren't jealous of each other's professional associates. They never criticize each other's work until the film is finished. They pool their money, but each reserves a small separate account for minor expenditures. And—this

Figure 16. Rod La Rocque photographing his wife. Source: *Photoplay*, July 1932.

is most important—they never both lose their tempers at the same time."[35] As if to validate the sheer perfection of their lifestyles, the spread included iconographic evidence: photographs of both spouses working in their separate offices and relaxing together in their Hollywood home. In this quasi-pastoral narrative—remaining firmly in place for the subsequent years of Bánky's career—the star assumed the role of expert on the complicated art of marriage. In their relentless rehearsal of Bánky's performance as a wife, the fan and popular press drew from her link to the image of ideal white womanhood, promoted in the initial two years of her work in Hollywood, the symbolic status of which I discussed at length in the previous chapter. What makes Bánky's recommendations on marriage legitimate, authoritative, and worth adhering to was not her long-term experience in the matter (one needs to remember that at this stage, she was still a newlywed) but the connotations of whiteness she carried. The authority assigned to her stemmed from the combination of her ethnicity, nationality, gender, and social station.

I have already examined how, in drawing a parallel between white skin and superior inner qualities, the contemporaneous debates favored conspicuously white immigrants—Swedes, Germans, the English, and in this case, a Hungarian—over other Europeans, such as Spaniards and Italians, regarding the former as more intelligent and virtuous and, perhaps most importantly, more likely to adopt the protestant decorum and way of living. Furthermore, as shown by Julian B. Carter, among others, the discourses of whiteness and heterosexual marriage are inherently linked[36] and are mobilized in the textual and extratextual sources of Bánky's stardom. Such concepts mutually address the Anglo-American normality, invoking the conceptualization of matrimony as vital to the development of carefully regulated white, middle-class civilization. Although it is a long-standing Christian principle, an argument relating marriage to white identity (with its ethics of self-discipline and progress) resounded particularly loudly in the United States in the early 1900s.[37]

Numerous magazine features described the La Rocques as a perfectly matched couple who shared many treasured moments. Just four months after Bánky's marriage to La Rocque, *Picture Play* published a long feature describing the immense happiness shared by the newlyweds. On this occasion, Rod La Rocque described himself as a man who craves inspirational, feminine companionship, admitting he is "no bachelor by nature" and that no man "knows the essence of real living until he marries."[38] Such strong statements are ironic, given that only four months earlier the actor was reportedly denouncing marriage as overall unsuitable for a male movie star.[39]

In January 1929, *Motion Picture Classic* ran an article investigating one of Rod's hobbies, the expensive and relatively new leisure pursuit of photography (figure 16). "What best do you like to photograph, Mr. La Rocque? The sea, the sun, the stars? June mornings or April nights?" "Landscapes and Vilma," answered the actor. "But mostly Vilma. Vilma in mood capricious. Piquant Vilma. Vilma glad. Vilma any way, and always."[40] With its reliance on companionship, mutual understanding, and affection, and with simultaneous dismissal of overt sexual passion, the Bánky/La Rocque union epitomized the newly emerging idea of marriage governed by love and empathy, which required cultivation to flourish (figures 17a and 17b). It corresponded to the debates led by *Photoplay* and *Picture Play*, concerned with re-defining the existing definition of marriage as a traditional ritual. In the contemporary Hollywood setting, a family unit must feature partners who "work together and play together, have a happy home and get along splendidly," wrote Frances Marion, a successful screenwriter and outspoken public figure.[41]

The preoccupation with love, a trend so characteristic of fan magazines of the 1920s, "was elaborated within a carefully controlled discourse centered on the stars' domestic bliss as happily married heterosexual couples."[42] What is missing from the write-ups of Bánky and La Rocque's relationship is any indication of desire between the spouses, at least in its most explicit forms; this is particularly evident when one compares their union with the construction of other liaisons, such as Pola Negri's romance with Rudolph Valentino. Juxtaposed to the stories of Negri's affairs, summarized by extravagant gifts, lavish parties, and great passions (and even greater tragedies), Bánky's love life appears uneventful and static, but also stable and comforting. This is due to the ambivalent attitude toward the staging of whiteness and heterosexuality in the context of modernity. While "companionate love" required erotic sensitivity, it also demanded social respectability. Henceforth, the key to a successful white marriage lay in a calibrated amalgam of desire and self-control."[43] According to *Photoplay*, the volatile excess of Negri-style romances cannot be sustained in the long run, however exciting: "You hear of so many [Hollywood] engagements that never reach the altar," lamented the magazine in 1925.[44] The notion that romance is fleeting and does not guarantee happiness in marriage long-term is further confirmed in the interview with Adolphe Menjou, another popular actor of the period: "With marriages that last an emotion grows up between the man and a woman. It may be friendship. It may be gratitude. It may be mutual dependence. But it is neither romance nor love. These two always depart early."[45]

In her seminal study on the history of women in American society from the 1890s to the 1970s, Banner claims that the vast majority of suffragettes and early feminists did not question the imperatives of beauty and romantic love, sharing common sentiments regarding the inherent value of marriage as a social institution. Banner also labels the supposed sexual rebellion of the 1920s as quite arbitrary. The threat ascribed initially to the flapper waned, as she would eventually find herself a husband and settle for a conventional life within the realm of domesticity.[46] In her essay on the position of women in the 1920s, Freedman also re-examined the popular notion of the flapper as radical and independent, arguing that young urban women did not aim to shake up the existing order; instead, they still dreamed of getting married.[47] Like Banner, Freedman casts a shadow of doubt on the nature of alleged female revolt, which she considers no more than a temporary phase in the lives of young women of the period. In a similar vein, Greg M. Smith points out that women of the 1920s could pursue their ambitions insofar as they remained single. Whatever professional aspirations they had, they would always be subservient to a "higher" calling: marriage, family, and domestic submission.[48]

For the contemporary wealthy classes, the idea of women choosing a career over housewifery was not a popular one; the leading cultural debates saw the financial dependence on a male as a source of pride. Gaylyn Studlar deliberated how the fan press and women's magazines approved of work outside the family, as long as it was framed as a prelude to marriage, not as a career in its own right.[49] In her monograph on the history of female labor in the American landscape, Alice Kessler-Harris also observes that the still revered nineteenth-century ideal of the nonwage "lady of the house" was out of tune with modern social shifts, especially the rise of female professionalism in the 1920s.[50] Moreover, the principle that married women should not engage in paid work "except in cases of dire need" went hand in hand with the lack of practical support: no day care, no concept that men should share domestic chores, and no family leave.[51]

The studio system was, therefore, caught in a dilemma. Some of the stars it created and subsequently promoted—Mary Pickford, Colleen Moore, and Constance Talmadge, to name a few—were married women, which rendered the negotiations of discursive boundaries of family and female identity increasingly

Companionate

Vilma Banky and Rod they reconcile domes-

By Ruth

Rod takes care of their investments. The La Rocques frankly own up to an ambition to make and save plenty of money

WE have heard about the girls who are "Dodging the Wedding Ring" in the Cinema City. We have read Francis X. Bushman's advice "Don't Marry" given to young men with screen aspirations. Now let us spend an evening with two stars who failed to heed such words of warning, who just went out and were married.

Rod La Rocque and Vilma Banky.

You know, I am glad I had not chanced to meet these two stars until, some eight months after their world-renowned marriage, I went out to talk to them about it. Glad that I was not prepared, had no inkling as to whether they were really happy or already half-tired of their bargain.

As we sat down to dinner, it was Rod who remarked casually, "We've never missed a dinner together. Not one, since we were married."

And Vilma who added, "We usually eat alone. We don't like company for dinner." Then said hurriedly, "That is, we don't mind one or two, but we don't like to be in a crowd for dinner."

"But how do you manage your schedules?" I queried. Although there seemed little doubt that they were, indeed, happy, yet, to one used to the early hours, the night hours, the location hours of the motion picture schedule, it just didn't seem that matrimony between stars could run as smoothly as this surface-taste promised.

"We have two," they both answered. "One when we're working and one when we're not."

The working schedule is as follows:

Rise at eight. "When the studio is good to me," Vilma interjected. "When it's not, up an hour earlier."

Breakfast together.

At the studio by nine.

Luncheon together, when they're both working. When Vilma is working and Rod isn't, which is the case while this story is being written, Rod sees Vilma off, takes an hour in his gymnasium with his trainer, then comes into the house, reads the morning papers and checks up the amount they have lost or have made on the rise or fall of the stocks they have purchased. If it's a rise, he orders his car and dashes to the studio and lunches with Vilma to tell her how much money they have made since yesterday morning.

If they have lost, he telephones her and says, "Dear, I have to go down town and talk to our brokers about it." And even though they have won, when he leaves her after luncheon, he goes into Los Angeles to talk with his business advisers to see if they can sell anything at a profit and invest where they can make even more profit!

THEN home to dinner, together, alone, and out to a picture show in the evening.

Yes, a picture show is what they insist is their favorite recreation. Oh, they have to go to parties once in awhile, but not any oftener than is professionally and socially essential. For they are movie "fans" pure and simple. And I doubt if there is a picture you could mention, that they haven't seen and discussed together.

There is a neighborhood theater around the corner, where they see most of their pictures. Independent productions, comedies, whatever hodgepodge is offered. Once in awhile, downtown to a big theater, or to Cecil B. De Mille's private projection room, or some other producer's.

Home early and to bed, where they read, usually, O. Henry.

"You know," Rod said, "I had heard Europeans, as a rule, do not appreciate our O. Henry. Imagine my surprise and my joy

HERE are some of the rules that Vilma Banky and Rod La Rocque apply to keep peace in the family:

They eat dinner together.

They go to parties together.

They aren't jealous of each other's professional associates.

They never criticize each other's work until the film is finished.

They pool their money, but each reserves a small separate account for minor expenditures.

And—this is most important—they never both lose their tempers at the same time.

48

Figures 17a and 17b. Bánky and La Rocque explain how to "reconcile domesticity with careers" on the pages of *Photoplay*. Source: Ruth Biery, "Companionate Stardom," *Photoplay*, March 1928, 48–49.

Stardom

La Rocque tell how ticity with their careers

Biery

Vilma keeps the family budget. She runs her home far more economically than many housewives with nothing better to do

when I found Vilma loves him. We read him over and over, and the other day I caught Vilma telling her maid an O. Henry story!"

In one respect, at least, it is a very modern marriage. They have separate bedrooms and separate baths, too. This arrangement, Balzac once said, is the sign either of a completely happy marriage or a completely disastrous one. In this particular case, it is the sign of a completely congenial marriage.

They are happiest, they both agree, when neither happens to be working, when they are both "on vacation" at the same time.

"Our schedule is wonderful! We do exactly as we please!" Vilma described it.

Since their marriage, their "fan" mail has increased twenty per cent, which shows that the public approves of the match

They go to parties only when they are not working, and they go only together. They don't even dance with others—"unless we can't help it," Vilma explained.

"Are you ever jealous of each other's leading men and leading women?" It's a dangerous question, but I asked it.

"Why, we never think about it!" Rod answered, calmly.

"But, isn't it true the world wanted Vilma to marry Ronald Colman?"

ROD leaned across and answered quietly, "Our fan mail has increased between fifteen and twenty per cent since we married, and there has never been a suggestion that Vilma should have married Ronald Colman."

"Do you criticize each other's pictures?" I thought it time to change the subject.

"And how!" Vilma promptly aided in switching the conversation.

"But not while they are being made. Not until they are finished do we talk about them," Rod added.

Aside from their love and their profession, money is the most important question between them.

"We want to be very rich," Vilma announced frankly.

Rod laughed. "You know, I realized I was marrying a star, and I was prepared to make allowances. I did not [CONTINUED ON PAGE 92]

difficult. There was no universal schema when it came to the reconciliation of images of stars as homemakers and stars as figures of professionalism. Constance Talmadge was presented as a proponent of partnership in marriage, a position also taken by her equally forward-thinking sister Norma, who thought a star should find herself a husband who "tried sincerely to aid his wife in her profession."[52] Accounts pertaining to Colleen Moore sought to authenticate her image as a wife by accentuating the dual role of her husband and agent, John McCormick, producer of Moore's films until their divorce in September 1930.[53] The descriptions of Mary Pickford's labor, meanwhile, were often linked to a homely atmosphere sustained at the studio, a "veritable refuge" where all the employees are "one big family."[54]

Bánky's publicity likewise tried to resolve the tension between what, on the surface, appeared as two irreconcilable elements of her stardom—employment and marriage—by downplaying the importance of her independent status and showing her involvement in the industry as a natural extension of the family role she played. The fan press was replete with stories implying that Bánky knew the inner workings of the studios. This helped her sympathize with the problems faced by her husband, consequently strengthening their relationship: "And it is vary [*sic*] important that we both understand our work," she explained. "Moving-picture work many times is terrible trying and irritating, and would upset household if husband or wife were not sympathetic."[55] The revelation at the center of the aptly titled piece "Lessons in Love" was of a similar nature, with Bánky stating that understanding each other's point of view is one of the most essential requirements for a happy marriage. "Our careers do not separate us, perhaps because we are both doing the same kind of work. And yet I think we would understand each other as well if Rod were in a bank and I were a milliner."[56]

Bánky allegedly verbalized her desire to leave Hollywood to enjoy what was viewed as a woman's privilege: to relish the life of a housewife. Margaret Reid's piece explained that the star intended to retire from the movie screen after marriage, yet her plans of becoming a homemaker full time were cut short by La Rocque's domestic service, which did not allow the mistress of the house to partake in any of the domestic work.[57] Given the lack of immediately pressing duties, Bánky decided to continue with her acting work. The column oscillated between tradition and unconventionality, betraying the ambivalent positioning of Bánky-the-star, who was "trying to speak to and for a large audience but whose own situation demanded a constant negotiation between contradictory positions and ideologies."[58] In reality, when such stories made it to the pages of the gossip columns, Goldwyn's star was still bound by the five-year contract she had signed with the studio in 1925.

However, the limits to Bánky's tenure as a public figure did not apply to all of her press coverage; one daily newspaper implied, for instance, that she viewed marriage as not only compatible with but also beneficial to the advancement of her career: "Marriage, if successful, means a new sense of responsibility—it affords a new incentive for hard work, a new reason for achievement." In completely revolutionizing her outlook on life, marriage would positively affect Bánky's screen work to come, making it more refined.[59] Goldwyn's publicity machine perpetuated the rhetoric of presenting Bánky's star role as secondary to that of a wife, by making her voice her traditional views. "There is a great deal of nonsense talked of careers," she claimed in an interview with *Motion Picture Magazine* in 1929, revealing herself as a homemaker at heart. "I try not to be the actress in my home, but just the wife."[60]

While the columns were integral in "toning down" Bánky's career ambitions, attitudes placing equal stress on domesticity were not upheld with the same ferocity by all female movie players. Despite confessing to prioritizing motherhood over career, Leatrice Joy also admitted to detesting housework ("drudgery, unless a woman likes it") and cooking. Joy described herself as adamant about what she termed as the "resurrection of old platitudes." "In our mother's youth, a girl's sole ambition was to be a competent housewife. Home was her horizon," she explained, emphasizing that female aspiration was no longer curtailed, that modernity furnished women with a plethora of opportunities, be they financial or creative ones, and that it would be "ridiculous" not to take advantage of them, especially when domesticity and a career "can be hitched together without quarrelling too much."[61] Confronted with such descriptions, the stance taken by Bánky as a homemaker, first and foremost, appears fairly old-fashioned.

Through representing the new Mrs. La Rocque primarily as a wife, the studio underscored some of the already established, nonthreatening aspects of her persona, further highlighting the fact that she was not reconfiguring her life beyond the conventional patriarchal structures. Constructed in opposition to the more flamboyant Hollywood personalities, Bánky was portrayed as an introvert who preferred reading over attending extravagant parties.[62] One of the ways in which her persona perpetually re-enacted the ideas of female subordination was to refer to her conventional upbringing. For instance, when asked about one's ability to juggle household duties and a full-time job, Bánky explained: "I am very fortunate because my mother brought me up to be a wife. I never thought I should become an actress, but if I had a daughter who showed talent for some career, I should nevertheless teach her housekeeping first of all. Do not be misled by all this talk of feminists. Women were meant to be wives and make homes. My work is very dear to me. I take it seriously. But my home is dearer. I could never have been happy without it."[63]

Resonating at the core of this interview is a sense of hostility toward contemporary feminist ideals and a readiness to submit to a patriarchal ethos, features that operated to align Bánky with the prevalent ideology. Banner argues that the second half of the 1920s witnessed increasing disappointment in women's liberation, which in turn gave rise to a new form of antifeminism. The popular press became proficient in featuring revelations by (self-confessed) ex-feminists whose stories concluded that even liberated women found it difficult to work and have a family. Former feminists depicted by these accounts often regretted their association with the movement, contending that in gaining their rights they had to give up their privileges. Said privileges amounted to middle-class leisure, self-indulgence, and freedom from paid labor.[64] Karen Sternheimer notes that this pre-suffragette logic gained prominence as a means of counteracting the growing financial independence of women, at a time when their opportunities outside the family began to expand.[65] In this paradoxical dynamic, the narrative of Bánky's life operated as an ideological tool to promote female self-control and Puritan ethics, effectively encouraging women to limit their involvement in the professional sphere in favor of domesticity.

On one level, commentary assigned to Bánky tends to undermine women's engagement in paid work, drawing a clear line between what is represented as oppositional in modernity, between the domestic and public spheres. On another level—and this is an argument put forward by Shelley Stamp, developed convincingly by Anke Brouwers—such narratives are complex and can be viewed as an attempt to reconcile customary spheres of femaleness with emergent incarnations of female autonomy.[66] In commenting on the issue of combining marriage with careers, the fan press of the period supported the novel concept that professionalism and domesticity could co-exist, even if the former should be prioritized. Perhaps, it is significant to remember that a complete endorsement of professionalism would have been extremely hard to attain for a woman immersed in the dominant discourses of the 1920s. Brouwers contends it was a stepping stone that enabled women to "carve out a workable and socially acceptable space," a refuge that was "both defined and undermined by contradictory values and desires."[67]

If the short piece published by *Photoplay* is to be relied on, Rod La Rocque did not expect his wife to be any good at housekeeping; her exceptional ability to run a household came to him as a pleasant surprise. However, as Bánky explains, her husband forgot she was raised in Europe, where it is customary for women to be taught their domestic duties before embarking on any professional or artistic endeavor. By her own admission, Mrs. La Rocque knew how to keep a house before she knew anything about acting.[68] Somehow atypically of columns investigating housework, good housewifery is presented here as a desirable skill that needs to be learned and acquired through noninstitutionalized forms of education, rather than an innate female knowledge. It is interesting to note how, in the context of domesticity, the *Photoplay* article implemented a policy of equating Bánky's home country of Hungary with traditional, patriarchal ways of living. Amid the influx of foreign-born newcomers—actors and directors—

the image of Europe remained open to varying projections, ranging from the continent as a stable bulwark of gender convention to Europe as a paragon of debauchery and bohemia. This goes to show the degree of malleability contained within its cultural associations. The polarization between western and eastern parts of the continent is not without significance here; while the former region was linked to decadence, the latter held stronger ties with traditional patriarchal structures. The distinction, nevertheless, proved to be flexible throughout the 1920s, depending on the star as well as the specific national and ethnic undertones referred to. Pola Negri, most often conflated with being a gypsy, and hence connoting ideas related to eastern Europe, was hardly synonymous with images and ideals of domestic restraint.

Bánky's persona offers a useful case study in the shifting discourses of housewifery, which occupies an ambiguous, liminal site in the burgeoning culture of professionalism. It is at once *included in* and *excluded from* the paradigm of specialization because, while constituting a separate type of work, it simultaneously refers to an untrained form of labor.[69] Fanzines engaged with the construction of housework as concurrent with waged work, in the sense that both forms of labor required certain qualities that had to be exercised over time for ultimate achievement. No account of Bánky's married life at the time was complete without a remark celebrating her managerial skills in governing the family income and expenditure, thought of as a female responsibility. "[Bánky] runs her home far more economically than many housewives with nothing better to do," contended *Photoplay*, adding that the star was "so domestic, indeed, that she has her Viennese cook prepare their luncheons and their assistant chauffeur bring them to the studio, hot, in containers; not only because the taste is better, but because it is just a little cheaper."[70] Efficient, highly rationalized housework was integral not only to the establishment of female roles as wives but additionally to the fulfillment of their duties as aspiring American citizens. Such metanarratives functioned selectively to frame Bánky's talents (frugality, restraint, and organization) to demonstrate her "fitness for companionate marriage" and, by extension, for good citizenship.[71]

Bánky's image, celebrated for its close alliance with a Mary Pickford–esque brand of wholesome femininity, was vital in navigating the apparent incompatibility between the increasing professionalization of women and conservative gender norms. Visually, her traditional image is most evident in a number of features that offered the fans an insight into her living quarters, into what Simon Dixon calls "the domestic mise-en-scène of stardom."[72] The choice of the term is not coincidental, because articles that display stars in their domestic environment treat such spaces as settings marked by their screen presence, "an external stage, not a place but a *location*."[73] The relevance of Dixon's claim manifests itself through the comparison between pictures capturing the La Rocques' home, with its modest but classic furniture, and pictures showcasing the grandeur and opulence of houses belonging to stars acclaimed for their eccentricities, such as Gloria Swanson or Pola Negri.[74]

"In a Little Love Nest for Two" is a short feature consisting of photographs of the La Rocques in their abode. The article has no interest in elaborating on the peculiarities of the design, or the way in which they reflect the tastes of the two movie stars who inhabit them. Instead, the uncluttered interiors are used as a backdrop for a variety of domestic activities. They portray supposedly intimate scenes that any reader of gossip columns familiar with either the Bánky or La Rocque persona would, no doubt, expect them to perform, such as enjoying a meal together and reading. For example, the picture of the spouses eating while looking at each other is captioned: "The artful Rod is telling Vilma that he much prefers looking at her to eating," highlighting the romantic feelings between them.[75] "Rod interrupted Vilma in her boudoir to tell her how beautiful she is—and Vilma doesn't seem to mind," explains the description accompanying a picture of the star posing in front of her dressing table. Another conflation between the discourses of domesticity and companionate marriage is mediated through the photograph in the center, where Bánky is shown wearing an apron, with her husband kneeling in front of her, as if to confess his love.

Becoming American

Diane Negra has shown how ethnic female stardom denoted the promise of American pluralism, and "proved the desirability of the American dream" by providing either an example of triumph or a negative object lesson.[76] Bánky's biography, no doubt, bore witness to the former. While becoming Mrs. La Rocque did not change the legal status of the star—marriage to a U.S. citizen was no guarantee of American citizenship at the time—it did foster an opportunity to accentuate her loyalty toward her adopted country. The gender-based imaginary propagated by the star system functioned to reaffirm Bánky's position within patriarchal and nationalist theories; marriage to an all-American husband emphasized her readiness to integrate into U.S. society.

To use the framework developed by Antonella Palmieri in reference to another star, Italian-born Alida Valli, in the 1940s, Bánky's persona underwent a transition from European stranger, to "exemplary foreign guest" learning American ways, to the final stage of a "*good immigrant* who has proved she deserves acceptance and can enjoy the social, cultural and material benefits of successful assimilation."[77] Dorothy Donnell, a contemporary observer, wrote about this transformation:

> When Vilma Banky first came to Hollywood, she exclaimed vehemently that nevair, nevair [*sic*] would she remain here to marry an American man. She did not like our houses, our cooking, our amusements. She kept to herself, in

> a daze of homesickness, and shed tears at the thought of far-away Berlin where she had found fame. But when she married Rod La Rocque, his country became her country, his people her people. "Now I am more American than Hungarian", says Vilma, with only the faintest whisper of an accent. "More American than most Americans, I think. When I take out my final citizenship papers, I have learned the Constitution by the heart. Most of my native-born friends know only the first line. I made Rod learn at the same time—we two, we are both good Americans, and if I ever have any children, they will be born here."[78]

The process of her gradual Americanization was visualized through the ways in which Bánky embraced the customs of the New World, especially by starting to play golf and tennis, sports of strong elitist pretentions.[79] Both games have been the domain of the wealthy since the 1870s; both underwent a rapid surge in popularity in the 1920s and 1930s, with the middle-class demographic using their disposable income to mimic the activities of the most affluent families (such as the Vanderbilts, Carnegies, and Astors), through the acquisition of memberships in country clubs.[80] As pointed out by Arne Lunde in relation to Greta Garbo, being American appears to correlate inversely to the themes of freedom, and thus to physical vitality and athleticism.[81] Other theorists of globalization and Americanization also chart such links, placing sport within the context of common or lived culture.[82] While professional players commanded neither high prestige nor impressive salaries, the American psyche revered amateur ones, as they constructed "admirable models of athletic fitness, moral character, and honorable spirit."[83] Again, the link between assimilation and ability to participate in leisure activities is not incidental, as it also relates to the homogenic vision of Americanization, where all markers of American life are, by definition, synonymous with middle-class, gentile status. Therefore, interest in outdoor activities confirmed one's allegiance to a specific class. Paired with Bánky's impending retirement from public to the private sphere, such narratives created a safe identity for the Hungarian star.

This is not to say that attempts to manufacture Bánky as American were not made before her relationship with La Rocque. For example, Edwin Schallert and Elza Schallert reported that shortly before their engagement was made public, Bánky applied for American citizenship.[84] The act was dictated, as the article explained, by her extreme appreciation for all the privileges granted to her by her rise to Hollywood stardom. "Eet iss [*sic*] not lack of love for my country. . . . Eet iss appreciation of-f all thees country has done for me."[85] "Must they become American?" asked *Picture Play* in an article titled with the same question, concluding that—however controversial the issue—the effort undertaken by some foreign stars to obtain American citizenship is an admirable, if only symbolic, gesture of gratefulness. Bánky in particular earns an honorable mention as one of the first actresses in a foreign colony to seek her naturalization papers.[86] Fashioned as a continual invocation of the American dream, columns of this nature indicated the overriding concern of the star system with providing audiences with the most desirable models of civic behavior. References to other foreign players frequently appeared alongside discussion of Bánky and her exceptional willingness to adapt to the American way of life. As suggested by William McKegg, "where other European importations flared over the cinema horizon, flashing temperamental wings of egotism, Vilma remained quiet and essayed to learn the manners and ways of the people she had come to live among."[87]

In 1929, *Motion Picture Classic* confirmed that the star had taken out papers to apply for American citizenship, because "she wants Uncle Sam for a genuine relative, not as an in-law acquired through her marriage to Rod La Rocque."[88] Even so, marriage was one of the central tenets that manifested her putative transformation from a European girl to an all-American wife. According to a long feature published by *Picture Play* in June 1929, she was not a shy girl from Hungary but a fully Americanized woman who could no longer associate herself with Europe.[89] The transition from being a guest in Hollywood to being a citizen was made evident in her fluent, confident use of English, which resembled a New York accent.[90]

The role of exemplary whiteness in this highly publicized quest for social acceptance, supported by the simultaneous erasure of Bánky's Hungarian identity, cannot be underestimated. After all, ethnic identities—including those placed at the bottom of internal, ever-shifting hierarchies of whiteness in American culture, exemplified by Italians, Spaniards, or eastern Europeans—were considered a burden, a problem to overcome.[91] Through her morphing into a representative of movie royalty, Vilma La Rocque was restored to the aristocratic privilege her former self, Vilma Bánky, purportedly enjoyed in the prewar Europe. She regained her throne through Hollywood success, within the transformative tale where one's life in America is an authentic realization of one's full potential.

"Vilma Banky La Rocque announced recently and very firmly that she was through, that she was going to stay at home and be the little house frau she has always longed to be, that she would go in for kiddies in Big Way and be a proper wife to Rod," proclaimed *Motion Picture Classic* in October 1930.[92] Bánky's contract with United Artists had expired in April of that year and was not extended, which effectively marked the end of her illustrious work on American screens. According to the evaluation provided by Schildgen, the reasons behind her retirement were likely to differ from those cited by fan magazines, at least to some extent.[93] In fact, it can be argued that the coming of sound curtailed the progress of Bánky's career; like so many other silent movie players, she was unable to solidify her position in the changing market of the 1930s. Such hardheaded considerations were touched on in the previous chapter, specifically in relation to one of her last cinematic works, *This Is Heaven* (1929). On a broader, ideological plane, the gradual limitation of Bánky's public visibility can be understood as a sign of abiding by Puritan rules, where her eventual disappearance into the domestic sphere marks a culmination of the trajectory of total assimilation.

Conclusion

By the time of Bánky's marriage to La Rocque, her star persona had already been shaped in favor of traditional female values, such as modesty and a desire to settle down. She did not challenge the received wisdom that a woman should find a man in order to feel complete. Samuel Goldwyn publicized the private activities of his chief star to increase her visibility and further perpetuate the conflation between her filmic image and the characteristics she emblematized off-screen. This was achieved, quite explicitly, first by drawing attention to Bánky's wedding and then by painting the relationship between "Vilma and Rod" as exceptionally happy and romantic, but not overtly erotic, and therefore affiliated to the most esteemed attributes of whiteness.

All stars embody a narrative tension, whether consciously or not.[94] In Bánky's case, this paradox can be located in her roles as both wife and star, as someone inhabiting both the private and the public spheres. Many feminist scholars argue that, despite the widely held notion of the 1920s as a decade that saw significant changes in gender roles, the prevalent ideology continued to see full-time housewifery as the most suitable occupation for middle-class women for whom paid labor was not a fiscal necessity, even if they were allowed an initial period of independent adulthood and financial agency.[95] The incongruous aspects of Bánky's image were reconciled through a repetitive affirmation of her intention to prioritize marriage over her acting career. Domesticity became a facet that anchored Bánky's image to the prudish standards of the American hinterlands; in framing her primarily as a wife to another film star, the studio system made sure she conformed to the dominant cultural climate. As a result, she not only retained her association with conventional white femininity but also enhanced her position in the narrative of assimilation.

Although the star discourse belittled Bánky's professional success—so it could be presented as concomitant with the institution of marriage, rather than constituting a direct threat to it—her juggling of professional and private lives can be read as a positive departure from the status quo. In keeping with the argument put across by Stamp and Brouwers, although such stories were problematic, they also initiated a small but significant step toward a stronger sense of female independence.

CHAPTER 6

Jetta Goudal and Exoticism

"SHE LOOKS LIKE A BEAUTIFUL COSSACK. SHE LOOKS LIKE AN ORIENTAL PRINCESS"

Jetta Goudal, a rising actress of Dutch origin, first appeared on the silver screen in a small role in Richard Barthelmess's historical drama *The Bright Shawl* (1923). Her portrayal of Pilar—half-Chinese, half-Peruvian—immediately brought the actress to the attention of *Picture Play*, which called Goudal "a picturesque newcomer" and "one of the most unusual and interesting screen debutantes."[1] The same year saw the release of *The Green Goddess* (1923), where she was cast as an Indian servant of the raja. In his forecast for 1924, Edwin Schallert listed the performer as one of the most noteworthy personalities to look out for in the upcoming season.[2] According to the description penned by *Motion Picture Classic*, Goudal was a French native with a particularly Oriental slant to her beauty: "Notwithstanding her intriguing type it was some time before she gained recognition. Her first picture is *Martinique* [*The Bright Shawl*], with its locale in the tropics, where passions are like cloud bursts and the niceties of life are swept away in the flood."[3]

A brief overview of Goudal's cinematic oeuvre illuminates the workings of a prevailing Western logic, according to which "The Orient" is not defined in any rigid terms. Culturally, the notion of Orientalism is not attributed to any specific geographic setting; therefore, Goudal—like many other European actors of the period—shifted freely among playing heroines of Hispanic, Russian, or Peruvian origin. This type of imagery underpinned many of her incarnations on celluloid, especially those crafted at DeMille's studio. Thus, the role of a "wicked half-caste" from her cinematic debut set a precedent for the types of female representation Goudal would come to embody.[4] She went on to portray a Mexican dancer in the lachrymose melodrama *White Gold* (1927), was cast in the role of a French woman four times in her career, and appeared as Russian, Italian, Spanish, and Indian heroines in other productions.[5] This chapter interrogates the exotic aspect of Goudal's star persona by exploring the ways in which her image fed into American projections of the Orient. It discusses how certain elements of the star's physique were used to fetishize the idea of ethnic difference and how the star system framed Goudal's alleged non-whiteness as a consumable pleasure in a process that Ella Shohat has termed the "spectacle of difference."[6] Publicity stills and other extrafilmic materials embraced the performative possibilities of costume to nourish fantasies of exoticism, presenting Goudal draped in kimonos, feather gowns, and attire that unmistakably underlined her position of otherness in relation to white American culture.

The Star Body as a Spectacle

Edward Said identified the fantasy of the East as "almost a European invention," which "had been since antiquity a place of romance, exotic beings, haunting memories and landscapes, remarkable experiences."[7] Said theorized the Orient as devoid of any specific topography; the cultural imagery of the West places it above geographical settings to create a realm where neither space nor time matters. Exotic lands are constructed as outposts of legends. They are thrilling, ready-made spectacles for colonial consumption. In her theoretical development of Said's ideas, Karla Rae Fuller showed how, depending on the historical period, the American notion of the Orient encompassed places as distant as the Arabian Peninsula and Asia, especially China, Japan, and India.[8]

Commentary gleaned from the pages of fan magazines imbued Goudal with the representational characteristics of the Middle and Far East. Those periodicals often relied on potent symbols of exotic flowers and starry nights. Descriptions deployed by *Motion Picture Classic*, for instance, spoke of embodiments familiar from post-enlightenment visual arts, which had become conventional constructions in filmmaking by the 1910s: "Jetta Goudal is rather a fantastic person whose strange beauty intrigues the imagination. Surely from no commonplace background came that dance, those long pale hands, *like lotus buds that float*. Surely there are memories of old customs and silken loves, of dances to outlandish instruments, of burning days and deaths that ordinary people do not die, behind those inscrutable eyes of Jetta."[9]

This short passage is pregnant with a variety of tropes: from dance and lotus flowers to expensive fabrics, all of which speak of the non-Western world as a rich, vibrant setting beyond time.[10] It succeeds in creating a sense of a liminal zone where thrills and passions await. Popular discourse of the 1920s constructed the Orient in terms of its binary opposition to attributes of the West—to rationality, modernity, and masculinity. The imagery of the East was employed to evoke the phantasmagoria of the long-lost ancient world and to suggest a degree of mysticism. One reflection of this attitude is introduced by William McKegg, *Picture Play*'s columnist, according to whom Goudal obtained her mysterious, bewitching powers by means of reincarnation, "when she first came to earth, many thousands of years ago in Egypt."[11] The association with the land of the pharaohs enabled the journalist to draw on the nineteenth-century rhetoric of timelessness and the conquest of death.[12] It also mirrored the current craze for all things Egyptian—so-called Egyptomania—that swept America and Europe in the aftermath of the discovery of Tutankhamen's tomb in 1922.

The definition of the Orient as lacking both precise geographical and historical specificity influenced the construction of Goudal's persona, because her own, supposedly Oriental heritage remained in the realm of hearsay. That is, she was simultaneously presented as French, although rumored to have Mongolian, Cossack, or even Javanese blood.[13] When Goudal began to rise in prominence in 1924, *Motion Picture Classic* noted that "she looks like a beautiful Cossack. She looks like an Oriental princess. She looks like . . . well, whatever it is that has changing hazel eyes that slant at the corners; that slumber and drowse; then blaze with fires."[14] Two years later Margaret Reid wrote in *Photoplay* that Goudal looks neither French nor Dutch but could be reasonably mistaken for a Eurasian, "with maybe a trace of hindoo [*sic*] blood somewhere."[15]

Drawing on postcolonial theory, Fuller argues that the term "Oriental" supersedes national and racial classifications, "and thus, allows for shifts, transformations and reconfigurations over time due to its flexible boundaries."[16] It is in this context that we should understand fluctuating perceptions of Goudal's ethnicity. The similarly imprecise characteristics of exoticism fill out this cultural dynamic, as demonstrated by *Photoplay*'s claim that "being exotic is more a question of charm and personality and allure than of any regular style of beauty."[17]

In a similar vein, *Picture Play*'s piece "Never an Emerald without a Flaw" discussed the physical features of stars in great detail, eventually locating the charm of many foreign players in something that goes beyond their often-imperfect looks: in their magnetic aura and personality. The description of Goudal in this account focused on her mysterious appeal, highlighted by "high cheekbones, slightly flat nose and oblique eyes."[18] Her face was deemed appealing but "certainly far from beautiful." Such a portrayal stands in great contrast to the terms used to describe Janet Gaynor, a blonde star born and raised in Philadelphia, who occupied the other end of the representational spectrum and was lucky enough to have "no greater irregularities." Her charm, according to the column, lay in "her freshness and her naiveté."[19] Given the promulgation of whiteness as both an aesthetic and a spiritual ideal in the Anglophone world, *Picture Play*'s veneration of Gaynor's innocent qualities is hardly surprising. Within a culture that considered whiteness to be the apex of human virtue, Gaynor's blonde hair and fair skin served as compelling ciphers of radiant beauty and spiritual wholesomeness. Fair skin, and other physical attributes associated with it, is not only "a mark of perfection in human form"[20] but also a signifier of positive mental characteristics. Set against this construction of whiteness, ethnic difference expressed itself through association with darkness; Goudal had, in the words of one of her fans, "mid-night hair and mysterious, smoldering eyes" [*sic*] that were only accentuated by her dark makeup.

What does juxtaposing Goudal to Gaynor teach us? Richard Dyer has shown how explicit comparisons between the colonial other and the white subject were means of making whiteness, in its apparent invisibility as an ethnicity, more pronounced.[21] They also functioned to inculcate and reinforce racial tactics, fostering identification with Anglo-Saxon American culture in the magazine's readership. In being a supposedly exotic star, Goudal could be deemed fascinating or mysterious but not beautiful, because her looks did not conform to the prerogatives of white femininity. A moviegoer whose musings were published by *Picture Play* spoke in awe of Goudal's "piquant features" and "bewitching personality."[22] Margaret Reid of *Picture Play* joined the common sentiment by claiming to be unable to establish if Goudal was beautiful or not. She was certain, however, that the star was one of the most captivating, electrically magnetic women she had ever seen on the silver screen.[23] Accounts like this are a reminder of the central role played by ethnicity in the cultural construction of female beauty, where whiteness occupies the position of a universal ideal to which everyone should aspire or adhere to. As such, they follow tropes accelerated in the aesthetically embraceable image of Vilma Bánky, examined in the previous case study.

While vamp star types had to be juxtaposed to white American stars to conjure up an image of difference, the dominant ideology did not differentiate between the various ethnicities of the exotic other. As a distinctive strategy of the star system in the period, this dynamic allowed nonwhite ethnic identities to be interchangeable. In that respect, Said's model of Orientalism could extend to Mediterraneans and eastern Europeans. Indeed, Hollywood's publicity expanded the boundaries of the Orient to continental Europe; the Polish gypsy Pola Negri, Americans Nita Naldi and Natacha Rambova, as well as Franco-Dutch Goudal all fall under the category of Orientalism through their association with exoticism, regardless of their respective nationalities or ethnicities. Fan magazines promulgated a discourse that embraced the notion of a sensual allure inherent in exotic female types. All these female stars came to be cast as sexually provocative women on-screen. Goudal herself was "a vamp with a soul," a "composite of all the shady ladies history offers" (such as Bella Donna and Lucrecia Borgia), and a star of similar disposition to Negri and Alla Nazimova.[24]

Many scholars have contextualized the ways in which popular culture—and cinema specifically—persistently assigns women to the position of objects of display, reducing sexual difference to a form of spectacle.[25] This "to-be-looked-at-ness,"[26] as Laura Mulvey famously termed it, re-emerges with special force in relationship to star bodies. Jackie Stacey's groundbreaking study of female spectatorship, *Star Gazing*, points out that, in an ongoing process of commodification, every facial feature and every detail of a star's appearance can be dissociated from its context and abstracted ad infinitum, potentially becoming a powerful symbol on its own.[27] The body of the star therefore constitutes a cultural image that goes beyond the sum of its parts. In the 1920s, *Picture Play* took the lead in publishing articles that explained the meaning behind every aspect of star physiques. Jetta Goudal's face specifically was "of the Oriental mold—high cheekbones, a nose which one might term Mongolian, an oval face, oblique eyes. These suggest, first impassivity, then wisdom. And great reserve force."[28]

Stacey argues that the body of a female star is "infinitely commodifiable" because apart from being a commodity in itself, separate elements of her body (such as her hair, and particularly parts of her face) also go through the process of objectification. Hence, star bodies gain prominence within the realm of visual culture, becoming commodified fetish objects. Ella Shohat and Robert Stam have discussed how the colonial discourse of the exotic other tends to resurface in relationship to star bodies, mostly focusing on the bodies of women.[29] The objectified function of the star bodies in what Marguerite Rippy calls "a cycle of fantasy, performance and commodification"[30] is accentuated further if the star body represents ethnic otherness. Francesca T. Royster refers to the process of accentuation and circulation of fetishized body parts in the public realm as "the trade in celebrity bodies," noting that such trade is "necessarily but also unpredictably influenced by race."[31] Therefore, in the framework constructed by white culture, Goudal's supposedly exotic body went through the process of double objectification: first, as the body of a female star, and second, as the body of someone marked by racial difference, and whose body is "offered up for aberrant pleasure."[32] The ideas incorporated in the concept of Orientalism are thus aligned with other Western constructions, such as the dichotomies of race, ethnicity, and gender.[33] Consequently, Goudal's star narrative became a site of confluence for both a broader gender dynamic and the colonial imagery.

The appeal of exoticism was harnessed not only by stylized descriptions of star looks but also through the decorative qualities of the costumes worn by Goudal in her films, publicity stills, and other extratextual sources. Gaylyn Studlar sees the period between 1919 and 1926, some of the years during which Goudal remained active professionally, as the time when the deployment of an Eastern iconography in Hollywood reached its peak.[34] For Gundle and Castelli, the Orient is an ideal that provides the opportunity for aesthetic exaggeration; it is a manner of embellishing commodities with elements of dream and escapism, rather than a rigid aesthetic style.[35] Within the bourgeoning consumer culture, American visions of the East became a consumable phenomenon, sold to the general public in the form of ornamental, fashionable accessories and garments.[36]

In his study of Orientalism and its impact on the history of Western fashion, Adam Geczy argues that, contrary to common belief, Oriental themes were not popular in everyday wear during the interwar years, with fashion designers favoring simple, angular forms over ornamental opulence.[37] Lucy Fisher concurs with that view, adding that the aesthetic of art nouveau made an impact on the cinematic medium at a time when it was, ironically, declining in other artistic forms.[38] Through Geczy's perspective, a vogue for garments evoking the exotic lands of Asia maintained its most vibrant influence in the medium of film, where it worked in conjunction with classical narrative strategies to support the escapist imperative.

Beyond the silver screen, fashion was used as a fruitful locus of Oriental fantasy that rendered its famous wearers as extraordinary individuals. Promotional images of stars dressed in Japanese kimonos, Russian sarafans, and other types of ethnic costumes proliferated, reproduced on a previously unknown scale. Staged, consciously costumed, and framed, these photographs were performative activities, a form of racial masquerade that indicated the element of fluidity contained within the notion of exoticism. By 1923, fan periodicals featured an average of eighty-eight stills per issue, with head shots and half-length formats of female idols "dominating the pictorial field."[39] Silent movie players often posed in ensembles reflecting the current taste for Orientalist tropes, thus creating mutable identities;[40] some, including Pola Negri (as we have seen in relation to her occasional embodiment of Spanishness), Rudolph Valentino, and Alla Nazimova,[41] a Russian-born designer, performer, and producer, were distinguishable for a stylistic appropriation of this type. Valentino, for instance, was often pictured in various ethnic costumes, rehearsing aesthetic incarnations as varied as that of Native American chief (figures 18a and 18b), Mexican gaucho, or Indian raja.[42]

Culturally, clothing works on many levels, situating the wearer within broader aesthetic trends of the era while also communicating their cultural capital and status. Throughout the late nineteenth and early twentieth centuries, fashion's role as an indicator of personal taste had been increasing in stature. It is therefore notable that one of the very first features that introduced Goudal (then a newly emerged starlet) to the readers of *Picture Play* in late 1923 focused on the "cosmopolitan, continental air" apparent in the way she dressed. Through the choice of accessories—she wore a flowing afternoon gown, complete with the scarlet straw hat, "cascading earrings and the dim native peacock fan"[43]—Goudal was placed outside the discourse of practical fashion and mainstream femininity. She entered the realm of glamour. Such press coverage was often accompanied by photographs that accentuated non-Western sartorial styles and garments, simultaneously securing Goudal's reputation as an ethnic other and a dangerous vamp. As a graphic strategy, it draws back from the cultural and stylistic tropes of fin de siècle, where the "fatal woman" is a figure "indelibly associated with a rising fashion for a certain kind of exoticism in which we find (both) a concern for exact historical reconstruction, and a desire for escape into the nowhere land of dreams."[44]

Figures 18a and 18b. Racial masquerade. Valentino in Native American costume and Goudal wearing a kimono. Source: Valentino as an Indian, photograph by Russell Bell, *Motion Picture Magazine*, December 1923, 40; Goudal wearing kimono, German postcard by Ross Verlag, no. 3332/1, 1928–1929. Photo: DPC.

Feathers, furs, and animal prints all feed into the mythology of the Orient as an opulent, extravagant, decadent world created in opposition to the strict laws of modernity. Yet, these materials are more than indicators of exotic excess and primitivism, with Gundle and Castelli contending that attire festooned with feathers also conjures the ideas of a refined society.[45] Feathers of Asian birds were

a part of the imagery attached to exoticism in its most sensual and lavish version. Allegorically speaking, plumage has a strong relation to a certain type of threatening femininity, as it is one of the most easily appropriable symbols of seduction in the animal kingdom.[46] Such connection is especially evident in silent film's take on mythical temptresses: from Blanche Sweet's biblical Judith, seen in a giant peacock tiara, through Theda Bara's Cleopatra, festooned in feathers, or again, Nazimova's Salomé, who, in the screen adaptation of the same title, appears in front of Herod in an ornate peacock headdress.[47]

Animal-based garments featured prominently in publicity-generated, consumable images of Goudal. An undated, unattributed photograph of the star frames her face with a layer of ostrich feathers, feasibly another allusion to the decadence of art nouveau. For one, this kind of representation also ties Goudal to the vocabulary of Egypt (already present in fan magazines), to the aesthetics of giant feather fans, lotus flowers, and nemes crowns.[48] The complex iconography of pearls in the photograph, seen in the embroidery of the headdress and as strands of the necklace, adds to the richness of representation on offer here. Pam Cook interprets pearls as carriers of multiple meanings related to female sexuality, ranging from purity and elegance to the explicitly sensual.[49] The jewel's Eastern origin and striking symbolic connotations of female genitalia are both noteworthy in creating overtones of both the exotic and the corporeal.[50] In representing Goudal amid fetishized artifacts, in a manner conveying powerful associations of the Orient, photographs like this became key texts through which her star phenomenon associated itself with the specter of the exotic. Fashion further confirmed her unique position on the Hollywood firmament, transforming Goudal into a semi-mythical, glamorous creature driven by primal passions.

Exoticism On-Screen

As previously noted, Goudal's role as Pilar de Lima in *The Bright Shawl* constituted the beginning of efforts to define her star status in terms of ethnic masquerade and iconographic otherness. Here, the rising starlet—referred to mistakenly as "Miss Goodell" by the writer of *Motion Picture Magazine*—incarnates a vamp whose menacing charms lure one of the male protagonists to his death.[51] Though of relatively small narrative significance, the part was elaborated on by many journalists, who saw Goudal as perfectly suited for its physical requirements. As "an exotic little being" herself,[52] the actress was able to create a convincing performance of the racialized other, described by the film's literary source as a woman of enigmatic charm (largely arising from the fact that her features were, to a marked degree, identifiable as Chinese).[53] The cinematic version of Pilar de Lima is a "suave, smiling and sinister tool of the Spanish secret service."[54] Her identity as half-Peruvian, half-Chinese, represents a tendency of the era to imbue people of mixed ethnic origin with negative connotations, often linked to deception. The crossing of racial lines inherent to miscegenation echoes other transgressive elements of the character, such as Pilar's position as a special agent.

A broadly defined version of Orientalism was exploited in a bid to advertise the production. *Motion Picture Classic* and *Picture Play* provided their readers with evocative portraits of Pilar in headdresses reminiscent of Russian tradition, evidencing the degree of interchangeability between different forms of Oriental fashions (figures 19a and 19b).[55] Indeed, the visual culture of the United States mixed elements of Egyptomania, Japonisme, Chinoiserie, and Style Russe, creating an intoxicating style that, in losing its national specificity, denoted little more than opposition to aesthetic traditions of the West.[56]

Goudal was offered her first lead in the adaptation of Anzia Yezierska's novel *Salome of the Tenements* (1925), in which she starred as Sonya Mendel, a Russian-Jewish immigrant. Faced with the daily struggles of living in the poor community of the Lower East Side of New York, she sets to run away from "the blackness of poverty" and rise to higher social standing through marriage.[57] It is worth noting that even the title of the film—and the literary source it has been adapted from—reveals a strong association between its protagonist and an irresistible appetite for power. Drawing on the biblical figure of Salomé, "a craven seducer and a destroyer of men,"[58] the text establishes its heroine as a cipher of seduction, a modern siren, and a dangerous vamp. The enthusiastic review of the *New York Times* drew on this long-established lexicon rather explicitly, calling Goudal's character "a saucy little specimen" with "implicit confidence in her power to conquer men."[59] Sonya's courting of the gentile banker and philanthropist John Manning is marked by deception from the start: she manages to conceal her working-class origin by obtaining an expensive designer dress free of charge, therefore constructing and maintaining a fabricated class identity. Her efforts culminate in success as she wins his heart and the couple marries, but their happiness is soon threatened by financial trouble. In one columnist's words, "Of course the disaster must threaten her before the picture has ended. It does. In a note she gave a pawnbroker. But *Manning* [the husband] settles him and all is well."[60]

The core of the story depicted by *Salome of the Tenements* lies in the thematization of social boundaries and class distinction. It is about power. Even though Sonya's "vamping exploits"[61] testify to the dangers of gaining one's love through dishonesty, her endeavors do not offer a cautionary tale. In other words, the implications of her achievements do not correspond to the established pattern of rags-to-riches stories rehearsed by vamp characters, where a woman's ascent to the higher echelons of class is punished if the transformation does not go hand in hand with virtue.[62] Many historians have argued that moral uprightness is a crucial component of class ethos in the United States, which hails "honesty, or honest economy and toil, integrity [and] charity" as necessary for anyone wanting to move up the social hierarchy.[63] The American Dream moralizes social mobility, in the sense that it deems it achievable only by individuals whose motives align themselves with the dominant perception of moral probity. At the outset of Yezierska's novel, Sonya exhibits a conspicuous lack of any of these positive attributes, being described as "an egoist with a driving force that will carry her anywhere."[64] Instead of being punished, she triumphs—a fact that alarmed some literary critics. To them, *Salome of the Tenements* was ethically reprehensible.[65] The *Educational Screen* thought the picture play's storyline of cross-class,

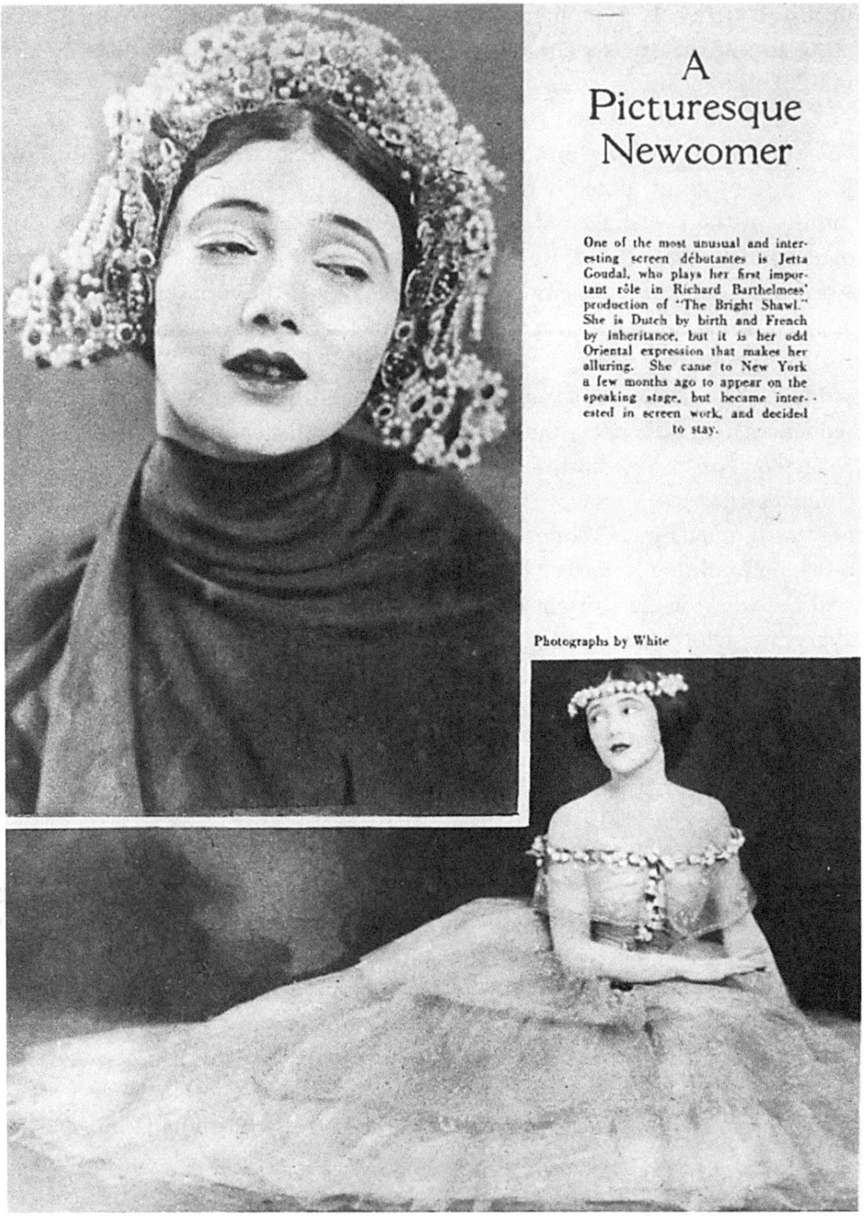

A Picturesque Newcomer

One of the most unusual and interesting screen débutantes is Jetta Goudal, who plays her first important rôle in Richard Barthelmess' production of "The Bright Shawl." She is Dutch by birth and French by inheritance, but it is her odd Oriental expression that makes her alluring. She came to New York a few months ago to appear on the speaking stage, but became interested in screen work, and decided to stay.

Photographs by White

Figures 19a and 19b. Features advertising *The Bright Shawl* (1923). *Picture Play*, July 1923, and *Motion Picture Classic*, June 1923.

interethnic romance was predictable, noting it depicted "the usual wicked schemes of the enemies of both [parties]."[66]

Was such representation extended to *The Coming of Amos* (1925), Goudal's first feature made under a new contract with the esteemed director and producer Cecil B. DeMille? Her character, Princess Nadia Ramiroff, is first introduced to the plot as "the exiled Princess Nadia of Russia—who has played havoc with many European hearts, including the Scandinavian." The intertitle works with visual information—Nadia wears a kokoshnik, an opulent diadem-shaped headdress—to convey a sense of exotic and potentially dangerous thrills. Visually, her appearance corresponds to the attractions of the Orient institutionalized in popular culture, and specifically its taste for luxury, overindulgence, and a penchant for excess.[67] The traditional tiara, combined with a cloche hat, has been featured in photographs of Aileen Pringle, Dolores Del Rio, Florence Vidor, Anna May Wong, and many popular female movie players, epitomizing the vogue for Russian-inspired garments.

Reflecting the perpetual deployment of exoticism as an opportunity to create spectacle, Nadia's costume makes her at once desirable and threatening, glamorous and inferior. Some of the stylized images included in fan magazines also depicted Goudal wearing a kokoshnik, which is an illuminating example of how the star system could utilize fashion to bridge the gap between on-screen and off-screen narratives of stars.

Soon enough, though—and despite such a bold introduction—the storyline reveals that the princess is no femme fatale in the traditional sense of the term; as a character, Nadia has no active engagement in bringing doom to the men that fall for her. Rather, she is a signifier of trauma perpetuated directly by Garcia Ramirez, her evil admirer. Nadia's love for the main protagonist, Amos (Rod La Rocque), is not a scheme devised to obtain social or financial advantage.

However, the purity of her intentions means very little in the eyes of the immediate threat posed by the jealous Ramirez, who is determined to kill anyone who lays eyes on his beloved. Initially, Goudal's tragic heroine appears to be bound to her disastrous fate. Sensing the romantic tension between the woman he desires and the newly arrived Amos, Ramirez cautions her: "You seek your happiness so far afield, Madame. I am the voice that calls you home." Once the princess realizes that three men who were linked to her died recently in mysterious circumstances, she tries to distance herself from Amos in order to save him. What ensues is a series of dramatic fights between the vicious Ramirez and the titular character that all end in victory for the former. In the final scheme of things, Goudal's Nadia is unable to determine her own fate and becomes a token of victory for the hero.

Another noteworthy concern of the film, interwoven with questions of gender and nationality, is the representation of class relations. Amos is a salt-of-the-earth, working-class type whose lack of savoir vivre sets him apart from his aristocratic uncle and his milieu. He might be socially inept, but his naïveté—alongside his superior skill in throwing a boomerang—renders him morally superior to the luxurious but corrupted lifestyle of the wealthy inhabitants of the French Riviera. In her discussion of the star persona of Alida Valli, Antonella Palmieri argues that the eventual acquisition of a European woman by a deserving and righteous American in film symbolizes the inherent vulnerability of Europe and its need for U.S. protection.[68] *The Coming of Amos* seems to share a similar, patronizing approach toward interclass and international relationships, even despite Amos's identity as an Australian.

Two of the pictures Goudal made during her tenure at DeMille's studio, *Three Faces East* (1926) and *The Forbidden Woman* (1927), deal explicitly with the pernicious myth of women in espionage, drawing Goudal's respective characters in bold outline. The former depicts the inner workings of the German and British Secret Service, and Goudal is cast as a "fascinating woman of intrigue" whose position between two conflicting powers is not revealed until the final scene.[69] *Photoplay* assured its readers of the sophisticated nature of the story and its potential appeal to female moviegoers: "It's about the war—but don't let that or anything else keep you away from this picture. It is not the conventional war play. There are no trenches or barbed wire or dead soldiers."[70] Meanwhile, *Picture Play*'s reviewer concentrated on the glamorous allure of its "pictorially perfect" lead.[71]

In *The Forbidden Woman*, Goudal portrays Zita, a Moroccan spy and daughter of the sultan, who is forced to marry a French colonel to serve her country in obtaining military secrets.[72] On her journey to Paris, Zita meets a famous violinist and, to her despair, becomes entrapped by her romantic feelings for the man who soon turns out to be her brother-in-law. When the colonel catches the lovers red-handed, he sends his brother to Morocco; Zita falls victim to her convoluted circumstances and eventually confesses to treachery.

The two brothers are reconciled over the subsequent conviction and execution of Goudal's character.[73] The storyline places Zita in the position of an intruder, a figure of unbridled conceit that disrupts the stability of the relations between the two male protagonists. It is only when she is declared dead that their relationship regains its status quo. Initially, the plot creates a dual desire to both condemn and pity the double dealings of its heroine; the final sequence, however, invites little more than straightforward denunciation.

The unique mixture of the ingredients brought by Goudal's on-screen presence injected new life into the symbol of the vamp, making Zita a peculiar hybrid between a fatal siren and a woman desperate to be loved. Visually, the mutual imbrication of patriarchal and Orientalist discourses comes to the forefront in the publicity stills promoting *The Forbidden Woman*, where Goudal is bathed in dramatic lighting, wearing a rich Oriental headdress and heavy earrings.[74] Yet, there is something ambiguous about her soulful gaze, which can be read as both threatening, and thus symptomatic of her performance as a spy, and vulnerable, hence indicative of the film's narrative, where her character yearns to love and be loved.

Overwhelmingly, the opinions generated by the film speak of the currency of Goudal's image as a consolidated symbol of otherness. "Seldom has the exotic star been better cast," wrote *Moving Picture World*.[75] Joining the accolades, another review suggested that "La Goudal is perhaps the most luminous and exotic actress on the screen."[76] Interestingly (but not surprisingly), *Photoplay* remarked on the resemblance between the role of Zita and the one incarnated by Goudal in her previous picture, *Three Faces East*, as a variation on the same type.[77]

Rosie White argues that female spies confound the binary understanding of gender in patriarchal society because they are active, a quality not traditionally assigned to femininity.[78] Their engagement in obtaining secret information, often through sexual means, made them dangerous individuals defined in opposition to traditional ideals of womanhood centered on concepts of passivity and innocence. White also suggests that spy fictions are wired to the fear of national identity being in peril.[79] Likewise, Julie Wheelwright views spy fictions as metathemes that flourished in historical periods when the perceived independence of women in society was growing. "The lingering fear" that accompanied the changes in gender dynamics of the 1920s "was often found in the predictable plots of spy novels," she writes.[80]

The boundary-crossing nature of the spy archetype, as well as its reliance on images of national identity, makes it compatible with the figure of the Oriental temptress.[81] Another motif implicit within the chameleon-like persona of both the exotic seductress and the female agent is their function in intensifying anxieties of sexual difference. Writers and filmmakers seized the myth of the female spy, creating fictional portraits that spoke of passion, Orientalism, and, ultimately, of deceit being punished by death (figure 20). By setting up an equation between the Oriental other and potentially lethal deception, *The Forbidden Woman* reinstates the cultural images of mythical temptresses, such as Salomé, Jezebel, and Cleopatra. One of the posters for the film brings the danger carried by the film's protagonist to the fore, picturing Goudal's character leaning forward and holding a dagger, in a visual manner that connotes vamps of the early silent film, or even that of the fin de siècle. The appropriation of such imagery—the absent gaze of the woman, the attire that suggestively reveals her shoulders and décolleté—is apparent in earlier images, for instance in the promotion for Theda Bara's 1918 vehicle *The She-Devil.*

The Bright Shawl, *Three Faces East*, and *The Forbidden Woman* all capitalized on the association between Goudal and the Orient by placing the star within a narrative of deception and romance. They fed into the rich symbolism of exotic villainess to underpin her characterizations of a double agent with disruptive connotations. Furthermore, Zita's use of sex for personal gain emblematizes what underwrites the poetics of the femme fatale; as a female agent she is licensed to use aggressive methods to extract military secrets from her opponents.

Picture Play was one of several fan magazines that encouraged a textual conflation between the Oriental archetypes presented in both Goudal's oeuvre and discussions of her personal life. The October 1927 issue featured a long article that painted Goudal as a near-mythical creature whose screen allure does not lose any of its impact in real-life confrontation. "Jetta is one of those slender, sloe-eyed foreigners, galvanizing the lobby-lookers into staring unabashedly. She looks like her name. Whoever decided to call her Jetta Goudal had a precocious gift for title writing. Indeed, one might say, succinctly and finally, of this svelte, exotic creature. . . . The *Jetta* suggests her black hair with the glossy high lights, the dark eyes, somber as night, glinting as steel."[82] The interviewer reported that

Figure 20. Mysterious gaze. Goudal in a publicity still. Source: Austrian postcard by Iris-Verlag, no. 5187. Photo: Paramount.

Goudal looked equally impressive in person and in broad daylight as she did in her movie vehicles: "Her high cheekbones, slanting eyes, full lips, slim figure all serve to present an arresting picture."[83] One critic described Goudal as a "vivid exotic type, a blending of Latin street *gamine* and the international vamp."[84] This is not to say fanzines assumed Goudal shared the immoral qualities intrinsic to some of her heroines; rather, that blurring the lines between her portrayals on celluloid and what she stood for off-screen was, in this case, limited largely to the visual. Emphasizing her eyes as a marker of ethnic difference was a method of rendering Goudal compatible with her film characters.

Her Man O'War and *White Gold*

The critical response that met Goudal's portrayal in *Her Man O' War* (1926) attests to the link between her persona and the notion of Orientalism. Released in the period when films about the Great War reached the apex of their popularity,[85] it is set in Alsace and concerns the trials and tribulations of two American army men on a quest to locate and destroy a powerful German weapon. To succeed, they pose as prisoners of war and are effectively assigned to work on two farms run by Cherie Schultz (Goudal) and Big Bertha (Key Deslys). Jim Sanderson (William Boyd), one of the spies, falls in love with his host; despite reciprocating his feelings, Cherie sees through his disguise and reports him to a German colonel. Jim is about to be executed when he is rescued by American troops. In the opinion of the majority of the critics, the image of cultivated sophistication and Oriental charm that shot Goudal to stardom was at odds with the character of Cherie Schultz, a sympathetic but relatively simple farmer. *Picture Play* described the picture as a "tale of Alsatian peasant and American dough boy," considering it enjoyable but not well tailored to Goudal's talent.[86] Another, more elaborate article from the same publication expressed similar concerns.[87]

In miscasting Goudal in the role of a French peasant, *Her Man O' War* formed a radical departure from the representational schemes set by *The Bright Shawl* and consequently failed to function effectively as a vehicle for its chief star in the eyes of at least some contemporary critics. Such opinions reverberated with the critique aimed at Bánky's involvement in *This Is Heaven* (1929), discussed in chapter 4. In both instances, film magazines found it hard to negotiate between the film's diegesis and the extratextual layer of meanings and expectations brought to the story by the persona of its chief star. With her naïveté and her simple ways, Cherie Schultz stood in stark contrast to Goudal as a quintessence of complex exoticism; her character encapsulated everything that Goudal the star was not.

White Gold (1927) offered Goudal a sought-after opportunity to showcase her dramatic range in the portrayal of Dolores Carson, a Mexican woman and a former dancer married to a sheep rancher in the American West, Alec Carson (Kenneth Thompson). In a sense, the film is a continuation of some representational qualities of *Her Man O'War*, with Goudal playing, once more, a woman of the land. Directed by the renowned filmmaker William K. Howard, and inspired largely by German art cinema,[88] the film is exceptional in its partial acknowledgment of the problematic nature of ethnic stereotyping. Chosen alongside *The Forbidden Woman* as one of the best pictures of 1927 by the National

Board Preview of Motion Pictures, it was met with wide critical acclaim, especially for its realistic performances.[89]

At least in visual terms, Dolores does not conform easily to any representational schemes; she has the black hair of the femme fatale, but her simple attire lacks the ornamental qualities familiar from Goudal's previous pictures. Her characterization as a Latina runs against the grain of most silent film portrayals, where South American origin was often a satisfactory alibi for hot-blooded sexuality and where, as Stephen Sariñana-Lampson points out, "Latinas were depicted as the heathen seductress with little morals, physically aggressive and with an insatiable sexual appetite."[90] Within the narrative, Goudal's hardworking Dolores is the antithesis of the "loose senorita" and "easy cantina girl." She is introduced to the diegesis first and foremost as the wife of Alec Carson, a loving man who is nevertheless unable to stand up to his oppressive father, and his continual disapproval of the relationship. Despite Dolores's best efforts, the patriarch does not miss any opportunity to emphasize his position within the household. "Can't you see we are talkin'?" he remarks, embittered, as Dolores brings the food to the dinner table. When Alec asks his father to show more respect for his young daughter-in-law ("You shouldn't talk to her like that, Dad"), the old man states his resentment toward her more explicitly: "Why shouldn't I?—She's nothin' to me."

Carson's hatred for his son's wife appears to be nothing more than a rampant manifestation of immature jealousy over his only child, mixed with a hint of racial prejudice: "I've been father and mother to that boy—and he belongs to me," he responds to the heroine, as she tries to assure him he should not feel threatened by her presence. With Dolores shown in white dress reminiscent of a habit and a veil, the scene reproduces an aura of innocence through costume. The woman's sole fault lies in the fact that she has unwittingly resurrected the sheepherder's irrational fears of losing his son to someone else.

One day a drifter offers to help at the ranch, and he is allowed to stay at the family's dwellings in exchange for his labor. The man immediately develops a sexual obsession with Goudal's character, which culminates in rape. The father becomes an accidental witness to the attack and interprets it as proof of Dolores's immoral nature. *White Gold* ends with a scene of Dolores walking into the wilderness, away from the household where she was constantly surrounded by hostility and suspicion; "tainted" by sexual abuse, she walks into the Badlands, exclaiming proudly, "at least it will be freedom."

The film acknowledges the role of prejudice in informing human judgment by pointing to the devastating effects it can have on individuals' lives. Even though *White Gold* seems to condone the bigotry exhibited by the family's patriarch, paradoxically, it fails to steer away from stereotyping in representing Dolores's fate. Rayna Green's evaluation of Native American womanhood, with its focus on indigenous women as the embodiment of tragedy in Western culture, is applicable to the character depicted here by Goudal, regardless of her Mexican identity. Green argues that to personify a "noble savage," Native American women must violate their own cultural traditions in order to live with white men, and, eventually, suffer from either social ostracism or death.[91] As an ideal, Anglicized Latina defined primarily through her relationship to her husband and father-in-law, Dolores is a carrier of the same tropes. In choosing to marry an American rancher she simultaneously chooses to exile herself from her own people and to inhabit an essentially hostile environment, where the visions of her past life continue to haunt her.

The film's emphasis on status and hierarchy, as well as its appraisal of familial and political relationships where progress is constrained by other, stronger people—or even higher power—and ultimately impossible, makes it reminiscent of Greek tragedy.[92] *White Gold*'s problematic message manifests itself in the film's ending: Does Dolores truly leave the ranch to find freedom—as suggested by the intertitle—or, rather, does she wander into the Badlands, heartbroken and with nowhere to go, to meet her tragic end? In its broadest context, the collective American psyche framed interethnic unions as a site of conflict that disrupts the boundaries of identity, often linking such relationships to "negative, destructive, and marginalising outcomes and experiences."[93] What is evident in the final scene is the notion that intermarriage is doomed to failure, a statement that reflects the dominant racist myopia of the times and society that witnessed the production of *White Gold*. Goudal's standing as an exotic symbol is not apparent in the film, where she seems to be cast against type, as a woman whose definition of the self is based on the identities she performs for others: a wife and a daughter in-law. Nonetheless, her Hispanic origin and the practice of intermarriage provide a connective tissue between the characterization of Dolores and Goudal's previous incarnations on-screen.

Conclusion

The role of Pilar de Lima in *The Bright Shawl* sketched the contours of Goudal's figure along the lines of ethnic and cultural difference, providing a blueprint for her future appearances on the silver screen. Consequently, the criticism leveled against Goudal's part in *Her Man O' War*, where she performed as a French peasant, resulted from the fact that the role overturned the prevailing typecasting. Connotations of exotic splendor are absent from the character description of *White Gold*, a film remarkably realist in tone, which also went against the grain of convention in casting Goudal as a Mexican sheep rancher during a drought. Her character's future, however, is decidedly marked by her ethnic origin.

In Western discourse, Orientalism offers the promise of a thrill beyond the limits of the Occident. Labeling Goudal as physically different from the ideals of white femininity conveyed a sense of allure and danger inherent to Oriental fantasy. Featuring the actress in highly stylized fashion spreads, the star system turned Goudal's body into a racialized, gendered spectacle. Her face was assembled out of unfamiliar yet titillating features of "eyes that slant at the corners," high cheekbones, and glossy black hair.[94] "She stared at me," recounted one columnist, "with those long, pale green eyes of hers, as unwinking as an Oriental's."[95] In many respects, the conceptual treatment of the bodies of women and the ethnic others are congruent with each other, as they both stand in opposition to normative standards, emblematized by masculinity and whiteness. For the plethora of accounts generated by fan publications, Goudal's beauty was as fascinating as it was unusual, helping to secure a seamless match between her on- and off-screen self. But most importantly, Goudal's image was viewed through the lens of Orientalism even beyond the cinematic realm. Specific material objects, sartorial choices, and aspects of her physiognomy contributed to the creation of consistency within her exotic star text.

CHAPTER 7

Jetta Goudal and Mystery

"A Riddle in the City of Eager Autobiographies"

Writing for *Picture Play*, Myrtle Gebhart reported that "Jetta Goudal surrounded herself with an aura of mystery. She is charming and gracious on her infrequent appearances in public, but she is also very, very reticent about herself and her affairs."[1] The image of Goudal as the great Hollywood unknown was founded on the scarce availability of information relating to her past, her present, or her future. Facts from Goudal's biography were rarely distributed, and most mentions were accompanied by doubts regarding their accuracy. Margaret Reid of one fanzine dubbed her "a riddle in a city of eager autobiographies,"[2] adding that "no one has the vaguest idea if anything is true or untrue about her. Her withdrawal from the life of the colony is absolute."

The studio sought to control every aspect of recruiting and launching stars, and to elicit specific responses to star images.[3] I argue that in founding Goudal's projected identity on secrecy, Famous Players-Lasky, her first contractor, was allowed to maneuver between the appeal of exoticism and that of continental sophistication. The previous chapter asserted that Goudal was promoted as an explicitly coded Oriental body; here I reflect on the ideological functions of her double identity as both an exotic object *and* a French native. The aura of mystery worked in conjunction with some tenets of Goudal's persona by underwriting her exoticism, and in turn making her image less problematic. As a French-Dutch star she was not as threatening to the main current of American culture as she would be if she were a Mongolian, Indian, or Javanese woman. Simultaneously, her alleged exotic features, such as her eyes and black hair, were emphasized to appropriate the attractions of Orientalism; the innuendo molded around Goudal's ethnicity served as a lure to moviegoers.

In my previous discussion of exoticism, I showed how Goudal—once thought to be one-quarter Mongolian, another time alleged to be half-Chinese—had the capacity to represent the idea of the Orient, with its mysticism and opulence.

What needs to be emphasized, nevertheless, is the fact that her Asian ancestry had to remain an insinuation, a mere hint. In an attempt to elude her image, these dispersed accounts teased their readership with the allure of exoticism without exclusively confirming or denying Goudal's ethnic heritage. What lay at the core of this tactic was the urge to both perform a "spectacle of difference"[4] and create room for a safe, westernized sameness within the representational persona of the star.

Scarcity of Information

Richard Dyer frames silent cinema as a medium particularly well suited to constructing stars as mysterious and unapproachable.[5] Dyer's argument is developed further by Michaela Krutzen and Joy Ramirez in their respective discussions of Greta Garbo and stars of early Italian films. In accordance with Ramirez's theorization, the absence of sound is an integral component for producing a silent star whose reality is plastic and transcendent. For Ramirez, stars have a mainly symbolic meaning and because of this they do not require language. In fact, they are "all the more effective as a result of its absence."[6] Because the screen idols of the 1920s were deprived of the ability to speak, they eventually appeared (to use Krutzen's words) "less real and more divine."[7] To put it simply, silent divas *are* divas because they are silent.

It is a valuable argument; however, it does limit itself to the screen images of the stars, without taking their press-driven, off-screen personae into consideration. The handling of Vilma Bánky's accent in the periodicals, for one, indicates how fan press and fans speculated about the star voices long before the arrival of talkies. Additionally, the theory does not account for the fact that not all silent stars were constructed as equally unapproachable. While Negri's love life was commented on in practically every single film periodical, Goudal's histrionics remained largely off the radar. This is where the exoticism embodied by the former differed from the aspects of exoticism that signaled flamboyance represented by the latter. Where Negri defied local mores by exuberantly flaunting her private pursuits, Goudal was marked as restrained and mysterious.

In an interview conducted by DeWitt Bodeen in the early 1970s, Goudal admitted to always being an intensely private woman, even at the pinnacle of her stardom.[8] Sean P. Holmes observed that Goudal's personal need for privacy constituted a challenge for her employers, who filled the void in the star image by fashioning her as a European diva prone to tantrums.[9] Still, studio documents suggest that her idiosyncratic traits were embraced and exaggerated; Goudal wanted a secretive life and film producers colluded with her, shaping that desire into a sense of alluring mystique. In 1927, one publicist expressed his approval for the policy of shrouding the star's past in the utmost mystery, also recommending that the scheme be rigidly maintained.[10] Goudal's supposedly abrasive nature was an integral aspect of her persona, but it did not serve as a counterpoint to her secrecy. Veiling Famous Players-Lasky's new star in mystery was evidently a conscious practice aimed at eliciting interest in the moviegoers, as it gave audiences the opportunity to fantasize about one of their screen idols and, to use Holmes's words, "colour in the blank spaces that surrounded her."[11]

The construction of star images is riddled with paradoxes, and one of them relates directly to the issues of on- and off-screen visibility. Simon Dixon writes that movie players strive for public recognition, as their professional and commercial value depends on it. At the same time, they often become outspoken advocates for maintaining their privacy and anonymity.[12] Film magazines were invested in presenting the secrecy that Goudal relished as a personal choice. She thus emerged from the pages of *Photoplay* as a woman who cherished her independence and indulged in loneliness, behavior that was understood to be extremely rare among her fellow movie stars. The reluctance to attend parties or participate in other social endeavors was framed as one of Goudal's main character traits, instead of being discussed—more accurately—as part of the politics of the studios that produced and utilized star images.

According to *Picture Play*, "on the screen, Goudal is a personage rare and unusual: personally she lives a life that is both individual and different—almost nun-like, it would seem, in its quietude."[13] One of *Photoplay*'s features claimed that the star lived outside Hollywood (although still in Los Angeles), greatly appreciating the air of mystery so becoming to her.[14] In addition, Goudal kept her icy, distant allure even on those rare occasions when she decided to emerge from her allegedly self-imposed solitude to enjoy a nightclub. Another article claimed the star visits all functions alone, without speaking to anybody, simply watching her environment: "The fact that she comes often must mean that she enjoys being alone, and being left alone. Jetta Goudal, sitting in all her silver-screen aloofness, seems to say, 'I am sad; you'll never understand!'"[15]

What many of these accounts have in common is their framing of solitude as something at odds with Hollywood living, an anomaly in "a city of eager autobiographies,"[16] where oversharing is the most common publicity practice. Constructed in opposition to the exuberance associated with her star lifestyle, Goudal's hermit tendencies suggest she is more authentic than many of her colleagues. She was presented as a victim of the system that preferred sensation over genuineness, rumor over truth. Goudal's status as an artist, as opposed to simply a star—that is, as an individual not only naturally more creative but also more sensitive than others—added credibility to her yearning for privacy. *Photoplay* journalist Francis Clark called the actress "abnormally sensitive," hence not fully equipped to lead her life in the Hollywood limelight. Indeed, she proclaimed that it was the fabricated stories of her temperament that made her shy in the first place.[17]

This is not to say that the constraint associated with Goudal was always framed as genuine. Numerous press features presented the star as perfectly aware of the commercial potential held by insinuation and mystery in the construction of one's stardom. But even when editorials recognized mystery as a useful publicity tool, they failed to acknowledge star images as products of the studio system. Magazine discourse invested stars with a sense of agency in creating their own images, although, in reality, they had very little power over the way in which their star personae were constructed and utilized.[18] The following account, published in 1929, is a good illustration of how such a narrative was deployed in practice:

> Even after ten years in this country Jetta maintains the secret of her past. "My work belongs to the world", says Jetta. "My life belongs to me alone." Wild rumours have circulated about the Goudal [*sic*], each purporting to tell the truth. One says that she is an East Side Jewess, and points to the way her exotic accent becomes plain American in moments of stress. Another whispers that she was born on a Wisconsin farm. Still a third insists that she is the daughter of a Chinese nobleman and a missionary. Jetta listens to these tales, and smiles her cryptic smile. She knows that mystery is becoming to her.[19]

The columnist identifies rumor as a powerful tool that can propel an aspiring actress into the spotlight. Yet, it does not place star images in the context of the film industry's promotional practices. According to the article it is up to Goudal—and Goudal alone—to decide which biographical facts to disclose. The July 1929 issue of *Picture Play* included a long piece on the mysterious appeal of three movie stars: Greta Garbo, Jetta Goudal, and Ronald Colman (figures 21a and 21b). The article sees the aura surrounding the stars in question as both a genuine reflection of their personalities and a part of their individual tactics in promoting themselves. Goudal benefits from the scarcity of information concerning her private life because she knows what to disclose and when to remain silent. "Some actresses, like the enigmatic Garbo, [and] the sphinx-like Goudal, are total strangers even to their film friends," contends the author.[20]

The column cautions any journalist who decides to approach Goudal that it is very difficult to get to know her. Such a warning in itself implicitly verifies the rumors. Potential interviewers are deemed to fail, because: "Goudal will look half smiling at you, just like the Sphinx. She makes you both believe and disbelieve; she suggests and denies, which usually causes one's ideas to go this way and that."[21] The article by *Motion Picture Magazine* is unusual, as it briefly addresses the role played by studios in constructing star identities. "Some of the life stories of film celebrities have been made out of white cloth—and colourful cloth—by their publicity men. There was Ricardo Cortez, for instance." The writer goes on to admit he had asked Cortez about his birthplace, to which the actor replied: "The publicity department hasn't decided that yet."[22]

The Three

Questions directed to Jetta Goudal, Greta Garbo, same results as efforts to draw the mysterious chatter, so far as their inner selves and

By William

Photo by Bell

The many-sided Jetta Goudal is the subject of rumors which evoke only a smile from her, although one of them hints of a rôle in a dramatic chapter of the World War.

ASK the cold Sphinx whence it came. Put question after question before it, and it will merely stare back at you with its inscrutable countenance. Never can you see behind its eyes. Go wild with rage, for all it cares, when you fail to get an answer. It should worry. It is doing very well. The Sphinx is world famous.

So are two women and a man in Hollywood who possess the same distracting, enigmatic qualities. *Unknown* is the middle name of Jetta Goudal, Greta Garbo, and Ronald Colman.

Goudal has attracted attention, because of the aura of bafflement she carries about with her. There is no stronger magnet to draw the human mind than mystery. Perhaps Jetta realizes this.

She flashed to success, as most people know, some years ago, in "The Bright Shawl," in which she played the rôle of a Eurasian spy.

Who was she? Where did she come from? People asked, but failed to get an answer. Rumor said her mother was French, her father Chinese. Other rumors of an exotic nature spread about.

Ask for verification of these rumors and Goudal will look half smiling at you, just like the Sphinx. She makes you both believe and disbelieve; she suggests and denies, which usually causes one's ideas to go this way and that.

Versailles, we are informed, is her birthplace.

A sphinx from Versailles. Why not?

Mention of Versailles recalls Vincennes. And Vincennes conjures up visions of Matahari, the half-caste Javanese dancer of exotic memory. Her real name was Margaret Zelle. Her father was a Dutch sea captain. During the war Matahari was a notorious spy for Germany, belonging to the *Wilhelmstrasse*. She was executed, presumably, by the French in 1916.

Greta Garbo quietly observes Hollywood through half-closed eyes, suggesting disturbances that at once charm and mystify the screen colony.

Photo by Louise

Matahari was fictionized after her announced death, by several novelists. Ibáñez portrayed her in "Mare Nostrum." Elinor Glyn forgot "It" for a moment and declaimed, "Thus perish all spies!" when she had her executed, in "The Price of Things." A few French writers dramatized Matahari in their novels, "La Chèvre aux Pieds d'Or" being the most famous.

Whether Jetta Goudal suggested "The Goat With the Golden Feet," when she appeared on the stage in New York, cannot be said. All the same, the book made a splendid film for her, as some profess to believe that she is Matahari herself. Secrets were supposed to have been let out. Those who know say this.

Was it true that the French government freed Matahari in return for some very important secrets, then gave out the report that she had been executed? Was it true that they let her escape to Holland, with a stern command never to set foot in France again? Was it likewise true that Jetta Goudal was really that

Figures 21a and 21b. Goudal, Colman, and Garbo described as enigmatic "three sphinxes." Source: William H. McKegg, "The Three Sphinxes," *Picture Play*, July 1929.

Sphinxes

and Ronald Colman have about the lady of the Nile into self-revealing personal histories are concerned.

H. McKegg

lady when she landed in America in 1918? Or was it all fabricated by some one who had taken his spy stories too seriously?

Of course there is no great resemblance between Jetta and photographs of the Mata-hari of twelve years ago. *La Goudal* also seems too young. Nevertheless, who could play the spy in "Three Faces East" and "The Forbidden Woman" with more conviction than she? None but a splendid actress, at least. She is a many-sided person, as her rôles have proved.

In any case, why is she such a sphinxlike personality? Why does she remain secluded from all Hollywood? She is a very remarkable person, with an intellectual brilliance that would surprise many who do not know her.

A gifted linguist, she speaks several languages. She has a slight French accent. Yet Goudal talks the purest English. Her French is fluent, too, but Jetta speaks it in a calm, steellike tone—hardly like a Parisienne. Of tremendous mental power, she knows more than any three people put together. Her personality defies definition—hence her mystifying ways.

Ronald Colman is not so mysterious as to antecedents as are Goudal and Garbo, but he possesses a baffling something in his personality. It is well known that he comes from a good family. He does not hide his background. He merely objects to dragging in his private affairs for publicity.

Photo [illegible]

Ronald Colman's antecedents are known, but since the war he has acquired something baffling in his personality which defies analysis.

Colman's sphinxlike quality is an acquisition. It was not always present. It has appeared only since the war. What caused that baffling, sorrowful expression that you see in his eyes when he believes himself unnoticed?

The war "got" those who were in it, and those just old enough to realize the slaughter of it all—that is, the young people of Europe. Colman's plans for the future were shattered on August 4, 1914. He was already in the reserves, and was one of the first to go to France. More than two years of horror passed before he was sent back to England, wounded.

He returned to the London of 1917. Every one was dancing amid the roar of near-by guns. To a returning soldier, the people must have seemed mad. One never knew when one went to bed whether one would be blown to fragments during a midnight Zeppelin raid. Soldiers on leave would have their "last fling" before returning to the death zone some forty or so miles away. Death had touched every family. People went about with a hideous mask of joy on their tear-stained faces, to conceal their terror.

The war snapped the cord that tied one to tradition. Many young people sought the stage. Colman was one of them. Poppy Wyndham, Lord Inchcape's daughter who also did splendid war work, was another. Colman and she acted together. This talented, beautiful girl was recently killed while attempting a flight across the Atlantic. The war had never left her.

Is it the war, now ten years gone, that causes Colman to smile so ironically at Hollywood's civilization? Or is it some sorrowful memory in his own life? To his personal friends Ronnie is no sphinx. He is humorous, honest, and straightforward. Still, he has a great sorrow for something—or is it some one?

Ronald Colman views his fellow men from a mountain of his own vision. He laughs at them for their vanities, well knowing the futility of everything that depends on material hopes. Yet in spite of his sphinxlike quality, Colman is the most sympathetic of men—that is, if one seeks his sympathy.

Greta Garbo has taken upon herself a sphinxlike personality. It is either because she has been advised to do so, or because she can't help it.

Where does Greta come from? Sweden, yes. But where in Sweden? Stockholm is given for answer,

Continued on page 114

In using humor, the anecdote illustrates how some details of Hollywood biographies are embellished or simply made up to sustain media interest. There is no concealment here for one of Hollywood's chief strategies: the production and circulation of star commodities. Even so, it is important to note that there is a limit to the transgressive abilities of fan magazines. More exaggerated displays of star behavior are criticized as not fully genuine or even dictated by the studios. The star images appealing to mystery, however, are never examined as artificial constructs conforming to a wider framework of power. If being mysterious is depicted as tactical, it is explained within the context of personal choices, rather than in terms of a studio-driven publicity scheme.

An article from *Motion Picture Classic* argues that film stars are a different species, naturally predestined to act strangely even when the camera is off. Female stars are depicted as more adept in the art of "overtime acting" in comparison with their male colleagues.[23] Greta Garbo "likes to walk by the *misty sea*" in the act of making herself appear more distant. Goudal, on the other hand, "is such a consummate actress that one can't tell when the actress ceases and Jetta begins."[24] According to the feature, mystery is a pose intended to create an air of world-weariness around young actors unable to attract attention simply by their artistic merit. In a similar vein—and in accordance with a gendered belief that women are prone to confabulation—another article holds Goudal's keen imagination responsible for the enigma of her origin.[25]

Nationality

The mid and late 1920s witnessed a construction of parallels between Goudal's and Greta Garbo's personae that concentrated on their representations as "mysteries" to be solved. Both performers rose to stardom around the same time: Goudal landed a leading role in Raoul Walsh's *The Spaniard* in 1925, whereby Garbo's first American moving picture, *The Torrent* (1926), was released the following year. One source that linked Goudal and Garbo in terms of their mysterious appeal was a letter published by *Picture Play* in 1929: "Isn't Jetta Goudal the most fascinating, mysterious, exotic, gorgeous personality on the screen? Greta Garbo looks stupid beside her,"[26] wrote one fan. After the initial attempt to promote Garbo as an athletic, wholesome type, studio executives decided to take a strategic turn and capitalize on her aversion to public appearances, consequently re-imagining the star as an enigmatic Swedish goddess. This turned out to be an excellent move. Sumiko Higashi explained that, in a manner not far removed from the dynamics of Goudal's publicity, Garbo achieved her godlike status by taking advantage of scarcity: "Since her elusiveness inflated her stature as an icon, she remained an unusual star in a modern celebrity culture designed to promote endless consumption."[27] Such statements are perfectly applicable to the construction of Goudal's star persona. In his analysis of Goudal's career trajectory,

Holmes argues that Famous Players-Lasky endorsed mystery as a strategy for Goudal after recognizing she was not interested in promotional matters.[28] The notion of mystery soon became intrinsic to the way she was represented by the star system, and effectively outgrew her personal politics.

Similar to Garbo's, Goudal's on-screen persona stretched far beyond any precise geography. In her work, Garbo portrayed characters of varying nationalities, from Spanish, French, and Russian women to a Polish aristocrat and Queen Christina of Sweden.[29] Vincendeau and Phillips point out that many émigré stars were allowed to move freely among depictions of different nationalities.[30] Sarah Berry also supports that view, adding that the extent of interchangeability between "ethnic" typecasting did not extend to the portrayal of characters of Anglo-Saxon heritage. A progression from "ethnic" to white roles was rare.[31] The dynamic could have a positive impact on the careers of foreign film stars, as their heroines could evade the code of conduct that applied more strictly to their wholesome American counterparts; consequently, these actors occupied a niche in the movie market, with the label of Europeanness granting them permission to become more versatile and play more challenging, complex parts.

Where the representations of Garbo and Goudal differ is in terms of their respective national identities. Garbo off-screen was decidedly marked as a Swede, which equated easy assimilation into American whiteness.[32] Goudal's persona, on the other hand, as we have seen, carried more complex—and often conflicting—ethnic and national connotations. According to the account penned by *Sunday News*'s columnist, observers were immediately struck by Goudal's appeal, which escaped straightforward classifications: "Some few months ago I was seated in the lobby of a hotel awaiting the arrival of a woman friend from the West. In a nearby chair a girl was sitting talking with an enraptured male. She fascinated me with her unusualness of beauty, her broken accent and air of mystery, which set me conjuring as to whether she might be a resurrected daughter of a decapitated Czarina, a recently impoverished Polish refugee or a French girl come to solicit funds for another devastated area."[33]

The "girl" turned out to be Goudal, and in the interview that ensued, the performer admitted to receiving a lot of attention despite her best intentions to remain unnoticed. She dresses simply to avoid being stared at. Yet, the unusual, mysterious aura she embodies makes it impossible for her to stay anonymous in the crowds. By her own admittance, Goudal is not pretty; hence, she puts such interest on the carb of her magnetic personality: "It's so strange. People to whom I have never been introduced will come up to me and ask me what nationality I am. I got so tired of it, yesterday when a woman stopped me and asked me that question, I said 'Chinese, but don't you tell anybody, will you?'"[34]

Although the exotic part of Goudal's nationality was not coded explicitly (and never verified), the continental European aspect of her persona was articulated as either Franco-Dutch (in 1923) or French (during the ensuing years of her career).[35] In a review of *The Bright Shawl*, her first credited feature film from 1923, Goudal is referred to as "a fascinating French-Dutch actress."[36] A short article published by *Picture Play* in the same year wrote of her in similar terms: "She is Dutch by birth and French by inheritance, but it is her odd Oriental expression that makes her alluring."[37] *Sunday News* introduced Goudal to its readership as an intriguing vamp type, "a Parisian-born actress and screen personage."[38] From 1924 onward, mentions of Goudal's Dutch ancestry began to be replaced with an emphasis on her association with French culture. According to the August 1924 issue of *Photoplay*, Goudal, a French actress, was a new thrill in Hollywood.[39] The interview conducted by *Motion Picture Classic* stays in line with that simulacrum, revealing that Goudal is "just French."[40] She might look like an Oriental princess, but regardless of the rumors, she does not have a drop of Indian or Mongolian blood running through her veins.

In the words of Harry Carr, Goudal combined "the French instinct for gesture and the French adroitness of suggestion" with the arresting, exotic beauty of Pola Negri and Barbara La Mar.[41] *Motion Picture Magazine* referred to some of the spreading rumors of her "exotic nature," according to which Goudal's mother was French and her father was Chinese,[42] yet, like many other magazines of the period, it played with pieces of gossip while ultimately steering away from verifying them.

Therefore, such sources go to show how Goudal's off-screen brand of foreignness was an amalgam of stereotypes associated with Frenchness and an undefined generic sense of Orientalism. Goudal's dual star text as both Oriental and continental subject is moreover illustrated through varying visuals, specifically the colorful covers of fan magazines (figures 22a and 22b). Gundle and Castelli maintain that exoticism percolates mass culture and that it requires to be constantly negotiated to release the tension between here and there, dream and reality, pleasure and utility.[43] The meta-narrative of Goudal's stardom placed her at the junction of these two extremes; she was a commodified spectacle, a carrier of Western ideas of the Orient, but not an "Oriental" herself. The association with France kept Goudal in the far more familiar realm of Europeanness, whereas the atmosphere of secrecy turned into a safeguard that at once authorized her whiteness and distanced her from it. As a result, Goudal gained cultural currency as a safe version of the exotic star.

An analysis of fan magazines suggests how mutable iconographic opportunities offered by fashion operated, at times, to confirm the French element of Goudal's constructed identity. This was due to the popular ideology viewing French women, unlike the women of the United States, as fluent in the language of haute couture. Paris started to acquire the title of world capital of fashion during the Second Empire, and continued to solicit its cultural hegemony during the early years of the twentieth century, attracting many foreign dressmakers.[44] Richard Marchand argues that popular American magazines of the 1920s were prolific in endorsing the image of Europe, and France more specifically, as places where a cultivation of a personal sense of fashion and style was kept in the highest regard.[45] A highly idiosyncratic taste in clothing accentuated the Frenchness embedded in the Goudal persona, and—as I will discuss in the next chapter—reflected on the narrative of temperamental demeanor. All of Goudal's dresses were reportedly imported from her native Paris, where they would eventually be re-distributed among the poor artists once the star deemed them no longer fashionable.[46] Paradoxically, the discourse promulgated by *Photoplay*, *Picture Play*, and their like often satirized the inexplicable extravagance of Parisian gowns; even Goudal "now and then . . . hovers on that far side of bizarre which is outlandish," becoming more a victim than a follower of fashion.[47] To the most ardent fans, the extravagant styles Goudal was privately fond of were "delightful creations" that "shrieked of individuality."[48]

At the end of the 1920s, numerous fan magazines started to question Goudal's status as a French native. *Motion Picture Classic* suggested that the star's French is not particularly good and that at times she "forgets" to speak English with a French accent.[49] In his description of Goudal's mysterious attitude, the ever-enthusiastic William McKegg argued that the star spoke several languages, including Italian, German, and fluent French. However, her composed, cool speaking voice lacked the authenticity and passion one would expect to hear from the tone of the Parisienne she claimed to be.[50] Meanwhile, a letter published by *Picture Play* "exposed" Goudal as Henrietta Goudeket of Amsterdam. "Most people insist that all Hollanders wear wooden shoes, wide trousers, and have blond hair and blue eyes. This is probably the reason why she keeps her nationality a secret," explained the fan.[51] Such a depiction pivoted to highlight the Netherlands as unsophisticated—especially in comparison with France—while simultaneously aligning Dutch nationality with a much broader "Aryan" Anglo-Saxon ideal gaining traction in the period, in both Europe and America. These denunciations were, nonetheless, single instances aimed to furnish the pages of fanzines with some mild controversy rather than to deconstruct Goudal's refined image. The popular press did not put the nationality of the star in doubt and continued to rely on her image as a sophisticated Frenchwoman. In 1931, an unidentified paper from Portland wrote of Goudal's appearance on the local stage: "Miss Goudal isn't a bit like one would expect, except for her decided French accent, which is decidedly [*sic*] charming. She's every bit as French as her accent and her birthplace, Versailles, proclaims her, yet different from most of the stars from the land of Lafayette."[52]

As a strategy, hiding Goudal's origin offered fan magazines the opportunity to constantly rewrite and debate over the star's past. The carefully crafted lack of information gave rise to many different biographies, some more embellished than others. A lengthy feature in *Motion Picture Classic* suggested Jetta Goudal was in fact the only surviving daughter of Mata Hari, the infamous spy convicted

Figures 22a and 22b. Exotic "other" or the modern New Woman? Two magazine covers present strikingly different versions of Goudal. *Picture Play*, January 1927, and *Photoplay*, November 1927.

of and executed for espionage in 1917 (figure 23).[53] The article drew on many common denominators between the figure of Hari and that of Goudal: their mysterious past, their affiliation with France, and the fantasy of the exotic femme fatale. Moreover, it linked Goudal's off-screen self to the filmic personae estab-

lished by *The Bright Shawl*, *The Forbidden Woman*, and *Three Faces East*, in all of which Goudal appeared in the roles of beautiful (and dangerously seductive) spies. The comparison illuminated different representational issues related to the narrative of Goudal and, given its relevance to some of the most integral facets of her star phenomenon, deserves a closer analysis.

For Rosie White, the potency of Hari's myth lies in the paradoxical mixture of attraction and repulsion toward both Orientalism and espial practices.[54] Born

The *Mistress* of Mystery

Does the Career of Mata Hari, the Spy, Bear Upon the Riddle of Jetta Goudal's Past?

By DOROTHY DONNELL

JETTA GOUDAL has been for years an unsolved mystery of the movies. The stories that have been written of her birth and early life are palpably fiction; she has not even bothered to make them agree upon the comparatively simple matter of her birthplace. A so-called autobiography, claiming Versailles as her native town and a French lawyer as a father, was written by her press-agent in despair of ever getting the true tale from the enigmatic Jetta.

I asked her once whether she had any brothers and sisters. She stared at me with those long, pale green eyes of hers, as unwinking as an Oriental's for frozen moments before she answered icily, "It mos' hurt you to have to ask soch impertinent questions."

Even after ten years in this country Jetta maintains the secret of her past. "My work belong to the worl'," says Jetta. "My life belong to me alone."

Wild rumors have circulated about the Goudal, each purporting to tell the truth. One says that she is an East Side Jewess, and points to the way her exotic accent becomes plain American in moments of stress. Another whispers that she was born on a Wisconsin farm. Still a third insists that she is the daughter of a Chinese nobleman and a missionary. Jetta listens to these tales, and smiles her cryptic smile. She knows that mystery is becoming to her.

Or is there perhaps some other reason for her silence?

Where is Mata Hari's Child

ONE year before Jetta Goudal came to America, a beautiful woman faced a French firing squad in the trenches of Vincennes. She was forty-four years old, though not a soldier there would have guessed she was thirty. Smiling gaily over the armful of roses she carried, she remarked lightly to those who led her to death that it was a pity they had executions so early in the morning, when one would feel ever so much more in the mood for them after breakfast—say at three in the afternoon. A fusillade of shots crackled through the thin spring sunshine and the woman fell among her roses. So died Mata Hari, the exotic dancer, the spy, with the cynical little smile still on lips that had been kissed by kings.

And dying, left behind her a daughter, the heiress to her strange exotic beauty, to her dazzling and dangerous career—and perhaps to her fate. For wars may be over, but the secret service of warring countries does not forget, and those who are known to be friends or relatives of spies are always in danger.

What has become of the beautiful child of Mata Hari? No one seems to know. Daughter of a dancer, herself convent-bred, taught to speak French

(*Continued on page 84*)

In the two upper corners are two views of Mata Hari, the half Dutch, half-Javanese dancer shot as a spy by the French. In the center is Jetta Goudal

22

Figure 23. *Motion Picture Classic* arguing that Goudal might be the lost daughter of Mata Hari, the infamous spy. Source: Dorothy Donnell, "The Mistress of Mystery," *Motion Picture Classic*, February 1929, 22.

as Margaretha Geertruida Zelle in the Netherlands in 1876, Hari rose to celebrity status at the beginning of the century in Paris, where she created—and capitalized on—the stage persona of a Javanese princess of high Hindu origin. From 1915 onward, the performer also started to operate and make her name as a high-class prostitute. During the Great War, she used her liaisons with military officials to obtain information for German intelligence. Hari's Oriental image, although entirely fabricated, sparked human imagination, but it was only once her identity as a spy had been revealed—and after her subsequent trial and death by a firing squad—that her figure achieved a semi-mythical status.

Although the iconic image of Hari as the deadliest woman spy has been debunked by recent scholars, she continued—and, in many instances, still continues—to denote a cunning woman who stepped outside male-controlled norms, a highly politicized and Orientalized version of the femme fatale.[55] As an exotic dancer, a courtesan, and a double agent, Hari stirred emotions and intensified fears of the shifting patriarchal paradigm.[56] Most importantly, the peculiar placement of Hari, the symbol, somewhere between the Orient and the Occident made her concomitant with Goudal's public narrative.

The article published in the February 1929 issue of *Motion Picture Classic* comparing Goudal and Hari claimed to explain the secretiveness Goudal became so famous for, while simultaneously enhancing her association with Orientalism. According to Dorothy Donnell, who authored the piece, no one seems to know what happened to Mata Hari's daughter after Hari herself was sentenced to death. Rumor had it the girl spent her childhood and early teenage years in a boarding school run by nuns, perhaps somewhere on the Continent, studying French.[57] She disappeared from sight in late 1916, just before her mother faced the firing squad. Is it a mere coincidence, asked the magazine feature, that Goudal arrived on the American shore "a trifle more than one year later, early in 1918 . . . mysterious, exotic, speaking flawless French?" Goudal, it reasoned, appeared seemingly out of nowhere. Unlike other émigré performers, such as Pola Negri, she did not establish herself in Europe before starting to appear in Hollywood productions. The lack of a creative past is seen by Donnell as another case in point: "No one has been found who remembers seeing the Goudal in Europe. Is that, perhaps, because she had spent her life behind convent walls?"[58] Donnell recounted:

> And dying, [Mata Hari] left behind her a daughter, the heiress to her strange exotic beauty, to her dazzling and dangerous career—and perhaps to her fate. For wars may be over, but the secret service of warring countries does not forget, and those who are known to be friends or relatives of spies are always in danger. . . . The daughter of Mata Hari would be about thirty or thirty-two today. Jetta does not pretend to be a girl. The daughter of Mata Hari could pass—as Mata Hari herself often did—for a native French woman. Jetta looks more like the Rue de la Pais than Hollywood Boulevard. The daughter of Mata Hari must, one would think, looking at her portraits, have those same long Oriental eyes, that same wide, cryptic mouth, those same slim and beautiful hands you may say of the Goudal [*sic*].[59]

The fact that Goudal was cast as a mixed-race spy in *The Bright Shawl* worked to collapse the distinction between her private antics and the ever-potent fantasy of Mata Hari. In her piece Donnell went on to look at Goudal's breakthrough act with suspicion, hinting that only a woman with genuine experience of espionage could fare so well with the task of portraying a spy on screen.[60] This was, undoubtedly, a statement aimed at rousing the imagination of her readership rather than a genuine comment, as numerous, standardized spy fictions differed drastically—if not entirely—from the realities of military service in espionage.[61] What emerges from that multitude of star texts is a sense of alignment between larger-than-life heroines and Goudal's off-screen identity.

Conclusion

The discourses of mystery in contemporaneous fanzines tended to affiliate it with varying degrees of authenticity. Oversharing stood in opposition to privacy; the detailed portrayal of Pola Negri's love affairs, for example, was disapproved of by moviegoers who saw it as excessive and artificial.[62] The Franco-Dutch star was shown as unapproachable and mysterious, something of a misfit in the film industry where oversharing was the norm, thus reinforcing the idea of ordinariness denied to other, more flamboyant stars. Secrecy was placed on the other end of the representational spectrum where, most often, it was not acknowledged as a mediated practice, and thus did not attract the same level of criticism. Dyer relates this dynamic to the way audiences engage with the notion of star authenticity, arguing that film fans seek what lies beneath the superficial layer of star images and take it to represent the real identity of the star.[63] In suggesting they were uncovering what lay below the surface of the constructed persona, fan magazines claimed to give audiences a sneak peek into the "true" nature of stars.

The Goudal depicted by these discussions was either shy off-screen or actively engaged in the fabrication of her own private persona. Notably, in both circumstances, such accounts pictured her as largely independent from the influences of the studio system, in a sense that they placed stars in position to exert control over their images. According to fan press, it was Goudal, not the studio executives, who sustained her enigmatic aura. This was a commercial, sellable fantasy of how stardom operated, a vision in which Goudal was given more creative autonomy than she could potentially have. In reality, Goudal's identity as a mysterious creature of unknown origin was itself a creation of Famous Players-Lasky, put in motion to generate interest in her star vehicles. Propagated by editorials of film magazines, the star's reluctance to speak about her past was a representational tactic characteristic of the studio system, a stratagem for which she could not be held personally responsible.

An aura of mystery also functioned as a way of reconciling the contradiction between exotic otherness and Western familiarity that lay at the heart of Goudal's persona. In her interpretation of Edward Said's *Orientalism*, Gaylyn Studlar explains how the fantasy of the East "was rooted in the comingling of fear and fascination that grew out of contact with Islamic culture," and thus created a paradoxical rhetoric where appeal and repulsion go hand in hand.[64] While American fans were lured by the exoticism that Goudal promised, the simultaneous references to western Europe had the power to defuse the fear of hostility and the conjecture of inferiority buried within the imaginary of the East. Mystery supported the image of Goudal as racially ambiguous. Therefore, by focusing on continental aspects of her persona—and in providing grist for the mill of gossip—the studio succeeded in both keeping the threat of Oriental "otherness" at bay, and still catering to the appetite for Oriental thrills.

CHAPTER 8

Jetta Goudal and Temperament

"THE MOST TEMPERAMENTAL ACTRESS"

Goudal's contract with Famous Players-Lasky was terminated eighteen months before it was due to expire, in March 1925, with the executives proclaiming her unprofessional and impossible to manage.[1] The performer sued the studio for a breach of contract—making it the second lawsuit of this kind under her belt[2]—and promptly made her next move by joining a small, independent company run by the renowned director/producer Cecil B. DeMille.[3] Despite being awarded judgment against Zukor's company, Goudal maintained the "reputation of being hard to manage."[4] DeMille, her next employer, subsequently ended their contract three years prematurely, which resulted in yet another legal suit. The producer countered that Goudal's irrational behavior on set resulted in delays in shooting and cost the studio a great deal of money, but, having no records to support this claim, he also lost his case. Although the outcome of the court battle was beneficial for Goudal, who was granted $31,000 in damages,[5] her image became deeply embedded in the cultural currency presenting European performers as prone to insubordination, which incurred considerable costs at her expense.

One of the contentions made in Barry King's study of stardom in the classical period is that stars function in "manoeuvrable space"; that is, despite the challenging nature of their contracts with the studios, they exhibit a degree of independence in their relations with employers unavailable to lesser performers.[6] Sean P. Holmes set out to examine this assertion by applying it to the trials and tribulations of Goudal, concluding that "manoeuvrable space is not inherent in the institution of stardom. Rather, it is something that has had to be staked out and defended by individual stars, often at considerable personal cost."[7] He observes that the maneuverability Goudal negotiated through various court cases against her employers was counterbalanced by the extrafilmic narrative of her life, which identified her with mental instability and immature impulsivity. Thus, it consequently meant she was denied "a space in which to articulate her concerns as a worker." This chapter draws on Dawson and Holmes's argument by interrogating the origin of Goudal's public image as a temperamental diva, and the subsequent impact it had on the perception of her suit against DeMille. The fight between the star and the celebrated director was widely reported in the media, with most mentions in the press relying on statements made by DeMille, citing Goudal's demeanor as the reason why matters were brought to a head.[8] I argue that in referring to such unruly persona, Goudal was not allowed to articulate her own stance in matters relating to the control of labor. Thus, the persona crafted during the star's tenure at Famous Players-Lasky was used against her when she started to demand her rights as a worker. To the public, she was no more than an ill-tempered star of the silver screen, which in turn deprived her of the opportunity to voice her concerns about the Hollywood power dynamic in an effective manner.

Famous Players-Lasky

The image of a highly strung, temperamental movie player was constructed by the Famous Players-Lasky's publicity machine to contextualize Goudal's femme fatale persona.[9] In the context of the strategic commodification of her image, the star's allegedly problematic behavior operated as a means of authenticating her status as a French national. Irrationality was included in the mélange of clichés relating to European female performers. What is more, the idea of a woman having temperamental tantrums also related to patriarchal constructions of femininity as intrinsically unstable in emotional terms.[10] Within patriarchy, rational thinking and logic are constructed in opposition to emotion and irrationality, the set of disvalued attributes traditionally assigned to women. Thus, Goudal's nationality and gender operated in tandem to mark her "temperamental" persona as "real"; the value of this rhetoric is crucial because, as Richard Dyer argues, star phenomena must appear authentic in order to be meaningful.[11]

Jan-Christopher Horak notes that the stereotype of émigrés behaving badly was rooted in the fact that film actors in Hollywood had a dramatically different standing from that which they enjoyed in Europe. In Berlin, for example, they belonged to the highest caste of intellectuals and artists. In America, however, they were incorporated into the meticulous workings of the studio system and no longer constituted members of the cultural elite.[12] Indeed, Stephen Gundle and Clino Castelli argue that the institutionalization of American cinema differentiated it from other national cinemas.[13] The star system did not develop in the same way in the European film industries, with movie players holding a greater degree of control over their images, particularly in comparison with their American counterparts. In keeping with the popular discourse, European actresses were predisposed to cause trouble because they were not used to having the lower status that came with working in the studio system, where they may have had enormous public visibility but were, in the end, simply highly paid laborers. In this new climate, individual performers had virtually no control over the roles offered to them, or over the ways in which their image was constructed for mass consumption.

Magazines that discussed temperament among the movie folk often listed the same (mostly foreign) names, with Jetta Goudal and Pola Negri taking the lead as the most challenging to work with.[14] *Picture Play*, for instance, proposed that film directors were largely helpless against the overdeveloped temperament of "Pola Negri, Lupe Velez, Mae Murray, Jetta Goudal and their ilk."[15] Such description assigns stars an unhealthy degree of power over the working conditions in the industry, which is paradoxical, considering that the realities of their contractual engagements with the studios meant they had very little control over matters of this kind. Another article stated that imported contract players were not accustomed to the organization and speed of shooting in America, noting that a feature that might take a year to film on the Continent hardly ever took longer than six weeks to shoot in Hollywood.[16] This was undoubtedly an exaggeration, however, and, as Horak notes, the methods of film production across the Atlantic were never as dramatically different; no film producer in Europe could afford to shoot over such an extended period of time.[17] In any case, the magazine column that made this claim grafted it on a prejudice that presents Europeans as lacking a proper (American) work ethic. The perceived lack of professionalism of matinee idols hailing from the Continent is seen as a reason for their temperamental outbursts. To an extent, and as I will argue, this approach applied with particular ease to women, where such perceptions were also a product of patriarchy.

Studio executives embraced the connotations of bad behavior to authenticate the European origin of their stars. One of the documents in the Jetta Goudal Collection at the Margaret Herrick Library provides a fascinating insight into the logic that governed the production of star images. The transcript of an undated meeting of thirty-one film people—studio executives and exhibitors—supports the assumption that those in charge of designing star images saw female temperament as an intricate part of being French. The vice president in charge of exploitation and advertising (identified by the initials J.P.E) led the discussion of Goudal's worth at the box office: "Where do these Hollywood writers get the stuff that stories about the stars' temperament hurt the stars? Goudal's publicity instead of hurting her has helped her. I agree that in the case of Garbo it may have done some harm because Garbo has never had any sympathetic publicity at all, whereas Goudal has and while we feel that Garbo is really 'a foreigner' the american [*sic*] public has always been strong for French actresses and temperament seems the rightful heritage and expression of the French star."[18]

Although J.P.E acknowledged the benefits of a carefully crafted publicity campaign, he also saw the potential dangers of that line of "foreign" branding. Although undated, the document's mention of Garbo and DeMille allows it to be situated in the late 1920s. I suggest, however, that this characteristic brand of temperament was conceived much earlier. The rumors regarding Goudal's diva-like behavior were planted in the press soon after she entered the arena of stardom in 1923, with the release of *The Bright Shawl*.

In the last months of 1923, *Picture Play*'s Malcolm H. Oettinger described his meeting with Goudal as both mesmerizing and very emotional. "She is foreign in a highly theatrical way. Not for ze [*sic*] one moment does she permit you to forget that she is an importation,"[19] he observed, mimicking and gently mocking her foreign accent. The ideological imperatives behind presenting Goudal's behavior as challenging were aimed to enhance her alignment with Europeanness. As noted by *Photoplay*, the actress refused to stay in a hotel booked for her by Famous Players-Lasky's executives when she arrived in Hollywood, on the account of it being "too much old lady." She was promptly accommodated in another, more suitable establishment.[20] Neither of these mentions uses the adjective that soon came to outline Goudal's entire persona—temperamental—but they did lay a foundation to the later claims of explosive moodiness. Hinting at foreign, continental attitude served as a prelude to labeling Goudal as problematic.

In 1924, *Motion Picture Classic* proclaimed Goudal "the most temperamental actress that has ever been on the screen" (figure 24).[21] In accordance with the gossip columns, her blatant manifestations of temper were not welcomed by the film crew, who had to handle the star with extra care so that she would not leave the set post-haste. Harry Carr reported that Goudal did not obey orders given by the directors: "When she is told to do something she doesn't want to do, she gives the director a sidelong glance and a queer little twisted smile and says sweetly: *Ah, no. Goudal wouldn't do that.* And a herd of cyclones can't make Goudal do it."[22]

Dorothy Calhoun of *Motion Picture Classic* described star temperament as one of the hidden costs of every feature film, arguing that the difficult behavior of some performers delays production and causes financial loses.[23] She compared producers' dealings with their employees to the dynamics between a hunter and a lion: "The producer's delight at capturing the prize is mingled with apprehension, like that of a lion hunter who has a splendid specimen by the tail, and there's nothing left to expect just to lead it home and coax it into a cage." Calhoun viewed stage stars and foreign actors as the most likely to cause trouble. They are the most exceptional but also the most dangerous "specimens"; they are wild lions in need of taming.[24]

Several issues emerge from the marketing tactics established by Famous Players-Lasky in the promotion of Goudal's "difficult" star persona. First of all,

Jetta and Her Temperament

By
HARRY CARR

Elle Est Française,
Mais Oui ! Et Ce
N'Est Pas Tout!

White

NOT since Pola Negri arrived from Germany with her five-carat diamond has Hollywood had such a thrill.

The lady's name is Jetta Goudal. She looks like a beautiful Cossack. She looks like an Oriental princess. She looks like . . . well, whatever it is that has changing hazel eyes that slant at the corners; that slumber and drowse; then blaze with fires.

But Jetta insists that she is none of these thrilling and exciting things. She says she is just French.

She came here from New York to play a vampish rôle in "Open All Night," which is being filmed at the Lasky studio.

White

Above is Jetta Goudal in the fascinating rôle of La Pilar in "The Bright Shawl," in which she first attracted the attention of the critics. At the top of the page, a late portrait and left, with Paul Bern, who directed her in "Open All Night"

Figure 24. "Jetta and Her Temperament," published by *Motion Picture Classic* in October 1924.

fan magazines drew a parallel between a propensity to misconduct and being foreign, so Goudal's apparent temperamentality served to reinforce her connection to Europe. It is worth highlighting here that beyond secretiveness, discussed in chapter 7, the presumption of difficult behavior constituted another tread linking Goudal to the way in which Garbo was portrayed later. A 1926 article in the *Los Angeles Times* reported on the Swedish actress and her impossible demands, while another noted the difficulties faced by the studio in accommodating for numerous outbursts.[25]

Second, they engaged with an implicit discourse on silent stars that placed high currency on the nineteenth-century understanding of creativity and talent. Goudal's star image deployed the signs of an erratic disposition because, within such a framework, extremely gifted artists were often assumed to suffer from social inadequacy, or to be moody and generally difficult to deal with. The romantic polemic popularized by Schopenhauer characterized geniuses as maladapted in the most mundane ways.[26] Conforming to the philosopher's ideas, which remained influential throughout the 1920s, the high development of one of the selected intellectual faculties resulted in the weakening of other emotional areas. The June 1928 issue of *Motion Picture Classic* featured a piece concerned with Alan Crosland, a movie director renowned for working with many difficult stars, which demonstrates this line of reasoning.[27] Crosland's fifteen years in the industry made him realize that although filming some difficult stars poses risks, the artistic results that can be obtained with them are worth the challenge. Admittedly, the director "prefers the temperamental ones to the good troupers, because they are almost always the artists—the ones who have something to give."[28] This account equates superior skills with the demanding characters of the actors who possess them. *Motion Picture Magazine* found that understanding of talent problematic, criticizing stars too eager to exercise their right to be moody and irrational: "It has long been a tradition that an artist must, of necessity, have temperament. Otherwise he was not a real artist. And temperament has been taken to mean that the artist every now and then must flare up in fits of wholly unreasonable and picturesque fury. The more unreasonable the fury, the more *artistic* the artist."[29]

In castigating the prevailing attitudes, the article provides an illustration of the dominant discourse on artistry. Four months later, in March 1928, the same fan title celebrated Goudal's talent, decreeing her "a good enough actress to be temperamental and get away with it."[30] For the columnist, the star managed to escape the constraints of typecasting by choosing to exist outside of Hollywood molds. Her volatile demeanor was presented as going hand in hand with artistic ability, and that, in turn, was often linked to Europe as a land of sophisticated artistic traditions, and as a place where stars were handled differently. Conversely, the American industry offered movie players handsome salaries and huge public visibility while also treating them like a form of privileged laborers.

The romantics entwined the notion of genius with the idea of an innate, nearly godlike privilege that cannot be achieved by means other than some supernatural bestowal. To possess genius meant to be blessed with an extremely rare gift that is beyond one's rational control. For Kant, a genius was able to produce original ideas without having to be taught them, or conceive works "for which no determinate rule can be given."[31] In a similar vein, the star system constructs stars as talented and unique. Stars of the silent period in particular were often presented as self-taught, partially because they worked in a relatively new medium that had not yet established its own professional or educational norms. The journalist Homer Currie suggested that Goudal was not familiar with the techniques of film acting when she first appeared in Hollywood, but in time her innate talent was polished in front of the camera and led her to screen success. This eventually made up for the lack of knowledge that, in Currie's words, "even an extra girl would possess."[32]

In "seeking enlightenment on this genius topic," another journalist, William H McKegg, decided to interview Jetta Goudal, feeling assured that his "visit would not be in vain." His account presented Goudal as a perfect spokesperson for the subject, emphasizing her own artistic sensibility:

> You cannot compare a—well, I shall say an artist—with an ordinary person. There is no comparison mentally. An artist—or a genius—cannot be normal. By normal I mean average, one going according to rule. All real artists—or geniuses—are abnormal. . . . An artist, a genius—which-ever you like—is first of all true to himself. He will not do what his inner self tells him is not correct or right for his abilities. He sees, feels, and hears things differently—with a far keener perception—entirely above the senses of an ordinary person.[33]

The excerpt illustrates how the dictum of genius gave Goudal a different type of validity and elevated her above the ordinary, in a way congruent with the treatment of talent in the romantic canon. In societal terms, artists are pictured here not as craftsmen but as creatures that carry the connotations of the spiritual realm, "essentially alienated from routine life."[34]

How can one make sense of this ethos of celebrities as extremely gifted, given that they are also perceived by their employers as mere laborers? Dyer squares these apparent opposites by arguing that one of the key issues at the core of the meta-narrative of stardom is the representation of stars as both ordinary and extraordinary.[35] In the light of such analysis, Goudal is crafted as "just like us" (a worker) while simultaneously being shown to possess some rare qualities (an artist); she is more creative, more sensitive, and more talented than the majority of people. Vera L. Zolberg adopts a slightly different approach toward the issue, underlining the ideological constraints intrinsic to the conception of performers as artists in romantic tradition, and performers as workers in modern understanding. In Zolberg's argument these two notions are inherently incompatible, as the former effectively excludes the latter.[36] Consequently, this paradox is echoed in the handling of Goudal's persona in contemporary fan texts; by integrating concepts of talent and uniqueness into the image, the general rhetoric moved Goudal away from a more "ordinary" status in a wider social category of workers and toward a greater sense of extraordinariness.

Speaking in retrospect, Goudal admitted that she met her fabricated off-screen identity with some reservations; nonetheless, her feelings on the subject remained irrelevant to the studio, which was determined to stick to its stratagem.[37] There is evidence to suggest the actress made attempts to single-handedly challenge the temperamental facet of the persona assigned to her by Famous Players-Lasky by contacting the media responsible for upholding such images. An unpublished letter addressed to one of the writers of *Picture Play* (known as "The Bystander") illustrates the unease Goudal felt in regard to her own image. She wrote:

> I read the reference to myself in your article in the last number [*sic*] of Picture Play with rather mixed feelings! I do not doubt that you had the best of intentions, but you really were not giving me the kind of publicity I am looking for nor the public true facts. When I buy seats myself, I have the intelligence to find out exactly where they are situated and that before accepting them. If I am invited I consider it due to good manners to suffer in silence when bad seats are our fate. . . . To prove [to] you that I really do not have as bad a temper as some very sweet and kindly disposed person must have told you, let me tell you that I did not even lose it when I read your remarks, although it might have furnished a nice opportunity for it.[38]

The reference greeted by Goudal with such horror was relatively short and harmless in comparison with what was still to come. The Bystander reported Goudal was often spotted in New York theaters where she never failed to display both her stunning looks and bad temper. "If she doesn't like the seats she gets she complains so violently that the show can hardly go on. Usually, in desperation someone changes seats with her."[39] Goudal urged the writer to correct his mistake in one of the following issues of the magazine. Her plea did not go unnoticed;[40] the editors of *Picture Play* admitted they were wrong, rectifying what she thought of as a denigration. This was a small, and perhaps even questionable, victory that had no bearing on her image at large. As an individual and a laborer, she had little, if any, chance of taking control of her representation in the press. In early 1931, Goudal recounted her reaction to being molded into a marketable commodity: "It was while I was at Paramount, and when I objected, horrified, they assured me that it was a swell stunt and it would be continued, no matter what my feelings on the subject might be."[41] In the context of the industry methods of the decade, the fabrication and manipulation of one's star persona by the studio represented a common practice. Goudal's approval, or lack thereof, would not have any impact on the route Famous Players-Lasky decided to take.

One of the most crucial assertions made by Holmes in his discussion of Goudal's labor in Hollywood is that the star tried to seize control over the choice of her film costumes so as to manage her own image.[42] Michelle Tolini Finamore's evaluation is aligned with Holmes's in the sense that she also acknowledges the high degree of independence the star exerted over her on-screen costumes.[43] Goudal's agreements with consecutive employers guaranteed that every "modern" ensemble worn by her character would have to get her personal seal of approval before filming; the proviso did not extend to period costumes, which lay in the competence of the wardrobe department.[44] The contract she signed before the production of *Lady of the Pavements* (1929), for instance, contained a clause that allowed her to have a final say in the matter of "design of clothes necessary . . . to be worn" in her part.[45]

In paying considerable attention to what was worn by her characters, Goudal attempted to reclaim her image. However, it is important to understand that fashion departments were not included in the structure of film studios until the early 1920s. Before this development, extras and actors alike were obliged to provide their own film costumes; and some major stars continued to administer their wardrobe even well into the second decade of the century.[46] Although Tolini Finamore notes the practice was on the wane by the late 1920s, Goudal continued to oversee the design of her on-screen gowns throughout her fruitful but short-lived career.[47] The terms and conditions of the agreement with Cecil B. DeMille Pictures Corporation stated that the services Goudal is due to perform are of intellectual and therefore of unique character.[48] DeMille himself recollected that throughout her employment the actress made many valuable suggestions regarding not only her own wardrobe but also other aspects of films she was cast in, such as set design and script.[49] With surprising tenacity, the star used fashion as an avenue through which she strengthened her continuous refusal to fully subordinate to the commands of the studio system, asking for respect of her creative rights as an artist.

In the previous chapters of this case study I investigated how fashion intersected with a number of discursive parameters implicit in Goudal's persona, namely with the notion of exoticism and her alleged Frenchness. In this context, the way in which studio managers—and, subsequently, the press—handled Goudal's personal involvement in the costume department is fascinating, and the public treatment of the subject speaks volumes about the conditions of commodification endured by film performers of the period. *Motion Picture Classic*, *Photoplay*, and other periodicals effectively integrated this facet of Goudal's professional activity into the narrative of temperament, implying that her interest in fashion verged on obsession. For example, one commentator claimed that Goudal tended to "register her displeasure at any gown she happened to dislike—and there were few that she did not dislike—by violently tearing the offending garment from her body, and ripping it into shreds."[50] Jesse L. Lasky, a film producer, allegedly compared Goudal to a Bolshevist who was impossible to work with, recounting she developed a habit of ripping the costumes that did not satisfy her aesthetic requirements.[51]

According to the study by Charles C. Benham, the first dispute between Goudal and Famous Players-Lasky's executives took place on the set of *A Sainted Devil* (1924), a Rudolph Valentino star vehicle. Goudal ostensibly disapproved of the costumes she was required to wear, and—despite the fact that her studio contract gave her the right to select her wardrobe—she was dismissed from the production.[52] In the public domain, the event was framed as a conflict between Natasha Rambova—Hollywood personality, costumer, set designer, and, most importantly, Valentino's wife at the time of filming—and the ill-tempered continental star. *Photoplay* informed its readers that the dissolution of Goudal's contract was caused, to an extent, by the frequent feuds she had with Rambova, particularly on the issue of costumes.[53] One of Valentino's biographers suggests that although Rambova commented on the aesthetic value of the mise-en-scène, the artistic influence she exerted over the shoot tends to be overstated. Goudal resented the intrusion Mrs. Valentino made on every department "with suggestions, criticisms, requests—and then demands for changes,"[54] and expressed that resentment loud and clear. The constant bickering, writes Robert Oberfirst, cost her a leading role.[55] This form of representation was grounded in a rhetoric that saw fashion as an essentially feminine occupation, with the perception of fashion-savvy women as highbrow, as well as self-indulgent and volatile. Professional and personal interest in couture operated as a recognizable component of Goudal's identity, and thus it was often constructed by the editorials as yet another indication of her obsessive, flamboyant nature.

Although less frequently, some sources described Rambova as sick with jealousy over the growing closeness between her husband and his attractive co-star.[56] Ultimately, Rambova succeeded in having Goudal replaced by Dagmar Godowsky, a good friend of her husband's.[57] Later commentators went further in implying that Goudal, in her dubious nature, was solely responsible for planting such fabricated stories. "Miss Goudal hinted that Valentino himself had become strongly attracted to her and that this has displeased Natacha so much that she had resorted to firing her out of retribution."[58] In referring to either scenario, the fan press capitalized on pre-established ideas that reflected on both Rambova and Goudal as imperious, strong-willed women. One can see how an impending romance between Valentino and Goudal seemed plausible, given that most moviegoers saw Valentino as the embodiment of the exotic, passionate lover. Like fan magazines of the era, the account written by Alan Robert Ginsberg demonstrates a reliance on the same discursive pattern, referring to the Goudal/Rambova incident as "a clash of divas." Ginsberg also adds that Rambova turned out to be "one rival prima donna . . . capable of battling and beating Jetta."[59]

Holmes notes that by recasting the tensions on set as a personal affair, the studio ensured that "a struggle between a performer and the studio that employed [Goudal] over the terms of her commodification never reached a wider audience,"[60] therefore using star phenomena not only as promotional tactics but also as means to subjugate actors to the demands of the studio system. In other words, instead of entering the public domain as an issue regarding professionals, the story morphed into an anecdote about female misconduct. Famous Players-Lasky also used the tensions as a means of justifying a contractual change, and after completing two more features, *The Spaniard* (1925) and *Salome of the Tenements* (1925), it dissolved Goudal's contract. Not surprisingly, Goudal saw the gesture as a violation of her contractual rights and insisted on seeking justice in court.

Recent research conducted by Ginsberg reveals that the legal fight against Famous Players-Lasky was not the first instance in which Goudal had appeared as plaintiff, although it was the first case of such nature that attracted public attention. Goudal's first multipicture contract was signed for an initial period of six months with Distinctive Pictures, granting the actress an attractive salary of $500 per week. On November 17, 1923, less than a month after commencing employment, the star's agreement was terminated by the studio. Goudal brought a lawsuit against it for the amount of $100,000, which included the remaining salary payments and a reimbursement for damages to her professional standing suffered as a consequence of sudden redundancy.[61] The proposed sum exceeded unpaid wages by $89,000, but, as argued by Goudal's attorney, the breach of contract significantly impaired the development of his client's career, casting a shadow of doubt on her professional ethics.[62] While the exact outcome of the lawsuit remains unknown—perhaps due to relatively low visibility of Goudal's status at the time, it was never evaluated by the press—Ginsberg notes that the lack of court documentation suggests that a settlement was reached.[63]

Famous Players-Lasky capitalized on the "temperamental" persona of its former star to protect its interest, and subsequently caused Goudal to fall victim to her constructed public image. In arguing that the performer was fired due to her poor conduct, the November 1927 issue of *Motion Picture Classic* reflected general attitudes. Goudal, it claimed, became infamous for disobeying directorial instruction: "When she was in a fury she would sit down when told to stand and would stand up in a scene which required her to sit."[64]

Motion Picture Classic had no sympathy for picture players who had reservations about the ways producers handled them. The magazine tended to emphasize the financial strain put on the studio by the ridiculous demands of big screen names, including Goudal herself. "Primarily, picture production is a strictly business affair. Temperament costs money and gives no tangible returns for that money."[65] Daily newspapers joined in expressing familiar sentiments, presenting foreign players as arrogant and insubordinate. One specific source deliberated whether putting a ban on émigré performers would be a welcomed development in Hollywood. After all, "they are all too much like Miss Goudal—temperamental and difficult to manage."[66] The fact that Goudal reached a full settlement in all claims against Famous Players-Lasky—and, most likely, Distinctive Pictures—was kept outside of public consciousness.

When interviewed, Goudal vehemently opposed the idea that she was temperamental or hard to manage. She maintained she was not thin-skinned but simply ambitious, and admitted to having no qualms about making her observations known to film producers and directors.[67] *Picture Play* described Goudal's strong reactions to the vaguest reference to bad temper as indicative of her emotional instability. According to Harry Carr, "When you ask Jetta about this [her temperament], her eyes wander up and down your personality: then they half close and she says with a tired little smile that she isn't temperamental at all; she just has her own ideas about things. She says otherwise she never would have been in America at all."[68] The conduct of the star during the interview conformed to her persona; paradoxically, in denying the rumors it only cemented Goudal's identity as a troublemaker.

At the height of Goudal's fame *Picture Play* ran an interview in which she, again, contested her bad reputation, calling all the stories of leaving Famous Players-Lasky's studio premises in a fit of dudgeon "base lies." The actress was clearly reluctant to see herself as more than a strong-willed individual with a vision. The article was published in October 1927, one month after the termination of her employment at DeMille's studio had been announced. Goudal blamed the media for ruining her professional standing. She refused to play "silly roles" or otherwise engage with projects that revolted her conscience as an artist; eventually, she was portrayed as hard to work with. "Now they try to break my contract. But they cannot. So they take it to court to prove how temperamental Goudal is. That is how you read those awful things! It is untrue, sir!"[69]

In general, fan magazines did not dare question whether Goudal actually exhibited sulky, diva behavior. Margaret Reid's account is one of the very few examples that employed a more sympathetic angle in describing Goudal's histrionics; to Reid, Goudal was just a cog in the machine. The journalist was astonished that "cold-officials" could disregard the insights of someone as gifted and intelligent as Goudal. According to the article, the widely discussed reputation Goudal acquired was pure fabrication and a harmful device, "a poisoned thorn in her olive-tinted flesh."[70] Therefore, it was not strange that the star fought for her rights but rather that she had so little room to maneuver in her dealings with the studio that she was forced to enter such battles. On one occasion, *Picture Play*'s writer William H. McKegg presented Goudal in equally positive light, explaining that she was labeled as volatile simply because she wanted her costume designs to follow her explicit instructions. "They say she is temperamental when she merely points out their obvious mistakes. Not a quarter of a fault escapes Goudal's artistic eyes."[71] Unfortunately, the seamstresses could not match the greatness of Goudal's artistic vision, sparking conflict. Such commentary merged the narratives of great sensibility and genius (as investigated before) with the notion of temperament; here, however, Goudal's behavior is motivated by appropriate considerations.

DeMille's Studio

The star's exchange value kept on growing in 1925. After being dismissed from Famous Players-Lasky, Goudal was offered positions at both MGM and the DeMille Picture Corporation, eventually opting for the latter. Neither the court case against Distinctive Pictures nor the one against Famous Players-Lasky was settled at the time.[72] The transfer from one of the most powerful studios to a firm led by DeMille—a director of considerably high status—attracted a great deal of attention in the industry and beyond. Numerous articles were devoted to the discussion of Goudal's infamous tantrums and speculation whether someone as capricious as her had a chance of lasting in the DeMille fold. *Photoplay* admired the producer for taking a risk in hiring Goudal, calling him a "lion tamer" and someone who "evidently knows how to handle these people with temperament."[73] The flighty connotations the star acquired while working for her previous studio were revalidated throughout her stay at DeMille's. In picturing Goudal as an irrational creature in need of training, her off-screen narrative followed the pattern of misconduct. The fact that she eventually ceased to cause problems, as some features suggested, was explained by the careful way in which DeMille managed her. *Picture Play* praised the exceptional skill of the producer, known to have dealt with more difficult players than anyone else in the industry. "He has tremendous tact, and he has mastered, somehow, the art of being impressive and inspiring respect in the most uncontrolled and emotional people."[74]

Other sections of the fan magazine discourse painted Goudal as a victim of gossip and a professional who fully recognized the potentially damaging repercussions her reputation could have on her career. Writing for *Picture Play*, William McKegg also defended her name by noting that Goudal, unlike many other film people, was pleasant to him during their meeting. The picture of the temperamental diva, so eagerly painted on the canvas of the press, has nothing to do with the real Goudal, he concluded, suggesting that "studio customers" were to blame for Goudal's unjustly earned reputation; what he meant by such "customers" remains somehow unclear.[75] In 1927, the actress looked back at her time after leaving Famous Players-Lasky as full of doubts and lost opportunities. According to the editorial, "the dreadful stories of her temperament" became a burden that kept her from getting any good parts; Goudal became so desperate to earn her living she immediately accepted DeMille's offer, "no haggling about money."[76]

The DeMille emerging from the pages of the contemporary press is a humble man who has not let the gossip influence his decision-making. In hiring Goudal—or in "taking a chance with the dynamite"[77]—he put himself at risk; he also gave the actress an opportunity she deserved. The sweeping financial success of *Three Faces East* (1926), a spy drama that capitalized on Goudal's mysterious appeal, proved that his decision was a good one.[78] Under her new management, the performer was ordained a major star. A year into the contract, fan magazines reported that Goudal not only managed to co-exist with DeMille in perfect harmony but had also started to refer to him affectionately as "Papa DeMille."[79] Her old, mercurial ways appeared to have gone.

Goudal's personal correspondence reveals that she was extremely conscious of her public persona and the challenges it posed. Indeed, on February 11, 1927 she asked DeMille for permission to hire her own publicity representative, which again speaks of her desire to take control of her stardom, or to maneuver for space, to use King's terminology.[80] DeMille agreed to the scheme, stating that such employee would of course have to cooperate with the studio "to avoid confusion." He also reserved the right to cancel the agreement as he saw fit.[81] In March 1927, Sig Schlager agreed to represent the actress in matters of "exploitation, publicity [and] counsel" and to take care of the further promotion of her career, for which he received a payment of $1,500 for two months of his services.[82]

In September 1927, the *Los Angeles Times* broke the news that the DeMille-Goudal working partnership was over. More than a year later, *Picture Play* concluded that Goudal's behavior was to blame for the court battle: "Tantrums on the set have won her realms of publicity, but they finally lost her a good contract."[83] DeWitt Bodeen quotes a salary dispute as responsible for the split. In accordance with his account, the contract signed by Goudal was divided into six monthly intervals, which necessitated a rise of $1,000 in the star's weekly wages. After the second year of their cooperation DeMille violated the terms and conditions by refusing to pay the increase, so Goudal pressed charges, demanding over $85,000 of financial compensation.[84]

By the time the trial commenced in late January 1929, Cecil B. DeMille Pictures Corporation was operating as part of Pathé Exchange, owing to DeMille's decision to sell the company a year earlier. DeMille's initial line of defense was to assert that Goudal was fired on the grounds of disobedience. His company had to incur extra production costs because its chief player repeatedly failed to show up for work on time, causing delays in shooting; on a more personal level, the producer had simply lost the patience to deal with Goudal's "spitfire temper."[85] The attorney who represented the actress suggested that the sudden termination of her services was motivated by financial difficulties faced by the studio at the time. In a desperate attempt to reduce spending, he explained, DeMille had to break an expensive star contract, even without a legitimate reason to do so.[86]

Working on behalf of the defendant, Neil McCarthy responded: "It does not make any difference what the motivation was. The only question is whether grounds exist for the discharge of this girl."[87] McCarthy's use of the term "girl" in reference to a woman of thirty-eight years of age is notable, given its connotations of adolescence and, therefore, of the misbehavior characteristic of this period of development. Goudal was aware of such patronizing attitude and its implications, testifying that a rationale of infantilization was deployed by DeMille during their partnership, as he expected to be addressed as "Papa DeMille," whereas he referred to the star as "a sweet child" and a "good" or "bad" girl, depending on circumstances.[88] In the light of tangible evidence provided by financial records of eight moving pictures Goudal filmed at the studio, the accusations of insubordination were found to be baseless. What additionally made DeMille's attacks disputable was the fact that the company exercised its right to extend Goudal's contract for a one-year term just four months before making her redundant. "If Goudal's behaviour had truly been unacceptable, why did the company keep renewing her contract?" asks Ginsberg, rather poignantly.[89] The judge ruled the plaintiff performed her duties accordingly.

Bodeen reports that in fighting her erstwhile employer, Goudal saw an opportunity to seize control over the image she acquired in the media.[90] However, correspondence between the two parties indicates that Goudal was ready to discuss the conditions of the proposed contract release without necessarily resorting to legal action. Her previous experience had taught her of the harm another dismissal would cause to her future employability. The existing letters also tend to strike a highly emotional note, suggesting that the star established a close relationship with her producer: "Don't you know that I have been sick and heartbroken over the whole matter [?] Don't you realize that I have been refusing to believe for nearly five months that you were aware of the unbusinesslike manipulating of your representatives [?]"[91] she lamented. At the same time, Goudal thought of her studio contract as a partnership, "a pact between equals, not an indenture binding a servant to a master,"[92] and, fully aware of the economic value she represented as a commodity, she sought to mitigate this professional setback through adequate compensation. Despite triumphing in the court of law, the incident failed to cast off her problematic persona. In fact, it achieved the opposite effect, as the popular press reveled in criticizing her for her bold actions. Facing a deluge of unfavorable comments and with her professional standing on the line, the indemnity of $31,000 must have seemed like scant consolation.[93]

Goudal's victory over the studio was greeted with a degree of suspicion, and most fan magazines acted in unison in criticizing the Los Angeles judge for his ruling. *Photoplay* smirked at the decision by saying that it sanctioned disobedience and gave Goudal "the right to be temperamental."[94] *Picture Play* went even further, seeing it as a threat to the workings of the film industry, where erratic women, from now on, would dictate their fancies.[95] Comments of this nature echoed the wider social reality where seeking to undermine existing structures of power—both within the star system and, on a wider scale, within patriarchy—was frowned upon.

One piece implied that Goudal's behavior in court was nothing more than a perfectly staged ploy. As reported by the Bystander, Goudal cried crocodile tears on the stand and generally behaved so slyly that one had to admire how tremendously well performed her act was.[96] Furthermore, the column advocated that Goudal's fashion choices were aimed to veil her true, authentic personality, effectively eliciting sympathetic responses from those following her trial with DeMille. The plaintiff used performative qualities of clothing to masquerade as someone she was not: "[Goudal] was wearing the outfit in which she had appeared in court for several days. It was probably the ugliest dress that any woman ever wore of her own free will. It was a muddy gray—covert cloth, or cravenette, or some such harsh, sensible material. Can you imagine a judge taking seriously the charge that La Goudal is temperamental, when she appears in a dress like that? No one with any temperament would wear it. That gives a fair illustration of how clever Jetta Goudal really is."[97]

Inherent in these comments is the notion that, as a female thespian, Goudal was bound to be dubious and manipulative. Virginia Wright Wexman theorized actresses as women who occupy a privileged position, in a sense that they inevitably come to symbolize "the role-playing that all women must inevitably perform within a patriarchal system."[98] With specified cultural attributes, femininity is in itself a performative state, an identity that requires continuous production and support.[99] Additionally, the role played by fashion in this fabrication further demonstrates the significance of Goudal's sartorial choices and their relevance in the construction of her star text. Drawing on dominant regimes of representation, interest in fashion is viewed as a specifically feminine quality, which enhances the connection between womanhood and the practice of deceitfulness.[100] Again, this worked on the assumption that the "real" star behind the facade is the incarnation of a European diva. *Picture Play* went on to describe Goudal's star image as an authentic representation of her true self, thus framing any inconsistency in it—epitomized here by an old-fashioned outfit—as suspicious. After all, Goudal's penchant for extravagant gowns both on and off the silver screen was well documented; her failure to conform to the image of a fashion enthusiast in court was read as a sign of ingenuity. The editorial connects her choice of simple attire to deception. This crafted trick, it reasoned, showed how "very shrewd"[101] the plaintiff was.

In a sense, this turn of events conformed to the narrative of temperament constructed in the initial years of Goudal's career; through that paradigm, her relatively "quiet," peaceful time at DeMille's studio was reframed as inauthentic, a mere performance. I have already mentioned how, in his groundbreaking work on stars, Dyer argues that a sense of authenticity is central to star texts.[102] This conceptual dynamic relates to the theorization of stardom as a constructed fiction in which audiences have access to a plethora of star sources, and where they can choose between those aspects they deem genuine. To quote from Clare

Whatling—who shares an ideological alliance with Dyer—"one image succeeds another in an infinite regress by means of which one more authentic image displaces another."[103] This is not to say that newly produced information on a star persona supersedes the old one, making it redundant. In the case of Goudal, the public discourse simply reverted to the old image of the star as a temperamental performer instead of developing a new narrative that would equate her with some form of agency.

The scrutiny that surrounded the actress's involvement in the trial stood in strong juxtaposition to the manner in which the star system treated her former employer. Cecil B. DeMille had a reputation for requiring a great deal of physical sacrifice from his leading cast, yet his autocratic behavior never had a derogatory impact on his image. An article in the *New York Times* from 1925 calls him an "imperious producer" and "a man with an iron hand," speaking approvingly of DeMille's strict directorial methods: "The other day I lunched with him in his delightful private studio suite, and I came out filled with admiration for Mr. DeMille's discipline, which is emulated by his subordinates."[104]

Gloria Swanson, who collaborated with DeMille on several films, echoed these attitudes in describing his somehow arrogant demeanor in equally positive terms: "If you didn't do the job he demanded of you, you got hell, no question about it. He stood for no nonsense."[105] Such reading of DeMille's persona was influenced by two subsequent factors. First, his actions were framed in the context of creative genius, as part of his pursuit of artistic perfection. Second, and more significantly, DeMille's position as a male producer meant that his personal conduct needed no excuses and that he had every right to challenge his employees; in fact, his disciplinarian filming methods were often venerated. Goudal's status as a mere worker and a woman meant that she was marked as problematic rather than admirable for ostensibly exhibiting the same manner of behavior. These social attitudes find their reflection in the "diva" term Goudal has been labeled with. According to the vaunting, collective hubris, perfectionism in men is to be praised; women who strive for perfection, however, are thought of as unprofessional at best, and downright unmanageable at worst.

It is telling that in the context of this paternal relationship Goudal lost her significance as a laborer. She was diminished to a disobedient child, ungrateful for the chance her "Papa" had given her. Her struggle was effectively recast as an argument between the artist and his muse, rather than a professional and legal dispute. The language used in the discussion of the court action often assumed a patronizing tone; in infantilizing her it further weakened her agency. *Picture Play* described the reason behind the court case as follows: "The company contends that she broke her contract by not being a good girl and obediently taking orders from her directors."[106] The Goudal that emerges from this discourse is not an actress, or even a grown-up woman; she is precisely a "bad girl" who behaves inappropriately in failing to respect her elders. The way fan magazines represented the Goudal/DeMille battle was hardly ever sympathetic toward the plaintiff, and the financial implications of the split failed to make a lasting impact on the public psyche.

In being insubordinate and thin-skinned Goudal exhibited features that were assumed to lie at the core of female nature. Not following the orders of Hollywood employers was, according to *Motion Picture Classic*, a common form of conduct among female stars. "Do Women Rule the Movies?" asked an editorial in 1928, pointing out that women exert a greater impact over movies than their male peers.[107] The bespoke influence is not earned because of their skill or status but is a result of childlike attitudes adopted by women to harass directors. Producers might try to protect their interests by hiring lawyers to put "threatening clauses" in star contracts, but the final say will always belong to the gorgeous screen ladies who "have ruled the movies by a tyranny of tears." The author of the article sympathizes with the studio executives who are presumably forced to fulfill the ridiculous demands imposed on them by their female employees. Corinne Griffith, Pola Negri, Gloria Swanson, Jetta Goudal, and Maria Corda are all listed as stars who notoriously ignore their professional obligations and behave in an irrational fashion to get what they want. The underlying assumption is that female players achieve their aims by a display of extremely unprofessional, immature conduct, but that they are also at their most authentic when in the throes of emotion. Consequently, *Motion Picture Classic* dismissed the objections raised by female stars against mistreatment as laughable.

Nonetheless, some parts of the debate regarding Goudal and her legal case started to change in the following years. Film magazines were not consistent in their treatment of gossip regarding film performers, and their stances on specific issues could change over time. In May 1928, for example, *Picture Play* disapproved of Goudal taking legal action against DeMille, noting that her contract had been canceled due to her "mannerisms" and alleged misconduct. Interestingly, a report published in the following year used a different tone, seeing defeat of DeMille as a welcome shift in the monolithic model of power relations in Hollywood and a victory of workers over the studio system. "The judge, in rendering the decision, indicated that artists have more rights intellectually than is ordinarily presumed, and that they can't be treated as menials and ordered about at pleasure," it reasoned, before concluding that the ruling "might be constructed as a blow to the so-called czarist methods that occasionally are advocated in the management of players."[108]

Besides witnessing the increased press coverage of juridical action against DeMille, the year 1929 saw the release of *Lady of the Pavements*, a United Artists production in which Goudal supported Lupe Vélez, a chief Mexican import. Similarly to fan magazines' handling of the previous incident featuring Natacha Rambova, Goudal was portrayed here as exhibiting an ostentatiously stuck-up attitude, consequently developing a long-standing feud with Vélez, whose propensity to tantrums and meltdowns matched her own. The spitfire temper—a locus of their respective star identities—was elaborated in *The Smart Set*, where the ongoing conflict between the movie players was compared to a tension that would inevitably arise if two tigers were to be put in the same cage. "What tigers say to each other is something fierce. And neither one ever gives in."[109] Their brawls stopped "just a fraction of this side of fisticuffs," informed *Motion Picture Classic*, considering it lucky—and somehow astonishing—that open, physical violence was averted on set. "Could their antagonisms have been translated into active weapons, not a stage would be standing on United Artists' lot and two little graves would probably be the sole remaining vestige of Lupe and Jetta."[110]

As noted before, Goudal's star image also partly enclosed her within the framework of romantic genius; hence, some of the voices that sympathized with her made use of the perceived notion of artistry to justify her actions. McKegg, who became an outspoken supporter of Goudal's fight, called attention to the fact that the judge presiding over the case against DeMille understood the implications of talent.[111] The greatness of artistic stature raised an individual above the ordinary, offering, in some instances, a form of immunity against the strict requirements of the studio system. In McKegg's words, "a real artist could not be expected to do the things expected of an ordinary person. That judge knew something. But he might have said *genius*—for such is Jetta Goudal in more ways than one."[112] In keeping with this line of argument, Goudal's qualities sanctioned her steely resolve. She had to object to some of the ideas promoted by her directors to retain her integrity as an artist; not to do so would degrade her to a position of a mere puppet. To betray one's vision was to commit one of the greatest transgressions any artist could commit.

In another piece, McKegg spoke equally highly of Goudal's professional competences, arguing that most of the disputes she became involved in arose as a consequence of her astute critical skills; she excelled in pointing out "mistakes and incongruities to the director, suggesting a far more logical or dramatic episode."[113] Despite the poignancy of Goudal's remarks, this form of professional involvement was not welcomed by the studio officials, presumably because of the existing gender alignment informed by patriarchy. No man feels comfortable being corrected by a woman, especially in the workplace, concluded the article. Overall, though, voices congruent with McKegg's in identifying the problematic nature of Goudal's professional status were vastly outnumbered by those that castigated her strong stance in matters relating to actors and ownership of labor.

The Aftermath

On the surface, Hollywood offered women a position of power incredibly hard to match in any other industry at the time. The machinery of the studio system elevated women to the spheres of recognition mainly as actresses, but also occasionally as screenwriters and filmmakers, and firmly placed them in the popular imagination. Paradoxically, the same industry closely controlled the images of the female celebrities it produced; the treatment they received in the press is a telling illustration of the constraints placed on stars by the studio system. Jeanine Basinger discussed how the attempts of stars to exert power over their own images were inherently doomed to fail,[114] understanding star power to be a saleable illusion that worked in the realm of popular culture but not within the film industry: "It was ironic that behind the scenes, seemingly powerful movie stars were not in a position to make any decision about how they were cast or used. . . . A star's only power lay outside the system, in the minds of the public and in the fans' response to their images."[115] Although Basinger might be overstating the case here—Goudal's carefully regulated influence over decision-making in the industry is the focus of this chapter—the statement draws attention to the imbalance between the perceived impact of stars and the very limited, concrete capacity they had to exercise actual power. Despite attempting to navigate her own authority, Goudal had little functional autonomy in the workplace.

In accordance with the discourse promulgated by fan magazines, stars had more power over their personae than they could ever hold in reality. In her research in the 1940s, Hortense Powdermaker also framed the studio system as a totalitarian structure that imposes its choices on stars, one of its chief commodities: "Its basis is economic rather than political but its philosophy is similar to that of the totalitarian state. . . . The basic freedom of being able to choose between alternatives is absent."[116] American production strategies were stronger than any individual, and Goudal laid herself on the line by challenging the status quo. Even though studios were in competition with each other, they often joined forces against performers who refused to fully adhere to their regime. Goudal's actions thus put her at risk of being permanently blacklisted by film producers.[117] After the DeMille court case, she made only two more films before retiring, her prosperous career brought to a standstill in the 1930s, partly because of the growing popularity of sound film, and partly because of her tenacity in fighting for her rights as a laborer. During the period of "studio bickering and feuds," Goudal was kept away from the camera for months, which effectively hampered her career. As stated in the press, her ongoing struggle to find work was self-inflicted. *Motion Picture Magazine* predicted that movie players who, like Goudal, "have let their ego run away with them, and who are in the habit of displaying that peculiar streak or personality known as temperament, will have to take off the high hat or join the great army of the unemployed."[118] "Directors no longer look upon temperament as a necessity and find that it is something they can do without," proclaimed *Photoplay*.[119] "Would you say that her behaviour is, as she describes, intelligent?" asked *Picture Play* rhetorically.[120]

In September 1931 Goudal had a brief stint working onstage in a production of *The French Doll* in Portland. Local newspapers hailed her talent, and were generally more understanding toward her peculiar position within the national film industry. One account explained Goudal's absence from the screen as a consequence of "a boycott, the result of a salary trouble with Cecil B. deMille [*sic*], which was decided in her favour, but which put her *in bad* with motion picture people, a situation just ended."[121] Nonetheless, the vehemence of criticism aimed at Goudal overrode rare voices of sympathy and understanding.

Conclusion

The issues that need to be foregrounded in the context of Goudal's image relate to her position as a European star, and thus someone presumably lacking the work ethic of the American-trained actor; somehow inconsistently, the apparent lack of professionalism was also incorporated into the extratextual performance of acting talent and a unique, God-given artistry. Like many other European players in Hollywood, Goudal's star image was built on the notion of temperamentality. As such, the infamous temperament was a marketable commodity imposed on Goudal by Famous Players-Lasky as a way of linking the star with the particular vision of Europeanness. Different aspects of her identity were intertwined with each other, creating a strong sense of highly emotional and "authentic" self.

In 1925, and in the court battle against DeMille that followed in 1928, Goudal's star persona was used at her cost. Her image was utilized first by Zukor's studio and then by Cecil B. DeMille as a tool to dismiss her refusal to subjugate herself to the workings of an exploitative industry. Instead of acquiring the status of an individual rightfully challenging the system—Goudal asserted limited independence through various avenues, such as supervising her costumes and hiring an impartial agent to represent her—she became a stereotyped caricature of the highly emotional woman who does not know how to behave and who needs punishment for bad conduct. The fact that her working relationship with DeMille was portrayed as paternal added fuel to the fire of controversy surrounding her decision to take the producer to court. In the eyes of contemporaneous moviegoers, her story was a cautionary tale of a woman who paid the highest price for being "a bad girl" and who had to sacrifice her career as a result. The strict reliance on her Famous Players-Lasky persona effectively moved Goudal's court case from the professional sphere to the realm of the personal, where her act of defiance lost its political meaning as a power struggle, depriving her of the opportunity to voice her concerns about the inner dynamics of the studio system. By framing Goudal's behavior as either insincere or childlike, the producers took control of the public account, ultimately relegating Goudal to the sidelines of the movie industry.

Conclusion

"Pola Negri returns from royal retreat more than ever *la femme fatale* of filmdom,"[1] announced a review of *A Woman Commands* (1932), Negri's first American talking picture. Yet, the star's return to the screen failed to attract moviegoers as much as the producers had hoped; recording a loss of $265,000,[2] the film became one of Negri's last Hollywood appearances.[3] The same year saw the release of *Business and Pleasure* (1932), which was to be Goudal's final professional endeavor. As an actress placed on the studios' unofficial blacklist, she struggled to keep afloat in the industry. In the following year, Bánky starred in *The Rebel* (1933)—the English-language remake of a Universal-Deutsche feature—which marked her fourth, and last, appearance in a sound film.[4]

It is notable that these three stars started to diminish around the same time, with the rising popularity of talkies. Indeed, the reception of their last ventures drew attention to their speaking voices; whereas Bánky's and Negri's pronunciation was described as problematic but subject to improvement,[5] Goudal's French accent was deemed too heavy to be easily understood.[6] Evidently, fanzines often saw the advent of sound as the culprit in terminating foreign careers: "Hollywood deemed pronto that accents wouldn't do. Emil Jannings, Pola Negri, Victor Cacroni, Vilma Banky, Jetta Goudal—oh, a sad exodus."[7] This is not to say that the growing domination of the talkies was the only reason halting their professional progress. According to Diane Negra, the failure of Negri's persona to achieve longevity was primarily ideological rather than aesthetic,[8] an assertion that can be extended to my two remaining stars. The economic crisis of 1929 marked a turning point in American history, and, while many societal gains were lost, the archetype of the all-American sweetheart began to occupy an important position in the collective consciousness. The type of representation both Negri and Goudal were known for—exuberant, irrational, and exotic—did not transfer successfully to the next decade. Janet Gaynor, often called "the child-woman," combined the simplicity of the silent era with a safe version of sexuality promoted throughout the 1930s.[9] Although some overtly sexualized stars, such as Mae West and Jean Harlow, were hardly representative of adolescent naïveté, they were also distant from the connotations of fatality carried by silent vamps. These were modern "blonde bombshells" whose Brooklyn and Midwestern accents bespoke of their American heritage.

In the latter half of the 1920s, though, Negri's, Goudal's, and Bánky's stars were a prominent fixture on the Hollywood firmament; my research has sought to understand the circumstances that allowed them to shine so brightly and then gradually fade out in the next decade. The animating question of such exploration related to the relationship between ethnicity and the construction of Europeanness, an integral element of stardom in the Jazz Age. Because the previous chapters consider Negri, Bánky, and Goudal separately, I conclude by focusing on issues that run across all three of the careers I have interrogated. Far from constituting a monolithic category, Europeanness was appropriated in these women's personae in various, often conflicting ways, demonstrating that the perfect vision of white womanhood included several characteristics, such as passivity, innocence, and obedience. The closer a given star came to emblematize those qualities, the more positive connotations were bound up in her public persona, and the higher her chances of long-lasting success. Clearly, conspicuously white, compliant foreign women represented less of a threat to the stock of national, protestant values and were seen as more likely to integrate into American society.

Relationships with Men

All three stars analyzed in this book were often discussed in reference to men, both professionally and privately, and the ways in which those relations were depicted spoke volumes about their reported ability to adjust to the American way of living. As an extratextual source, the nature of the interactions these women had with their superiors either aligned them with or juxtaposed them to the revered ideals of white femininity. Let us consider the relationships of two producers, Samuel Goldwyn and Cecil B. DeMille, and the stars they promoted. Throughout her American career, Bánky was presented as extremely grateful to Goldwyn for discovering her and bringing her to the United States, the land of opportunity, where she could flourish. The producer's involvement in Bánky's private affairs cast him as a paternal figure; indeed, in a letter to Bánky, Goldwyn stipulated that he had acted like a father to her.[10] The relationship between Goudal and Cecil B. DeMille initially operated on similar terms, with Goudal referring to her mentor as "Papa DeMille." While Goudal's affiliation with her producer/director eventually turned sour—she took him to court for a breach of contract, and won—Bánky's was sustained, as she never questioned Goldwyn's authority. Her status as a perfect embodiment of passive femininity can then be juxtaposed to Goudal's active, hence threatening, image.

Negri did not establish a strong relationship with any of her Hollywood producers, which is telling in itself; as we have seen, popular discourse presented her as an independent performer of strong character. Commentators often cited her creative partnership with the German filmmaker Ernst Lubitsch as the reason for the success she relished in Berlin. Some fans also criticized the low artistic merit of her American oeuvre on that basis, suggesting that, with artistic guidance equivalent to that of Lubitsch's, she might achieve new heights.[11] In Europe, Negri was a muse. In Hollywood, she no longer had a mentor ready to take her under his wing. Instead, it was the personal, not professional, relationships with men that formed the nucleus of Negri's narrative. From the onset of her international career, star discourse paid special attention to romantic alliances between Negri and several successful screen players. Affairs with Chaplin and Valentino enhanced her immigrant position as a star placed on the margins of the main current of society, where she came to symbolize the most dreaded aspects of modernity in the person of the exotic and uncontainable foreign woman.

Although very different from Negri's, Bánky's love life was also of great significance in sustaining her allegiance to idealized whiteness. Bánky's opinions were characteristically saturated in patriarchal metaphors, as she assured her fans, in interview after interview, that she saw herself mainly through the prism of domesticity, treating her star status as adjacent, if not secondary, to the status she gained within the institution of marriage. Where the description of Bánky's private life resonated with the dominant ethic of her era, indicating her conversion to the American way of living, Negri's did not.

Interestingly, the print media were not concerned with Goudal's romantic liaisons, which was a consequence of the way she was branded.[12] By being deliberately misleading, gossip and innuendo aided the constant negotiation between two contradictory components of her image: the attractions of the imagined East and ideas of French sensitivity. The alleged ethnic difference located Goudal on the precipice of the Occident and the Orient, which allowed the star to articulate ideas of national identity, Europeanness, *and* Orientalism.

Talent

The New World myth of emerging from obscurity to attain fortune—one of America's most enduring social paradigms—has been long concentrated "in the fresh, lively, popular art form produced in America's last frontier: Hollywood."[13] The short but lucrative careers of Negri, Bánky, and Goudal in the global film capital illuminate the characteristic features of such discourse. The ways in which the studio system framed Bánky's rise to fame as a fortunate coincidence were vastly different from those used to describe Negri's or Goudal's success stories.

As reported by *Picture Play*, Bánky was spotted by the perceptive producer, who recognized her as "the perfect embodiment of wholesome womanhood, and persuaded her to sign her name on a dotted line."[14] This particular way of approaching the success of female stars has been discussed by Virginia Wright Wexman. Women, Wexman writes, "have been spoken of as having been *discovered*, most frequently as a result of having exhibited themselves or their photographs in public places," which contrasts them to male stars, who are traditionally described as trained to master their craft.[15] While Bánky was encoded within a patriarchal storyline that placed the sense of agency on the producer rather than on his subject, the female star, the same cannot be said of Negri and Goudal, for whom—as publicity materials would have it—success was earned through talent, hard work, and extreme dedication. This key distinction, which lay in the notion of agency and talent, was extended to the depictions of performances of these three stars. The passive language used by fan magazines to describe Bánky's on-screen presence stood in contrast to the treatment received by Negri and Goudal, who were described as skilled and devoted artists. Where Bánky appears as simply beautiful and charming, the other two stars are gifted actresses and artists who put great effort into their roles.[16] Again, this serves as an indication of differences in their ethnically inflicted identities: the whiter the star, the more delicate she is, and the less agency she exerts. On the other hand, the more active the star's agency, the more exotic and dangerous she is.

Transformation

A third shared aspect of the three star trajectories under scrutiny here is their potential for successful assimilation. *Photoplay* and its ilk ascribed Negri with the fixed identity of an Old World diva, resistant to all attempts at Americanization. Despite the initial efforts to promote her career path as an embodiment of the rags-to-riches story—with the actress reportedly taking out citizenship papers in 1926—by refusing to conform to protestant norms, Negri failed to weave herself into the fabric of American society. The same idea applies to Goudal's star persona, which, on a basic level, remained static: she entered the star discourse as a French/exotic woman of temperament, and left the limelight as one too. Many elements of Bánky's off-screen life, such as the anecdotes of her struggles with mastering the English language, were central to upholding the idea that she is charming, nonthreatening, and, above all, aiming to transform herself. In keeping with ideas of American imperialism, Bánky's role as a wife to one of Hollywood's biggest stars—and, notably, an American—was portrayed as the pinnacle of her achievements, a real "happy ending" worthy of one of her film heroines. In a country with imperial aspirations, built on the foundation of protestant rhetoric where the American Dream fantasy was especially potent, stars could offer models of successful cultural integration. But they could also constitute the exact opposite: tales of failing to adjust to a genteel, middle-class ethos. Thus, where Bánky succeeded, Negri and Goudal failed.

In addition to the ongoing efforts at Americanization, emphasized continually in the extratextual materials that surrounded her, Bánky's roles functioned to further communicate a wholesome, passive image of femininity. Compare this with the casting of Goudal, who was usually given roles that underlined her ambiguous ethnic background, often conflating it with a range of broadly defined exotic types; as I have shown, she portrayed everyone from half-Peruvian/half-Chinese to Russians to Mexicans.[17] The heroines of *Forbidden Woman* (1927) and *Three Faces East* (1926) use sexual agency to commit a series of audacious transgressions, which are inevitably marked by tragic endings. In a similar vein, the fate of many of Negri's characters functioned as a parable of the "containment of female desire,"[18] illustrating the consequences of using sex to change one's class distinction, thus mirroring broader cultural fears related to upward mobility. These anxieties were indicative of issues that entered the dominant discourse in the wake of suffrage and the second wave of immigration. It is no wonder that in the context of America in the 1920s, threatening, foreign women were reenacted by actresses residing on the margins of whiteness.

Even though at first glance all three stars considered in this work would be classified as white, contemporaneous debates differentiated between their respective ethnicities, illustrating the degree to which prevailing attitudes tied different definitions of Europeanness to ethnic background. It is important to understand that the facets of star personae that go beyond the physical—romantic and professional relationships with men, acting agency, readiness to submit to patriarchal norms—are all interlinked to the construction of gendered whiteness.

Negri's off-screen narratives were interwoven with the persistent thread of sexual explicitness and lack of restraint, qualities often assigned to a woman claiming gypsy heritage. Bánky's persona relied on an imaginary known from myth and fable, where whiteness is brought into the racial dynamic through highly positive connotations. Her conspicuously white physical features came hand in hand with patriarchal relationships with men, lack of agency, and compliance with normative standards of femininity. Thus, Bánky could locate herself in a position ideologically far removed from the space inhabited by Negri and Goudal, both of whom were represented as ambiguously white, but also strong and talented women.

Once the movie industry and fan magazines, its supporting tools, came to structure and commodify what it meant to be European for a given star, the career of a movie performer became dependent on such specific, more rigid definitions. Artificially constructed images, alas commercially profitable, were also resistant to modification, often denying Hollywood actors a basic flexibility in their identities, which often curtailed their professional progress. Neither of these women could exert enough professional influence to drastically change their images once they had been ascribed to them.

In all three instances under examination, female star personae were overlaid with regressive gender norms. The infantilization applied so eagerly to Bánky in the early stages of her career was also applied to Goudal's persona, albeit to different effect. The mediated discourse of Bánky's adolescent behavior was put in motion to generate emotional warmth and highlight her cuteness. In Goudal's case, however, it acted to discredit her efforts in fighting the studio system and to undermine her maturity. Although not infantilized explicitly, the forms of representation assigned to Negri were also overlaid with versions of irrationality, overt emotionality, and lack of control, all traits associated with children.

Europeanness Today

Star and celebrity studies raise important questions about popular personalities, their bodies, performances, sexuality, and gender. Undeniably, the theory of whiteness as a culturally dominant and thus invisible ethnicity remains a crucial component of Hollywood-derived models of interrogating such mass phenomena. Does it mean then, as Sabrina Qiong Yu asks, that classical Hollywood stardom "is the last word on film stars?"[19] Although I have found many of the standard pronouncements of these disciplines useful and relevant—for example, the notion of assessing stars as capitalist products, or thinking of them in relation to ethnicity—I believe that star studies need to deepen their understanding of stars as texts carrying varying meanings for diverse audiences. For instance, it is possible that the images and films of Negri, Bánky, and Goudal spoke to African American audiences in ways that were different from the discourse filtered through Anglo-centered culture. This is just one of many perspectives that I did not engage with, but one that might potentially produce fascinating results. Nowadays stars function in an increasingly transnational, globalized landscape; therefore, research that examines them must be underpinned with the study of such contexts and with the perspectives of changing audiences.

What we can see at the core of these multiple star stories is that Europeanness is reliant on whiteness, and whiteness means more than what meets the eye. Beyond demonstrating some of the processes of image making, the problems illuminated by this book resonate with American culture of the 2020s, where the prerogative of whiteness continues to determine whether an individual is viewed as a nonthreatening immigrant subject. What Negri, Bánky, and Goudal teach us is that the ethnic underpinnings of such meta-narratives reflect the social and cultural landscape that produced them. But it is also clear that many of these potentially harmful notions prevail to this day. Decades after Negri and

Goudal descended from the Hollywood pantheon, many visual tropes deployed in their images, especially those that bespeak of exoticism, remain in use. Glamour photographs continue to appropriate costumes and makeup that position their wearers as semi-exotic subjects—that is, as white women carrying the specter of Oriental thrills.

It is enough to consider a handful of émigré stars who made it in the American film industry in past decades (Penélope Cruz, Monica Bellucci, Eva Green, and Olga Kurylenko) to see how they are tied to very specific personae, both on- and off-screen. Popular magazines tend to describe Cruz in gendered, highly racialized terms, as a Spanish woman whose beauty and voice are "exotic to Anglophone eyes and ears," a "screen siren."[20] Similarly, commentators use Bellucci's Italianness to explain her appeal.[21] "Like Sophia Loren, Gina Lollobrigida, Silvana Mangano, she has Italian film-star glamour—dark hair, voluptuous, a sensuous beauty," wrote *The Telegraph* in July 2017.[22] The attention paid by press articles to Cruz's "Spanish cadences,"[23] as well as rendering her English through misspellings, bears an uncanny resemblance to the handling of Negri, Bánky, and Goudal over ninety years ago. Revealingly, the actresses who speak with accents remain confined to the roles of femme fatales or sexualized women; such typecasting is avoided by those whose speech does not mark them as foreigners (think of Diane Kruger or Alicia Vikander).

In many respects, the issues inherent to the publicity of foreign-born stars in the 1920s find uncomfortable echoes in modern-day Hollywood. There is no doubt that the American film industry should shed its rigid notions of Italianness, Spanishness, and Frenchness, especially because its products reach over 2.5 billion people worldwide every year, contributing to the further promulgation of stereotypes across the globe. Even though the promotion of stars is based on little more than relatable fictions, such fictions achieve longevity. When, at the end of Negri's life, an eager journalist interrogated the former star about the long-standing rumors—that she was cursed by a gypsy and that all her lovers would die untimely deaths—she scoffed. "It was an invention of my publicity, *dahling*."[24]

Acknowledgments

Pola Negri's life story has fascinated me since my teenage years. I spent the summer of 2003 at the Baltic Sea reading Negri's biography by Wiesława Czapińska. Little did I know that a decade later I would be spending my professional life researching Negri and the mechanics behind her stardom.

Some parts of this book originate from the work I conducted during my masters course at the University of Bristol. I am grateful to those who helped me develop my interests in star studies, particularly Alex Clayton and Catherine O'Rawe. I would like to express immense gratitude to everyone who made this volume possible, from White Rose College of Arts and Humanities, which generously funded the project, to Andrew Higson. I thank Andrew for his brilliant comments and insights, as well as his trust in my ability as a scholar. I feel lucky to have had the opportunity to be involved in such a stimulating doctoral program, and that Clare Meadley and Caryn Douglas were always there to help with the administrative side of things. I am indebted to everyone who took the time to read this work and to those who encouraged me to do my best. From Rachel Schildgen, who gave me a copy of her own, inspiring book on Vilma Bánky, to my friends and loved ones; especially to Nicholas Hallows for all the time he spent proofreading, and for cherishing my successes. To Daniel Clarke, Francesco Chianese, Louisa Mitchell, David Morton, and Mike Samuel. I'm glad that our paths have crossed. To Francesca Arnavas for keeping me sane.

I also want to thank Michael Williams, whose scholarship I continue to admire, and who offered his unwavering support at various stages of this project. Another thank you is due to Rutgers University Press, particularly Nicole Solano, who was enthusiastic about this project from the get go. I appreciate the perceptive feedback I received from the anonymous reviewers of *Early Popular Visual Culture*.

Last but not least, to my family, especially to my parents Małgorzata and Zbigniew Frymus, who have always taught me I can achieve my goals, whatever they are. Dziękuję. To im dedykuję tą książkę.

Notes

INTRODUCTION

1. The term is used, for example, in "The Sheik Returns," *Motion Picture Classic*, June 1926, 54.

2. The career of a silent movie star lasted five years on average. See Norman L. Sper, "How Long Are They Stars?," *Motion Picture Magazine*, September 1926, 66–67, 97; and Dorothy Calhoun, "What If They Had Lived?," *Motion Picture Magazine*, December 1930, 28.

3. Jane Gaines, "White Privilege and Looking Relations: Race and Gender in Feminist Film Theory," in *Feminist Film Theory: A Reader*, ed. Sue Thornham (New York: New York University Press, 1986), 20.

4. Diane Negra, *Off-White Hollywood: American Culture and Ethnic Female Stardom* (London: Routledge, 2001), 68–69.

5. Tom Rice, *White Robes, Silver Screens: Movies and the Making of the Ku Klux Klan* (Bloomington: Indiana University Press, 2015), 229.

6. Richard Dyer, *White: Essays on Race and Culture* (London: Routledge, 1997), 129.

7. Harry Carr, "Jetta and Her Temperament," *Motion Picture Classic*, October 1924, 21.

8. See Sean Holmes, "No Room for Manoeuvre: Star Images and the Regulation of Actors' Labor in Silent Era Hollywood," in *Working in the Global Film and Television Industries: Creativity, Systems, Space, Patronage*, ed. Andrew Dawson and Sean P. Holmes (London: Bloomsbury Academic, 2012), 75–90.

9. See Mariusz Kotowski, *Pola Negri: Hollywood's First Femme Fatale* (Lexington: Kentucky University Press, 2014); and Sergio Delgado, *Pola Negri: Temptress of Silent Hollywood* (Jefferson, NC: McFarland, 2016), 26.

10. Jeanine Basinger, *Silent Stars* (Middletown, CT: Wesleyan University Press, 1999).

11. Rachel Schildgen, *More Than a Dream: Rediscovering the Life and Films of Vilma Bánky* (Hollywood, CA: 1921 PVG Publishing, 2010).

12. See Holmes, "No Room for Manoeuvre." See also Alan Robert Ginsberg, *The Salome Ensemble: Rose Pastor Stokes, Anzia Yezierska, Sonya Levien, and Jetta Goudal* (New York: Syracuse University Press, 2016).

13. Throughout this work, I use the terms "Exoticism" and "Orientalism" interchangeably.

14. The ideas relating to Goudal come from Cal York, "Studio News and Gossip—East and West," *Photoplay*, May 1926, 88. For the second mention, see Ivan St. Johns, "How Pola Was Tamed," *Photoplay*, January 1926, 53.

15. Richard Dyer, *Stars*, 2nd ed. (London: British Film Institute, 1998), 20.

16. Diane Negra, *Off-White Hollywood: American Culture and Ethnic Female Stardom* (London: Routledge, 2001), 24.

17. See Gaylyn Studlar's "The Perils of Pleasure? Fan Magazine Discourse as Women's Commodified Culture in the 1920s," in *Silent Film*, ed. Richard Abel (New Brunswick, NJ: Rutgers University Press, 1995), 263–297; and Studlar, *Precocious Charms: Stars Performing Girlhood in Classical Hollywood Cinema* (Los Angeles: University of California Press, 2013). See also Shelley Stamp, *Movie-Struck Girls: Women and Motion Picture Culture after the Nickelodeon* (Princeton, NJ: Princeton University Press, 2000); and Michael Williams, *Film Stardom, Myth and Classicism: The Rise of Hollywood's Gods* (London: Palgrave Macmillan, 2013).

18. Andrew Higson and Richard Maltby, introduction to *"Film Europe" and "Film America": Cinema, Commerce and Cultural Exchange 1920-1939*, ed. Andrew Higson and Richard Maltby (Exeter, UK: University of Exeter Press, 1999), 1–5.

19. Richard Koszarski, *An Evening's Entertainment: The Age of the Silent Feature Picture 1915–1928* (New York: Charles Scribner's Sons, 1990); Koszarski, *Hollywood on the Hudson: Film and Television in New York from Griffith to Sarnoff* (New Brunswick, NJ: Rutgers University Press, 2010); Janet Staiger, "The Hollywood Mode of Production to 1930," in *The Classical Hollywood Cinema: Film Style and Mode of Production to 1960s*, ed. David Bordwell, Janet Staiger, and Kristyn Thompson (London: Routledge, 1996), 88–244.

20. Richard Dyer, *Heavenly Bodies: Film Stars and Society*, 2nd ed. (London: Routledge, 2006), 4.

21. Cited in Koszarski, *Evening's Entertainment*, 193.

22. Negra, *Off-White Hollywood*, 55.

23. Sumiko Higashi, *Cecil B. DeMille and American Culture: The Silent Era* (Berkeley: University of California Press, 1994), 63.

24. The intersection between gender and ethnicity is also pointed out by Valerio Coladonato in "Italian-Americans' Contested Whiteness in Early Cinematic Melodrama," *Networking Knowledge: Journal of the MeCCSA Postgraduate Network* 7, no. 3 (September 2014): 5–20, accessed August 31, 2017, http://ojs.meccsa.org.uk/index.php/netknow/article/view/340.

25. Keisha Lindsay, "God, Gays, and Progressive Politics: Reconceptualizing Intersectionality as a Normatively Malleable Analytical Framework," *Perspectives on Politics*, vol. 11, no. 2 (June 2013): 448.

26. Kathleen Neils Conzen, David A. Gerber, Ewa Morawska, George E. Pozzetta, and Rudolph J. Vecoli, "The Invention of Ethnicity: A Perspective from the USA," *Journal of American Ethnic History* 12 (Fall 1992): 5.

27. See Edward W. Said, *Orientalism: Western Conceptions of the Orient* (Oxford: Penguin Books, 1995); and Dyer, *White*, 129.

28. See Sean Redmond, "The Whiteness of the Rings," in *The Persistence of Whiteness*, ed. Daniel Bernardi (New York: Routledge, 2008), 91–101; Lola Young, *Fear of the Dark: Race, Gender and Sexuality in the Cinema* (London: Routledge, 1996); and Tim

Bergfelder, "Negotiating Exoticism: Hollywood, Film Europe, and the Cultural Reception of Anna May Wong," in *Stars: The Film Reader*, ed. Lucy Fisher and Marcia Landy (London: Routledge, 2004), 56–75.

29. Ian C. Jarvie, "Stars and Ethnicity: Hollywood and the United States, 1932-1951," in *Stars: The Film Reader*, ed. Lucy Fisher and Marcia Landy (London: Routledge, 2004), 60.

30. Joanne Hershfield, "Dolores Del Rio, Uncomfortably Real: The Economics of Race in Hollywood's Latin American Musicals," in *Classic Hollywood, Classic Whiteness*, ed. Daniel Bernardi (Minneapolis: University of Minnesota Press, 2001), 140.

31. Michaela Krutzen, *The Most Beautiful Woman on Screen: Fabrication of the Star Greta Garbo* (Frankfurt am Mein: Peter Lang AG, 1992), 42.

32. Williams, *Film Stardom, Myth and Classicism*, 193.

33. Gene Charteris, "What the Fans Think," *Picture Play*, April 1928, 12.

CHAPTER 1 — POLA NEGRI AND ROMANCE

Chapter subtitle: "Ah love! It's not for me," E.G., comment on Edith Perrin, "What the Fans Think," *Picture Play*, February 1928, 12.

1. William K. Everson, *American Silent Film* (New York: Oxford University Press, 1978), 317.

2. Maximilian Vinder, "She Delivered the Goods," *Photoplay*, May 1922, 21.

3. Harry Carr, "Behind the Scenes with Pola Negri," *Motion Picture Magazine*, June 1923, 39.

4. Negra, *Off-White Hollywood*, 79.

5. Fan magazines used Chaplin's description of their first encounter. See Charlie Chaplin, *My Trip Abroad* (New York: Harper & Brothers,1922), 116.

6. Richard DeCordova, *Picture Personalities: The Emergence of the Star System in America* (Urbana: University of Illinois Press, 2001), 140.

7. Negra's book on ethnic female stardom in Hollywood, *Off-White Hollywood*, deals with the images of Pola Negri, Sonja Henie, Hedy Lamarr, and Colleen Moore. The term "off-white," central to Negra's work, refers to individuals who are white but who, according to the American conception of ethnicity in the early twentieth century, occupy lower strata of whiteness.

8. Negra, *Off-White Hollywood*, 64.

9. Martha Gever, *Entertaining Lesbians: Celebrity, Sexuality, and Self-Invention* (London: Routledge, 2003), 67.

10. "Who Is Married to Who: A Brief Pictorial Guide to Cupid's Fatalities in Celluloid," *Photoplay*, May 1917, 67.

11. Ellen Pullar, "*A New Woman*: The Promotional Persona of Anna Sten," *Celebrity Studies Journal* 1, no. 3 (2010): 283.

12. Gever, *Entertaining Lesbians*, 69.

13. Chaplin, *My Trip Abroad*, 116.

14. This is not to say that one cannot expect any points of convergence between the real, historical Negri and Negri's star persona. Indeed, many elements of stars' private existence informed the ways in which practices of studio system and film culture represented them.

15. Elza Schallert, "The Girls from Our Club," *Picture Play*, June 1923, 30.

16. "Pola Negri Jilts Chaplin after Engagement of Month," *Star Tribune*, MI, March 2, 1923, 1; "Pola Negri Jilts Chaplin; Make Up after 6 Hours," The *Post-Crescent*, WI, March 2, 1923, 1.

17. Harry Carr, "On the Camera Coast," *Motion Picture Magazine*, June 1923, 67.

18. Kenneth Schuyler Lynn, *Charlie Chaplin and His Times* (New York: Simon & Schuster, 1997), 274.

19. Agnes Smith, "Between Stars and You," *Picture Play*, November 1923, 20.

20. Marcia Landy, *Stardom Italian Style: Screen Personality and Performance in Italian Cinema* (Bloomington: Indiana University Press, 2008), 22.

21. Jeanine Basinger, *Silent Stars* (New York: Alfred A. Knopf, 1999), 255.

22. "Box Office Reviews," *Exhibitor's Trade Review*, December 6, 1924, 51.

23. Hal Erickson, synopsis of *Forbidden Paradise*, AllMovie, accessed August 23, 2019, http://www.allmovie.com/movie/forbidden-paradise-v92033.

24. Although the phrase is used by Robin Wood to describe one of the leading characters of *Sunrise* (1927), I find it applicable here. Robin Wood, *Sexual Politics and Narrative Film: Hollywood and Beyond* (New York: Columbia University Press, 1998), 39.

25. Richard Dyer, *White: Essays on Race and Culture* (London: Routledge, 1997), 39.

26. Dyer, *White*, 29.

27. Dyer, *White*, 29.

28. The phrase is Simon Dixon's in reference to star houses of the silent era, not *Forbidden Paradise*, but I find it applicable here. See Simon Dixon, "Ambiguous Ecologies: Stardom's Domestic Mise-en-Scene," *Cinema Journal* 42, no. 2 (Winter 2003): 8–88.

29. Sergio Delgado, *Pola Negri: Temptress of Silent Hollywood* (Jefferson, NC: McFarland, 2016), 84.

30. Anne Helen Petersen, "Scandals of Classic Hollywood: The Most Kissable Hands of Pola Negri," The Hairpin, November 14, 2013, accessed August 23, 2019, http://thehairpin.com/2013/11/scandals-of-classic-hollywood-the-most-kissable-hands-of-pola-negri/.

31. Cal York, "Studio News and Gossip—East and West," *Photoplay*, October 1924, 86.

32. York, "Studio News and Gossip," 86.

33. Scott Eyman, *Ernst Lubitsch: Laughter in Paradise* (New York: Simon & Schuster, 1993), 110; and Rachel Schildgen, *More Than a Dream: Rediscovering the Life and Films of Vilma Bánky* (Hollywood, CA: 1921 PVG Publishing, 2010), 82.

34. Eyman, *Ernst Lubitsch*, 110.

35. Valeria Belletti to Irma Prina, 10 March 1926, Valeria Belletti Papers, 1-f.4 Correspondence, January–July 1926, Margaret Herrick Library, Los Angeles.

36. The phrase comes from York, "Studio News and Gossip," 86.

37. Josephine Sheldon, "Signore Valentino Herewith Presents His New Leading Lady, Fraulein Banky," *Motion Picture Magazine*, November 1925, 24.

38. Edwin Schallert and Elza Schallert, "Hollywood Highlights," *Picture Play*, January 1924, 67.

39. Schuyler, *Charlie Chaplin and His Times*, 274.

40. Cited in Basinger, *Silent Stars*, 251.

41. Ruth Tildesley, "Time Limit Marriages," *Motion Picture Magazine*, June 1928, 88.

42. Gaylyn Studlar, "The Perils of Pleasure? Fan Magazine Discourse as Women's Commodified Culture in the 1920s," in *Silent Film*, ed. Richard Abel (New Brunswick, NJ: Rutgers University Press, 1995), 277.

43. Studlar, "Perils of Pleasure?," 270.

44. Herbert Howe, "Close Ups and Long Shots," *Photoplay*, April 1926, 43.

45. Allan R. Ellenberg, *The Valentino Mystique: The Death and Afterlife of the Silent Film Idol* (London: McFarland, 2001), 25.

46. Ellenberg, *Valentino Mystique*, 25.

47. "Reviews," *Exhibitors Herald*, October 27, 1923, 53. See also Natasha Rambova, *Rudolph Valentino: A Wife's Memories of an Icon* (Hollywood, CA: 1921 PVG Publishing, 2009), 66.

48. Lea Jacobs, *The Decline of Sentiment: American Film in the 1920s* (Chicago: University of Chicago Press, 2008), 239.

49. Gaylyn Studlar, "*The Perfect Lover*? Valentino and Ethnic Masculinity in the 1920s," in *The Silent Cinema Reader*, ed. Lee Grieveson and Peter Krämer (London: Routledge, 2004), 296.

50. Studlar, "*Perfect Lover?*", 291.

51. "Let Them Be Human," *Pictures and Picturegoer*, September 1925, 25.

52. The idea that Valentino was a subject of homoerotic desire is, of course, valid, if not a more difficult assertion to examine, given the scarcity of male fans willing to express their admiration for a male star. The responses generated by Valentino's male fans in Britain is interrogated, albeit briefly, by Michael Williams in *Film Stardom, Myth and Classicism: The Rise of Hollywood's Gods* (London: Palgrave Macmillan, 2013), 189.

53. Carr, "Behind the Scenes with Pola Negri," 39.

54. Joe Franklin, *Classics of the Silent Screen: A Pictorial Treasury* (New York: Citadel Press, 1959), 209. Franklin uses the expression in relation to Rudolph Valentino.

55. Stacey Abbott, "The Undead in the Kingdom of Shadows," in *Open Graves, Open Minds: Representation of Vampires and the Undead from the Enlightenment to the Present Day*, ed. Samantha George and Bill Hughes (Manchester: Manchester University Press, 2013), 100.

56. S. George Ulman, *Valentino as I Knew Him* (New York: A. L. Burt, 1927), 175.

57. Cal York, "Studio News and Gossip—East and West," *Photoplay*, May 1926, 88.

58. Brett L. Abrams, *Hollywood Bohemians: Transgressive Sexuality and the Selling of the Movieland Dream* (Jefferson, NC: McFarland, 2008), 78–112.

59. Alexander Walker, *Stardom: The Hollywood Phenomenon* (London: Michael Joseph, 1970), 126.

60. David Bret, *Valentino: A Dream of Desire* (New York: Caroll & Graff, 2007), 183.

61. Belletti writes about the romance in a letter to her friend Irma Perina: "The only dirt on the lot now is that Pola Negri drove to Albuquerque to meet Valentino. She has an awful crush on him. When Joe Scheneck heard about it, he wanted his press agent to drive after her and prevent the meeting because Scheneck is afraid there'll be some adverse criticism and scandal, but it couldn't be done so I suppose it will get out in the papers." Valeria Belletti to Irma Prina, February 2, 1926, Valeria Belletti Papers, 1-f.4 Correspondence, January–July 1926, Margaret Herrick Library, Los Angeles.

62. This is the title under which the film was released; however, the article refers to the film as *Naughty but Nice*.

63. Cal York, "Studio News and Gossip—East and West," *Photoplay*, October 1926, 104.

64. The Bystander, "Over the Teacups," *Picture Play*, July 1926, 93.

65. The reactions to Valentino's death and his elevated posthumous status are discussed at length by Williams. See *Film Stardom, Myth and Classicism*, 174–201.

66. Cited in Samantha Barbas, *Movie Crazy: Stars, Fans and the Cult of Celebrity* (New York, NY: Palgrave, 2001), 170. The *New York Times* estimated it was a crowd of 30,000. See "Thousands in Riot at Valentino's Bier. More Than 100 Hurt," *New York Times*, August 25, 1926, 1.

67. More recently, scholars have disputed the scope of Valentino "hysteria" as it was presented by the contemporary media. See Michael Williams, *Film Stardom, Myth and Classicism: The Rise of Hollywood's Gods* (Basingstoke, UK: Palgrave Macmillan), 175; Mark Lynn Anderson, *Twilight of the Idols: Hollywood and the Human Sciences in 1920s America* (Berkeley: University of California Press, 2011), 70–71.

68. Jeff Nilson, "How Rudolph Valentino Invented Sex Appeal," November 17, 2012, *Saturday Evening Post*, accessed August 23, 2019, http://www.saturdayeveningpost.com/2012/11/17/history/post-perspective/valentino.html.

69. "Crowds Still Try to View Valentino," *New York Times*, August 27, 1926, 3.

70. Richard Koszarski, *An Evening's Entertainment: The Age of the Silent Feature Picture 1915–1928* (New York: Charles Scribner's Sons, 1990), 298.

71. "Miss Negri Swoons at Valentino Bier," *New York Times*, August 30, 1926, 3.

72. Petersen, "Scandals of Classic Hollywood."

73. Cited in Ellenberg, *Valentino Mystique*, 56.

74. Margaret S. Stroebe, Wolfgang Stroebe, and Robert O. Hansson, *Handbook of Bereavement: Theory, Research and Intervention* (Cambridge: Cambridge University Press, 1993), 105.

75. Mary Ann Doane, *Femmes Fatales: Feminism, Film Theory, Psychoanalysis* (New York: Routledge, 1991), 3.

76. See Negra, *Off-White Hollywood*, 79; quotation in Howe, "Loves of Pola Negri," 38, cited in Negra, *Off-White Hollywood*, 80.

77. Myrtle Gebhart, "Hollywood's Latest Adventures in Matrimony," *Picture Play*, April 1926, 100.

78. Ruth Tildesley, "This Here Love Urge," *Motion Picture Magazine*, February 1928, 49.

79. Negra, *Off-White Hollywood*, 79.

80. Ellenberg, *Valentino Mystique*, 25.

81. Charles J. Maland, *Chaplin and American Culture: The Evolution of a Star Image* (Princeton, NJ: Princeton University Press, 1989), 95.

82. Delgado, *Pola Negri*, 117.

83. Pola Negri, *Memoirs of a Star* (London: Doubleday, 1970), 315.

84. Virginia Wright Wexman, *Creating the Couple: Love, Marriage, and Hollywood Performance* (Princeton, NJ: Princeton University Press, 1993), 24.

85. Wexman, *Creating the Couple*, 124.

86. "It's Miss Negri, Not 'Princess,' She Announces," *Billings Weekly Gazette*, MT, May 31, 1927, 5.

87. Elizabeth Greer and Dorothy Donnell, "News of the Camera Cost," *Motion Picture Classic*, July 1927, 122.

88. Gaylyn Studlar, *Precocious Charms: Stars Performing Girlhood in Classical Hollywood Cinema* (Los Angeles: University of California Press, 2013), 44.

89. Marquis Busby, "Overtime Acting," *Motion Picture Classic*, August 1928, 17.

90. Edith Perrin, "What the Fans Think," *Picture Play*, January 1928, 10.

91. E.G., comment on Perrin, "What the Fans Think," February 1928, 12.

92. Elizabeth Greer, "The Screen Observer Has Her Say," *Motion Picture Classic*, November 1926, 60.

93. James R. Quirk, "Close-Ups and Long Shots," *Photoplay*, July 1927, 74.

94. Quirk, "Close-Ups and Long Shots," 74.

95. DeCordova, *Emergence of the Star System in America*, 105–106.

96. Richard Dyer, *Stars* (London: British Film Institute, 1998), 52.

97. Studlar, "Perils of Pleasure?," 271.

98. In fact, my analysis of *Photoplay, Picture Play,* and *Motion Picture Classic* in 1927 finds only two articles linking Negri's wedding with the recent demise of her previous lover.

99. Schallert and Schallert, "Hollywood Highlights," 72.

100. Helen Louise Walker, "The Little Poses of the Stars," *Picture Play,* May 1928, 112.

101. E.G ., comment on Perrin, "What the Fans Think," 12.

102. Gladys Hall, "The Besetting Sins of Hollywood," *Motion Picture Classic,* March 1928, 17.

103. "Is Pola's Hubby a Fake Prince?," *Hollywood Vagabond,* July 30, 1927, 1.

104. In the article, the prince discusses his familial wealth in more depth: "When I was born, my family owned thirty-seven towns and four castles. . . . It would have taken many days to ride on horseback over all our possessions. We were a rich family—that is why we have always had the *entrée* everywhere in Europe. It takes more than a title alone to be received there." James Bagley, "The Truth about Pola's Prince," *Motion Picture Classic,* October 1927, 20, 67.

105. Wexman, *Creating the Couple,* 146.

106. "Paris, May 14. Pola Negri became a princess and Serge Mdivani the custodian of a $520,000 a year salary—the movie queen's income—at 5 o'clock this afternoon in the historic chateau at Seraincourt, thirty miles from Paris." Henry Wales, "Movie Queen Pola Becomes Prince's Wife," *Chicago Sunday Tribune,* May 15, 1927, 1. Mdivani family papers provide evidence that Serge Mdivani indeed mishandled his wife's $5 million fortune. See Mdivani Family Papers, Correspondence 1922-1985, Hargrett Rare Book & Manuscript Library, University of Georgia Libraries.

107. Helen Carlisle, "And This Is Her Husband," *Motion Picture Magazine,* May 1928, 124.

108. Greer and Donnell, "News of the Camera Cost," 122.

109. *Ogden Standard-Examiner,* May 29, 1927, 4, cited in Delgado, *Pola Negri,* 117.

110. "In and Out of Focus," *Motion Picture Magazine,* May 1928, 38–39.

111. Benedict Anderson, *Imagined Communities: Reflections on the Origin and Spread of Nationalism* (London: Verso, 2003), 5–8; Russell A. Kazal, "Revisiting Assimilation: The Rise, Fall, and Reprisal of a Concept in American Ethnic History," *American History Review* 100, no. 2 (1995): 440.

112. Kazal, "Revisiting Assimilation," 440.

113. Herbert Howe, "The Real Pola Negri," *Photoplay,* November 1922, 59. Cited also in Negra, *Off-White Hollywood,* 67.

114. See "Pola Swears Allegiance," *Motion Picture Magazine,* August 1924, 63; and "Uncle Sam's Adopted Children," *Photoplay,* January 1926, 68–69. The quote comes from Kazal, "Revisiting Assimilation," 437.

115. William H. McKegg, "*Must* They Become Americans?," *Picture Play,* May 1928, 66–67.

116. McKegg, "*Must* They Become Americans?," 66–67.

117. M. M., letter to the editor, *Motion Picture Magazine,* December 1927, 8.

118. Myrtle Gebhart, "Not So Dumb!," *Picture Play,* April 1928, 29.

119. Mariusz Kotowski, *Pola Negri: Hollywood's First Femme Fatale* (Lexington: Kentucky University Press, 2014), 115.

120. Walker, *Stardom,* 138–139.

121. Negra, *Off-White Hollywood*, 79.

122. Negra, *Off-White Hollywood*, 81.

123. In line with Negra, Marjorie Rosen also suggests that Janet Gaynor represented a new type of star, popularized as a response to the changing economic situation. Gaynor was "a symbol of the new, warmly loving, virginal-looking angel, a resurrection of the Victorian Madonna" whose "familiar values . . . comforted like an old fashioned balm on open wounds." Marjorie Rosen, *Popcorn Venus: Women, Movies and the American Dream* (London: P. Owen, 1973), 129.

124. "Uncle Sam's Adopted Children," 68–69.

CHAPTER 2 — POLA NEGRI AS THE VAMP

Chapter subtitle: "Temptatious Pola Assailed Picture Citadel by Storm," Dorothy Spensley, "Languishing Romances," *Photoplay*, September 1925, 110.

1. Tony Guzman, "The Little Theatre Movement: The Institutionalization of the European Art Film in America," *Film History: An International Journal* 17, nos. 2/3 (2005): 261.

2. "The Ogre Who Proves to Be a Pigmy," *Photoplay*, June 1922, 55.

3. Jan Christopher Horak, "Sauerkraut & Sausages with a Little Goulash: Germans in Hollywood, 1927," *Film History: An International Journal* 17, nos. 2/3 (2005): 247.

4. The titles of the films are those used for American distribution only. *Gypsy Blood* was initially released in Germany as *Carmen*, *Passion* as *Madame DuBarry*, and *One Arabian Night* as *Sumurun*. Because I look at the reception of Negri in the United States, I use the titles of American releases rather than the original ones.

5. Frederick C. Luebke, *Germans in the New World: Essays in the History of Immigration* (Urbana: University of Illinois Press, 1999), 173.

6. Two other German films with Negri were also released in the United States: *Sappho* (1921), retitled *Mad Love*, and *The Flame* (1922), known also as *Montmarte*. However, both productions came to America in 1923, when Negri was already working in Hollywood, and were therefore not instructive in shaping her early publicity.

7. For Diane Negra, Negri "revisioned" the vamp of the 1910s. See Diane Negra, *Off-White Hollywood*, 68.

8. Graham Petrie, *Hollywood Destinies: European Directors in America, 1922–1931* (Detroit: Wayne State University Press, 2002), 4.

9. Sergio Delgado, *Pola Negri: Temptress of Silent Hollywood* (Jefferson, NC: McFarland, 2016), 26.

10. *Photoplay*, March 1921, page unknown, cited in Delgado, *Pola Negri*, 26.

11. "Passion Sets New Record at Capitol; Rothapfel Holds It for a Second Week," *Moving Picture World*, January 1, 1921, 30. See also Scott Eyman, *Ernst Lubitsch: Laughter in Paradise* (New York: Simon & Schuster, 1993), 379.

12. *Motion Picture Magazine*, February 1921, page unknown, cited in Petrie, *Hollywood Destinies*, 14.

13. Barbara Wilinsky, *Sure Seaters: The Emergence of Art House Cinema* (Minneapolis: University of Minnesota Press, 2001), 48. For more information about German productions in the US, see Stefan Drössler's detailed article, "Ernst Lubitsch and EFA," *Film History*, 21, no. 3 (2009), Producers and Directors, 208–228.

14. Nick Smedley, *A Divided World: Hollywood Cinema and Emigré Directors in the Era of Roosevelt and Hitler, 1933–1948* (Bristol, UK, and Chicago, IL: Intellect, 2011), 157.

While Smedley expresses this in reference to Lubitsch's later films, the notion is applicable to the 1920s. See also Janet McCabe, "Regulating Hidden Pleasures and 'Modern' Identities: Imagined Female Spectators, Early German Popular Cinema, and *The Oyster Princess* (1919)," in *Light Motives: German Popular Film in Perspective*, ed. Randall Halle and Margaret McCarthy (Detroit: Wayne State University Press, 2003), 24–40.

15. Agnes Smith, "The Screen in Review," *Picture Play Magazine*, January 1921, 57.

16. Rick McCormick, "Sex, History and Upward Mobility: Ernst Lubitsch's *Madame DuBarry/Passion*, 1919," *German Studies Review* 33, no. 3 (October 2010): 615.

17. Thomas Elsaesser, *Weimar Cinema and After: Germany's Historical Imaginary* (London: Routledge, 2000), 277.

18. McCormick, "Sex, History and Upward Mobility," 604.

19. Scott Nye, "Scott Reviews Ernst Lubitsch's Madame DuBarry," Criterion Cast, September 14, 2015, accessed August 21, 2019, http://criterioncast.com/reviews/blu-ray-reviews/scott-reviews-ernst-lubitschs-madame-dubarry-masters-of-cinema-blu-ray-review.

20. The phrase is used by Petrie. See Petrie, *Hollywood Destinies*, 25.

21. Nye, "Scott Reviews Ernst Lubitsch's Madame DuBarry."

22. "Right Off the Grill," *Picture Play*, September 1921, 93.

23. The heroine is called La Carmencita in the surviving American version of the film. However, her character is based on Carmen (and even possibly called that name in the original version of the film), so I continue to refer to her as Carmen, in the interest of consistency.

24. Jess Sully, "Challenging the Stereotype: The Femme Fatale in Fin-de-Siècle Art and Early Cinema," in *The Femme Fatale: Images, Histories, Contexts*, ed. Helen Hanson and Catherine O'Rawe (London: Palgrave Macmillan, 2010), 47.

25. Mario Praz, *The Romantic Agony* (Oxford: Oxford University Press, 1970), 206–207.

26. Phil Powrie, Bruce Babington, Chris Perriam, and Ann Davies, *Carmen on Film: History* (Bloomington: Indiana University Press, 2007), 22.

27. Lola Young illustrates this dynamic when she suggests that the "oriental image has to be situated within its contemporary colonial discourse, as a part of politics that described non-white women in terms of hypersexuality and immutable difference." *Fear of the Dark: Race, Gender and Sexuality in the Cinema* (London: Routledge, 1996), 62.

28. Joy Ramirez, "Silent Divas: The *Femme Fatales* of Italian *Cinema Muto*," in *The Femme Fatale: Images, Histories, Contexts*, ed. Helen Hanson and Catherine O'Rawe (London: Palgrave Macmillan, 2010), 65.

29. Gustave Flaubert, *Salammbo* (New York: Mondial, 2006; first published 1862); and Oscar Wilde, *Salomé* (New York: Dover Publications, 1967; first published 1864).

30. Ewa Kuryluk, *Salome and Judas in the Cave of Sex. The Grotesque: Origins, Iconography, Techniques* (Evanston, IL: Northwestern University Press, 1987), 189.

31. Powrie et al., *Carmen on Film*, 32.

32. Sabine Hake, *Passions and Deceptions: The Early Films of Ernst Lubitsch* (Princeton, NJ: Princeton University Press, 1992), 46.

33. Powrie et al., *Carmen on Film*, 23.

34. Petrie, *Hollywood Destinies*, 3.

35. Richard Dyer, *Stars*, 2nd ed. (London: British Film Institute, 1998), 178.

36. Diana Anselmo-Sequeira, "Blue Bloods, Movie Queens and Jane Does: Or How Princess Culture, American Film, and Girl Fandom Came Together in the 1910s," in *Princess Cultures: Mediating Girls' Imaginations and Identities*, ed. Miriam Forman-Brunell

and Rebecca C. Hans (New York: Peter Lang Press, 2014), 185. See also Raymond Durgnat and John Kobal, *Greta Garbo* (London: Studio Vista Limited, 1965), 10.

37. Maximilian Vinder, "She Delivered the Goods," *Photoplay*, May 1922, 21, 109.

38. Samantha Barbas, *Movie Crazy: Fans, Stars and the Cult of Celebrity* (New York: Palgrave, 2001), 41. See also Herbert Howe, "They Can't Fool the Public," *Photoplay*, June 1922, 47.

39. "Reviews," *Exhibitor's Herald*, May 28, 1921, 28.

40. Barry King, "Stardom as an Occupation," in *The Hollywood Film Industry*, ed. Paul Kerr (London: Routledge, 1986), 160.

41. "Screen Hall of Fame: A Dozen Stars Name Their Favorite Role," *Motion Picture Magazine*, September 1926, 38.

42. *Variety*, May 13, 1921, 2; and *New York Times*, May 9, 1921, cited in Mariusz Kotowski, *Pola Negri: Hollywood's First Femme Fatale* (Lexington: Kentucky University Press, 2014), 26.

43. Vinder, "She Delivered the Goods," 20–21.

44. The review refers to two opera singers famously associated with the story of Carmen: Emma Calvé, a French opera singer who personified the heroine on stage, and Geraldine Farrar, another opera singer who starred in the screen adaptation in 1915. See Burns Mantle, "The Shadow Stage," *Photoplay*, June 1921, 52.

45. *Picture Play*, June 1921, page unknown, cited in "Gypsy Blood," Silents Are Golden, accessed August 21, 2019, http://www.silentsaregolden.com/gypsybloodreview.html.

46. "Ideal Cast Contest," *Motion Picture Magazine*, October 1921, 80.

47. *Photoplay* labeled the film as only "mediocrely successful" financially. See "Ogre Who Proves to Be a Pigmy," 55.

48. Edward Said, "Orientalism," in *The Post-Colonial Studies Reader*, ed. Bill Ashcroft, Gareth Griffiths, and Helen Tiffin (London: Routledge, 1995), 87.

49. Nassaer Al-Taee, *Representations of the Orient in Western Music: Violence and Sensuality* (Surrey: Ashgate Publishing, 2010), 272.

50. Richard McCormick, "Desire vs. Despotism: The Politics of *Sumurun* (1920), Ernst Lubitsch's 'Oriental' Fantasy: Rediscovering Germany's Filmic Legacy," in *The Many Faces of Weimar Cinema: Rediscovering Germany's Filmic Legacy*, ed. Christian Rogowski (Rochester, NY: Camden House, 2010), 69.

51. McCormick, "Desire vs. Despotism," 75.

52. McCormick, "Desire vs. Despotism," 76.

53. "One Arabian Night," *Picture Play*, November 1921, 47.

54. "One Arabian Night," 47.

55. Kelly Robinson, "Sumurun: Ernst Lubitsch and Pola Negri's Arabian Night," Silent London, April 2, 2013, accessed August 26, 2019, https://silentlondon.co.uk/2013/04/02/sumurun-ernst-lubitsch-and-pola-negris-arabian-night/.

56. Pamela Robertson Wojcik, introduction to *Movie Acting, The Film Reader*, ed. Pamela Robertson Wojcik (New York, NY, and London, UK: Routledge, 2004), 7.

57. Mary Ann Doane, "The Voice in the Cinema: The Articulation of Body and Space," in "Cinema/Sound Issue," *Yale French Studies*, no. 60 (1980): 33.

58. Ramirez, "Silent Divas," 65.

59. *Off-White Hollywood*, 68.

60. Richard Koszarski, *An Evening's Entertainment: The Age of the Silent Feature Picture 1915–1928* (New York: Charles Scribner's Sons, 1990), 298.

61. Cited in David W. Menefee, *The First Female Stars: Women of the Silent Era* (Westport, CT: Praeger, 2004), 25–26.

62. Adolph Zukor to Ralph Kohn, telegram, July 18, 1922, Adolph Zukor Correspondence, Correspondence 1922, 1-f.5, Margaret Herrick Library, Los Angeles. See also Ben Blumenthal to Adolph Zukor, June 30, 1922, in the same collection, accessed January 1, 2019, http://digitalcollections.oscars.org/cdm/compoundobject/collection/p15759coll3/id/364/rec/2. Blumenthal was convinced the professional pairing would "create a sensation in America, this being the first big foreign director with a reputation who has come to America."

63. The phrase comes from Hans Kafka, "What Our Immigration Did for Hollywood, and Vice Versa," *New German Critique*, no. 89 (Spring–Summer 2003): 185.

64. Sarah Berry, "Hollywood Exoticism," in *Stars: The Film Reader*, ed. Ludy Fischer and Marcia Landy (London: Routledge, 2004), 191.

65. Anne Helen Petersen, "Scandals of Classic Hollywood: The Most Kissable Hands of Pola Negri," The Hairpin, November 14, 2013, accessed August 21, 2019, http://thehairpin.com/2013/11/scandals-of-classic-hollywood-the-most-kissable-hands-of-pola-negri/.

66. Negra, *Off-White Hollywood*, 80.

67. Pola Negri, "Autobiography of Pola Negri. Part I," *Photoplay*, February 1924, 50.

68. Lois Banner, *American Beauty: A Social History through Two Centuries of the American Ideal, and Image of the Beautiful Woman* (New York: Alfred A. Knopf, 1983), 204.

69. See Delgado, *Pola Negri*, 11. Although Negri was certainly not from an affluent background, it is hard to establish whether she lived in poverty.

70. See Kristine Somerville, "Enemy of Men: The Vamps, Ice Princesses and Flappers of the Silent Screens," *Missouri Review* 37, no. 3 (2014): 87.

71. "Pola Negri in *One Arabian Night*," *The Standard Union*, October 9, 1921, 19. See also "Pity the Poor Dancer," *Albury Banner and Wodonga Express*, Australia, September 25, 1925, 14.

72. This part of Negri's public biography is, unlike most of the writing concerning her father and her time in Russia as a ballet dancer, factually accurate. Some sources anglicize the name of the production company to Sphinx. See Marek Haltof, *Polish National Cinema* (New York: Berghahn Books, 2002), 6–7. See also Delgado, *Pola Negri*, 44.

73. Sheila Skaff, *The Law of the Looking Glass: Cinema in Poland, 1896–1939* (Athens: Ohio University Press, 2008), 60–61. In her *Memoirs*, Negri claimed to have been born on the last day of the nineteenth century, but numerous sources suggest she was actually three years older. See Martin Votruba, Slovak Studies Program, University of Pittsburgh, accessed August 25, 2019, http://www.pitt.edu/~votruba/qsonhist/celebrities/negrip.html; and Kotowski, *Pola Negri*, 4.

74. Roger Butterfield, *The American Past: A History of the United States from Concord to Hiroshima* (New York: Simon & Schuster, 1947), 5.

75. Anselmo-Sequeira, "Blue Bloods, Movie Queens and Jane Does," 181.

76. Anselmo-Sequeira, "Blue Bloods, Movie Queens and Jane Does," 181.

77. Ernst Lubitsch, "My Two Years in America," *Motion Picture Magazine*, December 1924, 104.

78. William McKegg, "Uncensored Observations," *Picture Play*, July 1926, 48.

79. Holmes uses the description in relation to another star of the silent screen, Jetta Goudal, but it seems applicable to Negri here. For a discussion of Goudal's "temperamental"

image, see chapter 8. See Andrew Dawson and Sean P. Holmes, "New Perspectives on Working in the Global Film and Television Industries," in *Working in the Global Film and Television Industries: Creativity, Systems, Space, Patronage*, ed. Andrew Dawson and Sean P. Holmes (London: Bloomsbury Academic, 2012), 77.

80. Jeanine Basinger, *Silent Stars* (Middletown, CT: Wesleyan University Press, 1999), 239.

81. "Coast Critics Praise Bella Donna," *Exhibition Trade Review*, March 31, 1923, 891.

82. Jack G. Shaheen suggested that silent films engaging with Orientalist tropes served as a "repetition teaching tool" in perpetuating the notion of the Arab as savage and malicious. Jack G. Shaheen, *Reel Bad Arabs: How Hollywood Vilifies a People* (Northampton, MA: Olive Branch Press, 2009), 588.

83. Edwin Schallert, "The Elegy of Pola," *Picture Play*, March 1923, 77.

84. "Pola Negri in Her First American Production, Bella Donna," *Motion Picture News*, April 7, 1923, 1616, accessed August 21, 2019, http://archive.org/stream/motionpicturenewoomoti_o#page/1616/mode/2up.

85. "Pola Negri in a George Fitzmaurice Production *Bella Donna*," *Exhibitors Trade Review*, February 24, 1923, 27.

86. Adele Whiteley Fletcher, "Across the Silversheet: The New Photoplays in Review." *Motion Picture Magazine*, June 1923, 120.

87. *Variety*, April 19, 1923, 35, cited in Lea Jacobs, *The Decline of Sentiment: American Film in the 1920s* (Chicago: University of Chicago Press, 2008), 239.

88. *Photoplay*, August 1923, 44, cited in Delgado, *Pola Negri*, 60.

89. "We Interview Pola Negri," *Motion Picture Magazine*, January 1923, 23, 102–103. See also "The Negri in California," *Motion Picture Magazine*, February 1923, 22–23.

90. Grace Kingsley, "What America Has Done for Pola Negri," *Movie Weekly*, April 21, 1923, page unknown, cited in Kotowski, *Pola Negri*, 89.

91. The Klan was at its most active in protesting against films between 1923 and 1924. Tom Rice demonstrates how the organization was an influential force within national discourse during the period. See Tom Rice, *White Robes, Silver Screens: Movies and the Making of the Ku Klux Klan* (Bloomington: Indiana University Press, 2015), 71.

92. "Bella Donna-Bah!," *Fiery Cross*, April 27, 1923, 4, cited in Tom Rice, "Protecting Protestantism: The Ku Klux Klan vs. The Motion Picture Industry," *Film History: An International Journal* 20, no. 3 (2008): 370.

93. Charlotte Perkins Gilman, "Vanguard, Rear-Guard and Mud-Guard," *Century Magazine*, July 1922, 353.

94. Miriam Hansen, "Adventures of Goldilocks: Spectatorship, Consumerism and Public Life," *Camera Obscura* 8, no. 22 (1990): 64.

95. Roger Didier, "East of Suez Film a Race Film: Aims to Prove White Race Always Right," *Baltimore Afro-American*, February 28, 1925, A6.

96. Another two films mentioned by the column are *East of Suez* (1925) and *The Passion Flower*. Because the film with the latter title has never been made, it is safe to assume the film in question is actually *The Cheat* (1925).

97. Didier, "East of Suez Film a Race Film," A6.

98. Interestingly, in DeMille's version from 1915, the crook is portrayed as Japanese, which attests to the degree of interchangeability among "Oriental" villains in Hollywood. Jeffrey Richards, *China and the Chinese in Popular Film* (London: I.B. Tauris, 2017), 128. See also Sumiko Higashi, *Cecil B. DeMille and American Culture: The Silent Era*

(Berkeley: University of California Press, 1994), 111. For more recent work on the representation of the Chinese in the Hollywood film, see Sheng-Mei Ma, *Off-White: Yellowface and Chinglish by Anglo-American Culture* (London: Bloomsbury Academic, 2019).

99. Kotowski, *Pola Negri*, 64.

100. Janet Staiger, "*Les Belles Dames Sans Merci*, Femme Fatales, Vampires, Vamps and Gold Diggers: The Transformation and Narrative Value of Aggressive Fallen Woman," in *Reclaiming the Archive: Feminism and Film History*, ed. Vicki Callahan (Detroit: Wayne State University Press, 2010), 42.

101. "Pola Negri in the Cheat," *Motion Picture News*, July 1923, 4–5.

102. "Pola Negri in the Cheat," 4–5.

103. Delgado, *Pola Negri*, 64.

104. Rob Byrne, "Restoring *The Spanish Dancer*," *Moving Image* 12, no. 2 (2012): 161.

105. Byrne, "Restoring *The Spanish Dancer*," 161.

106. See *Motion Picture Magazine*, January 1923, page unknown, accessed August 21, 2019, http://www.silentsaregolden.com/spanishdancerreview.html.

107. It can be argued that this representational scheme remained unchallenged on celluloid until the late 1920s and early 1930s, when vamps and gold diggers started to be blonde. See Staiger, "*Les Belles Dames Sans Merci*," 41.

108. "In Comparison," *Motion Picture Classic*, November 1923, 48.

109. Richard Dyer, *White: Essays on Race and Culture* (London: Routledge, 1997), 129.

110. Harry Carr, "Behind the Scenes with Pola Negri," *Motion Picture Magazine*, June 1923, 33.

111. Kotowski, *Pola Negri*, 91.

112. Charles S. Sewell, "Newest Reviews and Comments," *Moving Picture World*, October 20, 1923, 668.

113. See Gaylyn Studlar, "*Out-Salomeing Salome*: Dance, the New Woman, and Fan Magazine Orientalism," in *Visions of the East: Orientalism in Film*, ed. Matthew Bernstein and Gaylyn Studlar (London: I.B. Tauris Publishers, 1997), 106.

114. Donnalee Dox, "Dancing around Orientalism," *Drama Review* 50, no. 4 (2006): 55.

115. Studlar, "*Out-Salomeing Salome*," 106.

116. Negri, "Autobiography of Pola Negri," 50.

117. Negri, "Autobiography of Pola Negri," 50–51. See also *Sheridan Enterprise*, WY, July 8, 1921, 3.

118. Negra, "Immigrant Stardom in Imperial America," 396.

119. Marcia Landy, "1922: Movies and the Changing Body of Cinema," in *American Cinema of the 1920s: Themes and Variations*, ed. Lucy Fisher (New Brunswick, NJ: Rutgers University Press, 2007), 109.

120. Steven J. Ross, *Working-Class Hollywood: Silent Film and Shaping of Class in America* (Princeton, NJ: Princeton University Press, 1998), 199.

121. Brian A. Belton, *Questioning Gypsy Identity: Ethnic Narratives in Britain and America* (Oxford: Altamira Press, 2005), 13.

122. Edward W. Said, *Orientalism: Western Conceptions of the Orient* (Oxford: Penguin Books, 1995), 208.

123. A columnist for the *New York Times* wrote about *The Charmer* (1925): "The idea of appearing as a Spaniard evidently appealed to Miss Negri, and there is no doubt that the costumes she wears in this production . . . suited her type." *New York Times*, April 6, 1925, cited in Delgado, *Pola Negri*, 88.

124. Matt Houlbrook points out that a female Apache dancer was "a staple role for the biggest stars of the silent movie era." In the same year that witnessed the release of *Shadows of Paris*, Gloria Swanson—Negri's chief rival—portrayed a similar character in *The Humming Bird* (1924). See Matt Houlbrook, *Prince of Tricksters: The Incredible True Story of Netley Lucas, Gentleman Crook* (Chicago: University of Chicago Press, 2016), 381. For more information on the Apaches as figures threatening the social order, and the ways in which French cinema represented them, see Richard Abel, *The Ciné Goes to Town: French Cinema, 1896–1914* (Berkeley: University of California Press, 1994), 123–129.

125. Interestingly, Negri claimed to be a countess through her first marriage to the Polish count Eugene Dombski, whom she married in 1919; they were divorced in 1922. Existing records prove their marriage was not a fiction. Dombski's aristocratic title, however, can be disputed.

126. Emmanuelle Dirix, "Birds of Paradise: Feathers, Fetishism and Costume in Classical Hollywood," *Film, Fashion and Consumption* 3, no. 1 (2014): 22.

127. Dirix, "Birds of Paradise," 22.

128. Stephen Gundle and Clino Castelli, *The Glamour System* (London: Palgrave Macmillan, 2006), 65.

129. Frank Elliot, "Shadows of Paris," *Motion Picture News*, January 26, 1924, 393.

130. "The Shadow Stage, a Review of New Pictures," *Photoplay*, May 1925, 56.

131. Negri, "Autobiography of Pola Negri," 51.

132. "Movie Encyclopaedia," *Motion Picture Classic*, October 1924, 74.

133. Myrtle Gebhart, "Up the Family Trees of the Stars," *Picture Play*, January 1928, 16–17.

134. Vinder, "She Delivered the Goods," 20.

135. Vinder, "She Delivered the Goods," 20.

136. Praz, *Romantic Agony*, 207–210.

137. Herbert Howe, "The Prodigal Daughter Returns," *New Movie Magazine*, October 1931, 59.

138. Carr, "Behind the Scenes with Pola Negri," 89.

139. Carr, "Behind the Scenes with Pola Negri," 89. See also Walter Ramsey, "Left Overs Hollywood Night and Day," *Motion Picture Magazine*, February 1929, 16.

140. Myrtle Gebhart, "Their Streak of Superstition," *Picture Play*, August 1923, 72.

141. Ramsey, "Left Overs Hollywood Night and Day," 16.

142. The other two are Gloria Swanson and Barbara La Marr.

143. Ben Lyon, "The Vampires I Have Known," *Photoplay*, February 1925, 28–29.

144. Negra, *Off-White Hollywood*, 80.

145. Kingsley, "What America Has Done for Pola Negri," page unknown, cited in Kotowski, *Pola Negri*, 89.

146. Herbert Howe, "Hollywood's Hall of Fame," *New Movie Magazine*, May 1931, 43.

147. Also referred to using the acronym WASP.

148. Donald H. Roy, *The Reuniting of America: Eleven Multicultural Dialogues* (New York: Peter Lang, 1996), 252.

149. H. H. Faulkner, "Character Readings of the Noses of Ten Famous Film Stars," *Motion Picture Magazine*, February 1923, 67.

150. The author suggests that "none of the famed beauties of history ever did. Each established a standard of her own that later became a model." Herbert Howe, "The Most Beautiful Women on Earth," *Photoplay*, August 1925, 111.

151. Howe, "Most Beautiful Women on Earth," 111.

152. Howe, "Most Beautiful Women on Earth," 111.

153. Myrtle Gebhart, "An Artist Talks on Screen Beauty," *Picture Play*, July 1926, 24.

154. B. Titko, "Brickbats and Bouquets," *Photoplay*, December 1925, 12.

155. The list also included Corinne Griffith, Florence Vidor, Greta Nissen, May Alisson, Alice Terry, Mary Astor, May McAvoy, Barbara La Marr, and Nita Naldi. See Howe, "Most Beautiful Women on Earth," 121.

156. Margaret Reid, "Brickbats and Bouquets," *Photoplay*, January 1926, 12.

157. Ellen Pullar, "*A New Woman*: The Promotional Persona of Anna Sten," *Celebrity Studies Journal* 1, no. 3 (2010): 275.

158. J. Malone, "Behind the Silver Screen," *Picture Play*, October 1926, 45.

159. Reid, "Brickbats and Bouquets," 12.

160. G. S. Sampson, "What the Fans Think," *Picture Play*, August 1923, 107.

161. Negra, *Off-White Hollywood*, 76.

162. Kathy Peiss, *Hope in a Jar: The Making of America's Beauty Culture* (Philadelphia: University of Pennsylvania Press, 1998), 316.

163. Ellen Tremper, *I'm No Angel: The Blonde in Fiction and Film* (Charlottesville: University of Virginia Press, 2006), 130.

164. Barnaby Conrad, *The Blonde: A Celebration of the Golden Era from Harlow to Monroe* (San Francisco: Chronicle, 1999), 39–40. See also Lois Banner, "The Creature from the Black Lagoon: Marilyn Monroe and Whiteness." *Cinema Journal* 47, no. 4 (Summer 2008): 12.

165. Pam Cook, "Because She's Worth It: The Natural Blonde from Grace Kelly to Nicole Kidman," *Celebrity Studies Journal* 7, no. 1 (2016): 12.

166. Negra, *Off-White Hollywood*, 76.

167. Cal York, "Studio News & Gossip—East and West," *Photoplay*, March 1926, 94.

168. Ann Sylvester, "There Are Styles in Stars Too," *Picture Play*, September 1928, 90.

169. See Melinda Szaloky, "As You Desire Me: Reading the *Divine Garbo* through Movement, Silence and Sublime," *Film History* 18, no. 2 (2006): 201.

170. Rosa Shpetner, "What the Fans Think," *Picture Play*, December 1929, 113.

171. Cal York, "Plays and Players," *Photoplay*, March 1921, 80.

172. Sully, "Challenging the Stereotype," 56.

173. Stacey Abbot, "The Undead in the Kingdom of Shadows," in *Open Graves, Open Minds: Representation of Vampires and the Undead from the Enlightenment to the Present Day*, ed. Samantha George and Bill Hughes (Manchester: Manchester University Press, 2013), 100.

174. Charles S. Sewell, "Newest Reviews and Comments," *Moving Picture World*, October 1923, 34.

175. *Photoplay*, December 1923, cited in "The Spanish Dancer," Silents Are Golden, accessed August 21, 2019, http://www.silentsaregolden.com/spanishdancerreview.html.

176. Negra, *Off-White Hollywood*, 78.

CHAPTER 3 — VILMA BÁNKY AND WHITENESS

Chapter subtitle: "The almost perfect Anglo-Saxon type, more English than the English," "Picture of Vilma. Vilma Banky Is the Almost Perfect . . . ," *Photoplay*, August 1928, 23.

1. Alastair Phillips and Ginette Vincendeau, "Film Trade, Global Culture and Transnational Cinema: An Introduction," in *Journeys of Desire. European Actors in Hollywood: A*

Critical Companion, ed. Alastair Phillips and Ginette Vincendeau (London: British Film Institute Publishing, 2006), 7.

2. The Extra Boy, "What the Fans Think," *Picture Play*, December 1927, 119.

3. Diana Anselmo-Sequeira, "Blue Bloods, Movie Queens and Jane Does: Or How Princess Culture, American Film, and Girl Fandom Came Together in the 1910s," in *Princess Cultures: Mediating Girls' Imaginations and Identities*, ed. Miriam Forman-Brunell and Rebecca C. Hans (New York: Peter Lang Press, 2015), 175.

4. Anselmo-Sequeira, "Blue Bloods, Movie Queens and Jane Does," 179.

5. Jerome Shorey, "Do You Believe in Fairies?," *Photoplay*, September 1918, 47, cited in Anselmo-Sequeira, "Blue Bloods, Movie Queens and Jane Does," 164.

6. Masha Orgeron, "You Are Invited to Participate: Interactive Fandom in the Age of the Movie Magazine," *Journal of Film and Video* 61, no. 3 (Fall 2009): 16.

7. "The Fame and Fortune Contest of 1921," *Motion Picture*, January 1921, 122.

8. Rachel Schildgen, *More Than a Dream: Rediscovering the Life and Films of Vilma Bánky* (Hollywood, CA: 1921 PVG Publishing, 2010), 43.

9. Cal York, "Studio News and Gossip—East and West," *Photoplay*, May 1925, 41.

10. Aileen St. John-Brenon, "Manhattan Medley," *Picture Play*, May 1928, 52.

11. Schildgen, *More Than a Dream*, 48.

12. See, for example, Myrtle Gebhart, "The Discovery of Vilma Banky," *Picture Play*, February 1926, 34.

13. Rob Baum, "After the Ball Is Over: Bringing *Cinderella* Home," *Cultural Analysis: An Interdisciplinary Forum on Folklore and Popular Culture* 1 (2000): 69–70, accessed August 19, 2019, https://www.ocf.berkeley.edu/~culturalanalysis/volume1/pdf/baum.pdf.

14. Tamar Lane, "That's Out," *Motion Picture Magazine*, April 1926, 59.

15. Myrtle Gebhart, "Not So Dumb!," *Picture Play*, April 1928, 29.

16. Gebhart, "Discovery of Vilma Banky," 34.

17. Dorothy Manners, "Second Mates," *Motion Picture Magazine*, July 1928, 78.

18. Cal York, "The Girl on the Cover," *Photoplay*, April 1926, 82.

19. Anselmo-Sequeira, "Blue Bloods, Movie Queens and Jane Does," 180.

20. Although she did not come from an aristocratic background, Pola Negri was reported to have become great friends with the last czar of Russia. See chapter 2, *The Spanish Dancer* and *Shadows of Paris*. Perry Meisel writes that in popular culture, stars are "an industrially produced aristocracy." See his *The Myth of Popular Culture: From Dante to Dylan* (Oxford: Wiley-Blackwell, 2010), 100.

21. Schildgen, *More Than a Dream*, 4.

22. The term is used by Anselmo-Sequeira. See Anselmo-Sequeira, "Blue Bloods, Movie Queens and Jane Does," 169.

23. Gebhart, "Discovery of Vilma Banky," 34.

24. Michael Williams, *Film Stardom and the Ancient Past: Idols, Artefacts and Epics* (London: Palgrave Macmillan, 2017), 194.

25. Edward Said, *Orientalism* (New York: Penguin Books, 1995), 240.

26. Gebhart, "Discovery of Vilma Banky," 34.

27. Josephine Shelodon, "Signore Valentino Herewith Presents His New Leading Lady, Fraulein Banky," *Motion Picture Magazine*, November 1925, 24.

28. Cal York, "Studio News and Gossip—East and West," *Photoplay*, May 1926, 38.

29. York, "Studio News and Gossip," 50.

30. Mildred Kenworthy, "Marry? I Zink Ya!," *Photoplay*, April 1927, 84.

31. Herbert Howe, "Hot Dickety Dog!," *Photoplay*, December 1925, 37.

32. Eugene V. Brewster, "Impressions of Hollywood," *Motion Picture Classic*, July 1926, 72.

33. Gaylyn Studlar, *Precocious Charms: Stars Performing Girlhood in Classical Hollywood Cinema* (Los Angeles: University of California Press, 2013), 19.

34. Gary Genosko, "Natures and Cultures of Cuteness," *Invisible Culture: Electronic Journal for Visual Style*, no. 9 (2005): page unknown.

35. Genosko, "Natures and Cultures of Cuteness," page unknown.

36. Aileen St. John-Brenon, "Manhattan Medley," *Picture Play*, March 1927, 61.

37. Brewster, "Impressions of Hollywood," 72.

38. D. Balch, "A Blonde from Pittsburgh," *Motion Picture Classic*, July 1926, 77.

39. E. Brown, "Brickbats and Bouquets," *Photoplay*, May 1926, 113.

40. Ellen Tremper, *I'm No Angel: The Blonde in Fiction and Film* (Charlottesville: University of Virginia Press, 2006), 130–131.

41. Karen Hollinger, *The Actress: Hollywood Acting and the Female Star* (New York: Routledge, 2006), 55.

42. Richard Dyer, *White: Essays on Race and Culture* (London: Routledge, 1997), 45.

43. Dyer, *White*, 71.

44. Antonella Palmieri, "Passport to the Dream Factory: Hollywood and the Exotic Allure of Female Italian Ethnicity" (PhD thesis, University of East Anglia, 2011), 11.

45. Francesca T. Royster, *Becoming Cleopatra: The Shifting Image of an Icon* (New York: Palgrave Macmillan, 2003), 97.

46. Edwin Schallert and Elza Schallert, "Hollywood Highlights," *Picture Play*, June 1927, 64.

47. "Picture of Vilma," *Photoplay*, August 1928, 23.

48. Elza Schallert and Edwin Schallert, "Hollywood Highlights," *Picture Play*, October 1925, 72.

49. Julian B. Carter, *The Heart of Whiteness: Normal Sexuality and Race in America, 1880–1940* (Durham, NC: Duke University Press, 2007), 40.

50. Dyer, *White*, 76.

51. Marian Brownridge, "Brickbats and Bouquets," *Photoplay*, February 1926, 12.

52. Brownridge, "Brickbats and Bouquets," 12.

53. Howe, "Hot Dickety Dog!," 98.

54. Cal York, Studio News and Gossip—East and West, *Photoplay*, March 1926, 94.

55. Dorothy Dandridge and Earl Conrad, *Everything and Nothing: The Dorothy Dandridge Tragedy* (New York: HarperCollins, 2000), 104, cited in Marguerite Rippy, "Commodity, Tragedy, Desire: Female Sexuality and Blackness in the Iconography of Dorothy Dandridge," in *Classic Hollywood, Classic Whiteness*, ed. Daniel Bernardi (Minneapolis: University of Minnesota Press, 2001), 201.

56. Manners, "Second Mates," 78.

57. Brewster, "Impressions of Hollywood," 44.

58. Brewster, "Impressions of Hollywood," 72.

59. Gebhart, "Discovery of Vilma Banky," 34.

60. E.M.H., "Brickbats and Bouquets: Frank Letters from Readers," *Photoplay*, March 1926, 133.

61. Shelodon, "Signore Valentino Herewith Presents His New Leading Lady, Fraulein Banky," 24.

62. William McKegg, "She Refuses to Glitter," *Picture Play*, June 1929, 64.

63. Gebhart, "Discovery of Vilma Banky," 34.

64. Sean Redmond, "The Whiteness of the Rings," in *The Persistence of Whiteness*, ed. Daniel Bernardi (New York: Routledge, 2008), 96.

65. Alistair Bonnet, "How the British Working Class Became White: The Symbolic (Re) formation of Racialized Capitalism," *Journal of Historical Sociology* 3, no. 11 (1998): 320.

66. Karen Sternheimer, *Celebrity Culture and the American Dream: Stardom and Social Mobility* (London: Routledge, 2011), 4. The quote comes from Gaylyn Studlar, "*The Perfect Lover*? Valentino and Ethnic Masculinity in the 1920s," in *The Silent Cinema Reader*, ed. Lee Grieveson and Peter Krämer (London: Routledge, 2004), 299.

67. Brewster, "Impressions of Hollywood," 72.

68. Paul McDonald, *The Star System: Hollywood's Production of Popular Identities* (London: Wallflower, 2009), 7.

69. Joe Franklin, *Classics of the Silent Screen: A Pictorial Treasury* (New York: Citadel Press, 1959), 122.

70. McKegg, "She Refuses to Glitter," 64.

71. Redmond, "Whiteness of the Rings," 93.

72. Alison Lurie, *The Language of Clothes* (London: Random House, 1981), 185.

73. Stephen Gundle and Clino Castelli, *The Glamour System* (London: Palgrave Macmillan, 2006), 125.

74. "Gossip of All the Studios," *Photoplay*, August 1927, 107.

75. Gundle and Castelli, *Glamour System*, 123.

76. Dyer, *White*, 110.

77. Gundle and Castelli, *Glamour System*, 133.

78. Eduard Morin, *The Stars* (London: John Calder, 2005), 4.

79. Dyer, *White*, 78.

80. Dyer, *White*, 76.

81. Stephen Fox, *The Mirror Makers: A History of American Advertising and Its Creators* (Chicago: University of Illinois Press, 1984), 101.

82. Redmond, "Whiteness of the Rings," 95.

83. Bánky, "The Question a Stage Woman Always Asks before Touching Her Face with Soap," *San Francisco Examiner*, May 22, 1927, 17.

84. Rosemary Wurdack, "What the Fans Think," *Picture Play*, December 1929, 94.

85. Dyer, *White*, 45.

86. William K. Everson, *American Silent Film* (New York: Oxford University Press, 1978), 196.

CHAPTER 4 — VILMA BÁNKY AS THE LEADING LADY

Chapter subtitle: "Bedecked in flowing gowns . . . and layers of pearls and jewels," Rachel Schildgen, *More Than a Dream: Rediscovering the Life and Films of Vilma Bánky* (Hollywood, CA: 1921 PVG Publishing, 2010), 3.

1. "The Confidential Guide to Current Releases," *Picture Play*, January 1926, 68.

2. "Stacey—Dark Angel," *Trenton Evening Times*, NJ, November 10, 1925, 16; "The Confidential Guide to Current Releases," *Picture Play*, January 1926, 68.

3. Virginia Wright Wexman, *Creating the Couple: Love, Marriage, and Hollywood Performance* (Princeton, NJ: Princeton University Press, 1993), 23.

4. A. Scott Berg, *Goldwyn: A Biography* (New York: Alfred A. Knopf, 1989), 130.

5. R. P. Levitt, "What the Fans Think," *Picture Play*, February 1926, 10.

6. Cited in Berg, *Goldwyn: A Biography*, 150.

7. Schildgen, *More Than a Dream*, 3.

8. Schildgen, *More Than a Dream*, 3.

9. Lea Jacobs, *The Decline of Sentiment: American Film in the 1920s* (Chicago: University of Chicago Press, 2008), 217.

10. Martin Schingler, *Star Studies: A Critical Guide* (London: Palgrave Macmillan for British Film Institute, 2012), 8.

11. David Bordwell, Janet Staiger, and Kristin Thompson, *The Classical Hollywood Cinema* (London: Routledge, 1996), 145.

12. Diana Anselmo-Sequeira, "Blue Bloods, Movie Queens and Jane Does: Or How Princess Culture, American Film, and Girl Fandom Came Together in the 1910s," in *Princess Cultures: Mediating Girls' Imaginations and Identities*, ed. Miriam Forman-Brunell and Rebecca C. Hans (New York: Peter Lang Press, 2014), 169.

13. Jeffrey Richards, *Swordsmen of the Screen: From Douglas Fairbanks to Michael York* (London: Routledge, 1977), 4.

14. Berg, *Goldwyn: A Biography*, 150.

15. Miriam Hansen, *Babel and Babylon: Spectatorship in American Silent Film* (Cambridge, MA: Harvard University Press, 1994), 269.

16. Laura Mulvey, *Visual and Other Pleasures* (London: Palgrave, 1989), 25.

17. Mulvey, *Visual and Other Pleasures*, 269.

18. Peter Bondanella, *Hollywood Italians: Dagos, Palookas, Romeos, Wise Guys and Sopranos* (New York: Continuum International Publishing Group, 2006), 139.

19. Although the film does not depict Negri as Catherine the Great explicitly—referring to her as the Czarina—it is clear that it draws from the same representational tradition.

20. Wood writes this sentence in reference to *Sunrise* (1927), but I find it applicable here. See Wood, *Sexual Politics and Narrative Film*, 39.

21. Bondanella, *Hollywood Italians*, 138. For a queer reading of Valentino's character in the film, see Susan Potter, *Queer Timing: The Emergence of Lesbian Sexuality in Early Cinema* (Urbana, Chicago, and Springfield, IL: Illinois University Press, 2019), 135–138.

22. The term is theorized by Slavoj Žižek in his *Metastases of Enjoyment: Six Essays on Women and Causality* (London: Verso, 2005), 89–91.

23. John Richardson, "The Neosurrealist Musical and Tsai Ming-Laing's *The Wayward Cloud*," in *The Oxford Handbook of New Audiovisual Aesthetics*, ed. John Richardson, Claudia Gorbman, and Carol Vernallis (Oxford: Oxford University Press, 2013), 300.

24. Jacobs, *Decline of Sentiment*, 181.

25. Mordaunt Hall, "The Screen," *New York Times*, November 9, 1925, accessed August 19, 2019, https://www.nytimes.com/1925/11/09/archives/the-screen.html.

26. Schildgen, *More Than a Dream*, 75.

27. Emily Wortis Leider, *Dark Lover: The Life and Death of Rudolph Valentino* (London: Faber and Faber Limited, 2003), 355.

28. Eve Golden, *Vamp: The Rise and Fall of Theda Bara* (New York: Vestal Press, 1996), 38.

29. The newspapers that published the same column include *Carbondale Free Press*, IL, January 19, 1926, 1; *Connellsville Daily Courier*, PA, January 18, 1926, 7; *Kingston Daily Freeman*, NY, 18 January 1926, 11.

30. "Couldn't Stand It to See Anybody Kiss Vilma Banky," *Pittsburgh Press*, February 28, 1926, 103.

31. Cal York, Studio News and Gossip—East and West, *Photoplay*, March 1926, 108.

32. Additionally, the anecdote emphasized the international appeal of Hollywood product, sending a strong message regarding the power and global influence of film. Moving pictures can create an illusion of love so great that audiences might be fooled by it; Imre Lukatz lost sight of the fine line between fiction and reality after watching Valentino perform as Bánky's lover. Who would not be tempted to see their on-screen romance, knowing it was convincing enough to provoke real-life havoc?

33. Gaylyn Studlar, "*Out-Salomeing Salome*: Dance, the New Woman, and Fan Magazine Orientalism," in *Visions of the East: Orientalism in Film*, ed. Matthew Bernstein and Gaylyn Studlar (London: I.B. Tauris Publishers, 1997), 100.

34. Jeanine Basinger, *Silent Stars* (New York: Alfred A. Knopf, 1999), 299.

35. Edward W. Said, *Orientalism: Western Conceptions of the Orient* (Oxford: Penguin Books, 1995), 208.

36. Richard Dyer, *White: Essays on Race and Culture* (London: Routledge, 1997), 142.

37. John Kobal, *Hollywood Glamor Portraits: 145 Portraits of Stars, 1926–49* (New York: Dover Publications, 1976), x, cited in Stephen Gundle and Clino Castelli, *The Glamour System* (London: Palgrave Macmillan, 2006), 71.

38. Dyer, *White*, 122.

39. Dyer, *White*, 124.

40. Studlar, "*Out-Salomeing Salome*," 103.

41. Chris Edwards, *The Son of the Sheik*, April 26, 2009, http://silent-volume.blogspot.co.uk/2009/04/son-of-sheik-1926.html.

42. Richard Dyer, *Only Entertainment* (New York: Routledge, 2002), 120.

43. Marina Warner, *From the Beast to the Blonde* (London: Chatto & Windus, 1994), 366.

44. Laura Mulvey, *Fetishism and Curiosity* (London: BFI Publishing, 1996), 29–34.

45. Lucy Fisher, *Shot/Countershot: Film Tradition and Women's Cinema* (Princeton, NJ: Princeton University Press, 1989), 74–75.

46. Cited in Adrianne L. McLean, *Being Rita Hayworth: Labor, Identity, and Hollywood Stardom* (New Brunswick, NJ: Rutgers University Press, 2004), 156.

47. Wexman, *Creating the Couple*, 71; and John E. Connor and Peter C. Collins, "Introduction: The West, Westerns and American Character," in *Hollywood's West: The American Frontier in Film, Television, and History*, ed. John E. Connor and Peter C. Collins (Lexington: University Press of Kentucky, 2005), 2.

48. See Berg, *Goldwyn: A Biography*, 157; and Schildgen, *More Than a Dream*, 122.

49. Cari Beauchamp, *Without Lying Down: Frances Marion and the Powerful Women of Early Hollywood* (Berkeley and Los Angeles, CA, and London, UK: University of California Press, 1998), 183.

50. Winona Howe, "Almost Angels, Almost Feminists: Women in *The Professionals*," in *Hollywood's West: The American Frontier in Film, Television, and History*, ed. John E. Connor and Peter C. Collins (Lexington: University Press of Kentucky, 2005), 198.

51. Sean Redmond, "The Whiteness of the Rings," in *The Persistence of Whiteness*, ed. Daniel Bernardi (New York: Routledge, 2008), 93.

52. Wexman, *Creating the Couple*, 16.

53. Dyer, *White*, 17.

54. Cecelia Tichi, *Shifting Gears: Technology, Literature, Culture in Modernist America* (Chapel Hill: University of North Carolina Press, 1987), 122.

55. Dyer, *White*, 35.

56. Tichi, *Shifting Gears*, 124.

57. Beauchamp, *Without Lying Down*, 181.

58. Elisabeth Gibson, *It Happened in Nevada: Remarkable Events That Shaped History* (Guilford, CT: Morris Book Publishing, 2010), 83.

59. Cal York, "Studio News and Gossip—East and West," *Photoplay*, October 1926, 102.

60. York, "Studio News and Gossip," 102.

61. Norbert Lusk, "The Screen in Review," *Picture Play*, March 1927, 64.

62. Advertisement for The Magic Flame, *The Film Daily*, August 17, 1927, 4.

63. Richard Dyer, *Stars*, 2nd ed. (London: British Film Institute, 1998), 109.

64. Dyer, *White*, 113.

65. Redmond, "Whiteness of the Rings," 92.

66. Valerie Preston-Dunlop and Glen Hilling, *Dance and the Performative. A Choreological Perspective: Laban and Beyond* (London: Verve Publishing, 2002), 5.

67. Stéphane Mallarmé, "Ballets," trans. Evlyn Gould, *Performing Arts Journal* 15, no. 1 (January 1993): 107.

68. "Photoplay Gets Its Reviews Months Ahead of the Other Magazines: Check Up and See," *Photoplay*, May 1928, 54.

69. Laurence Reid, "The Celluloid Critic," *Motion Picture Classic*, June 1928, 77.

70. "At the Regent," *Ottawa Citizen*, October 8, 1928, 9.

71. James Chapman, *Swashbucklers: The Costume Adventure Series* (Manchester: Manchester University Press, 2015), 259.

72. "A Picture of Vilma Bánky," *Picture Play*, March 1928, 15.

73. McLean, *Being Rita Hayworth*, 103.

74. "Photoplay Gets Its Reviews Months Ahead of the Other Magazines," 54.

75. Schildgen, *More Than a Dream*, 135.

76. Delight Evans, "Delight Evans' Reviews: The Magic Flame," *Screenland*, December 1927, 45.

77. "Hot Mamas and Papas," *Motion Picture Classic*, October 1928, 72.

78. Berg, *Goldwyn: A Biography*, 175.

79. Jacobs, *The Decline of Sentiment*, 217.

80. Richards, *Swordsmen of the Screen*, 1.

81. Lusk, "Screen in Review," 64.

82. "A Flapjack of All Trades," *Motion Picture Classic*, July 1929, 42.

83. Ana Salzberg writes that "heavy accents had hindered the success of stars like Banky and Negri." *Beyond the Looking Glass: Narcissism and Female Stardom in Studio-Era Hollywood* (New York: Berghahn, 2014), 28.

84. Donald Crafton, *The Talkies: American Cinema's Transition to Sound, 1926–1931* (Berkeley: University of California Press, 1999), 490.

85. Marie House, "Garbo-*Romance*," *Screenland*, July 1930, 116.

86. Nancy Kimball, "Brickbats and Bouquets," *Photoplay*, July 1929, 110.

87. Reprinted in "Captivates New York with Her Latest Success," *Variety*, May 28, 1929, 19.

88. Reprinted in "Captivates New York with Her Latest Success," 19.

89. Another reason that *This Is Heaven* did not achieve great popularity with moviegoers might be because it offered a very limited experience in terms of synchronized sound. With only three scenes of dialogue in the film, it did not seem technologically advanced in comparison with other talking pictures released in the same year.

90. Berg, *Goldwyn: A Biography*, 185.

91. Wexman, *Creating the Couple*, 22.

92. Stanley Cavell, "Reflections on the Ontology of Film," in *Movie Acting: The Film Reader*, ed. Pamela Robertson Wojcik (London: Routledge, 2004), 30.

93. "The Shadow Stage," *Photoplay*, May 1929, 56.

94. "Screen in Review," *Picture Play*, July 1929, 94.

95. Stephen Sharot, *Love and Marriage across Social Classes in American Cinema* (Cham, Switzerland: Palgrave Macmillan, 2017), 121.

96. Lois Banner, *Women in Modern America: A Brief History* (New York: Harcourt Brace Jovanovich, 1974), 18.

97. Sumiko Higashi, *Cecil B. DeMille and American Culture* (Oakland: University of California Press, 1994), 62–63.

98. Steven J. Ross, *Working-Class Hollywood: Silent Film and the Shaping of Class in America* (Princeton, NJ: Princeton University Press, 1999), 176.

99. Lisa Rose Stead, "*So Oft to the Movies They've Been*: British Fan Writing and Female Audiences in the Silent Cinema," *Transformative Works and Cultures* 6 (2011), accessed August 19, 2019, http://journal.transformativeworks.org/index.php/twc/article/view/224/210.

100. "Screen in Review," 94.

CHAPTER 5 — VILMA BÁNKY AND MARRIAGE

Chapter subtitle: "My mother brought me up to be a wife," Dorothy Donnell, "Lessons in Love," *Motion Picture Classic*, August 1929, 18–19.

1. Rachel Schildgen, *More Than a Dream: Rediscovering the Life and Films of Vilma Bánky* (Hollywood, CA: 1921 PVG Publishing, 2010), 155.

2. A. Scott Berg, *Goldwyn: A Biography* (New York: Alfred A. Knopf, 1989), 167–168.

3. Schildgen, *More Than a Dream*, 154.

4. Estelle B. Freedman, "The New Woman: Changing Views of Women in the 1920s," *Journal of American History* 61 (1974): 388.

5. Margaret Reid, "Vilma—As She Is," *Picture Play*, July 1928, 43.

6. Schildgen, *More Than a Dream*, 146.

7. Jan-Christopher Horak, "Sauerkraut & Sausages with a Little Goulash: Germans in Hollywood, 1927," *Film History: An International Journal* 17, nos. 2/3 (2005): 243.

8. Berg, *Goldwyn: A Biography*, 167.

9. Schildgen, *More Than a Dream*, 82.

10. Kristin Thompson, "The Formulation of the Classical Style, 1909-1928," in *The Classical Hollywood Cinema: Film Style and Mode of Production to 1960s*, ed. David Bordwell, Janet Staiger, and Kristin Thompson (London: Routledge, 1996), 341.

11. Katherine Lipke, "Rod Takes the Bitter with the Sweet," *Picture Play*, June 1927, 74.

12. "Please Stand By for Classic's Late News," *Motion Picture Classic*, June 1927, 8.

13. Dorothy Manners, "Looking Them Over Out Hollywood Way," *Motion Picture Classic*, July 1927, 33, 60.

14. Edwin Schallert and Elza Schallert, "Hollywood Highlights," *Picture Play*, July 1927, 55.

15. Elizabeth Greer and Dorothy Donnell, "News of the Camera Coasts," *Motion Picture Magazine*, July 1927, 50.

16. Grace Kingsley, "When Love Came to Stay," *Picture Play*, May 1928, 88.

17. Doris Denbo, "What Do Women Seek in Marriage?," *Motion Picture Magazine*, March 1927, 41.

18. Lois Banner, *Women in Modern America: A Brief History* (New York: Harcourt Brace Jovanovich, 1974), 257.

19. Jane Gaines, "War, Women and Lipstick: Fan Mags in the Forties," *Heresies*, no.18 (1985): 43, cited in Adrienne L. McLean, *Being Rita Hayworth: Labor, Identity and Hollywood Stardom* (New Brunswick, NJ: Rutgers University Press, 2004), 98.

20. Dorothy Manners, "Looking Them Over Out Hollywood Way," *Motion Picture Classic*, September 1927, 89.

21. "Streets Thronged as Film Stars Wed," *New York Times*, June 27, 1927, 1.

22. Samantha Barbas, *The First Lady of Hollywood: A Biography of Louella Parsons* (Berkeley: University of California Press, 2005), 112.

23. Alan Hynd and Dorothy Calhoun, "News of the Camera Coasts," *Motion Picture Magazine*, September 1927, 103.

24. Hedda Hopper to Sallie, July 13, 1927, Hedda Hopper Papers, Banky, Vilma f.674, Margaret Herrick Library, Los Angeles.

25. Stephen Birmingham, *"The Rest of Us:" The Rise of America's Eastern European Jews* (Syracuse, NY: Syracuse University Press, 1984), 196.

26. Elza Schallert, "Hollywood's Great Romance," *Picture Play*, October 1927, 54.

27. Both of Bánky's parents, however, were alive at the time. There is no evidence to suggest that any effort was made to invite them to the ceremony.

28. Schallert, "Hollywood's Great Romance," 95.

29. Malcolm H. Oettinger, "Please Don't Quote Me," *Picture Play*, November 1927, 20.

30. Cal York, "Gossip of All the Studios," *Photoplay*, September 1927, 44.

31. The film widely considered to be the first talking picture, *The Jazz Singer*, came out in 1927, but the industry's switch from silents to talkies was gradual.

32. Ben Lindsey and Wainwright Evans, *The Companionate Marriage* (New York: Boni & Liveright, 1927).

33. Christina Simmons, *Making Marriage Modern: Women's Sexuality from the Progressive Era to World War II* (Oxford: Oxford University Press, 2009), 122.

34. Dorothy Donnell, "Lessons in Love," *Motion Picture Classic*, August 1929, 18–19.

35. Ruth Biery, "Companionate Stardom," *Photoplay*, March 1928, 48.

36. Julian B. Carter, *The Heart of Whiteness: Normal Sexuality and Race in America, 1880–1940* (Durham, NC: Duke University Press, 2007), 9–11; Jenny Hockey, Angela Meah, and Victoria Robinson, *Mundane Heterosexualities: From Theory to Practices* (Basingstoke, UK: Palgrave Macmillan, 2007), 11.

37. Carter, *Heart of Whiteness*, 47.

38. Schallert, "Hollywood's Great Romance," 95.

39. See Lipke, "Rod Takes the Bitter with the Sweet," 74.

40. Dorothy Spensley, "Big Lens and Focus Men. Celebrities Who Are Always behind a Camera When They're Not before One," *Motion Picture Classic*, January 1929, 30–31.

41. "What They Think about Marriage!," *Photoplay*, April 1921, 20–22. The piece interviewed Cecil B. DeMille, Gloria Swanson, and Pearl White, among other celebrities.

42. Gaylyn Studlar, "The Perils of Pleasure? Fan Magazine Discourse as Women's Commodified Culture in the 1920s," in *Silent Film*, ed. Richard Abel (New Brunswick, NJ: Rutgers University Press, 1995), 270.

43. Carter, *Heart of Whiteness*, 40.

44. See Dorothy Spensley, "Languishing Romances," *Photoplay*, September 1925, 28–29.

45. Ruth Waterbury, "Why Women Like Sophisticated Men," *Photoplay*, May 1926, 32–33.

46. Banner, *Women in Modern America*, 150.

47. Freedman, "New Woman," 377.

48. Greg M. Smith, "Silencing New Woman: Ethnic and Social Mobility in the Melodramas of Norma Talmadge," *Journal of Film and Video* 48, no. 3 (Fall 1996): 4.

49. Studlar, "Perils of Pleasure?," 282.

50. Alice Kessler-Harris, *Out to Work: A History of Wage-Earning Women in the United States* (Oxford: Oxford University Press, 2003), 107.

51. Hillary A. Hallett, *Go West, Young Women! The Rise of Early Hollywood* (Los Angeles: University of California Press, 2013), 215.

52. "What They Think about Marriage!," 20–22. Such a statement has special relevance to Norma Talmadge, as the star was married to a film producer, Joseph Scheck, from 1916 to 1934.

53. Diane Negra, *Off-White Hollywood: American Culture and Ethnic Female Stardom* (London: Routledge, 2001), 37.

54. Although descriptions relating to Pickford came in the mid-1910s rather than the mid-1920s, their strategy is similar to that used in the press accounts of Bánky's work, particularly her nearly paternal relationship with her producer (discussed at length in the previous chapter of this case study). For more discussion on Pickford, see Richard Abel, *Menus for Movieland: Newspapers and the Emergence of American Film Culture, 1913–1916* (Oakland: University of California Press, 2015), 162.

55. Schallert, "Hollywood's Great Romance," 55.

56. Donnell, "Lessons in Love," August 1929, 18, 87.

57. Reid, "Vilma-As She Is," 43.

58. Anke Brouwers, "Letters from a Well-Known Woman: Domesticity and Professionalism in Mary Pickford's *Daily Talks* (1915–1917)," *Celebrity Studies* 3, no. 8 (2017): 432.

59. "Marriage Helps You Work Along, Aver Rod and Vilma, in One Voice," *Kokomo Daily Tribune*, IN, November 14, 1927, 12.

60. Donnell, "Lessons in Love," August 1929, 87.

61. Leatrice Joy, "Would I Want My Daughter to Be an Actress?," *Picture Play*, August 1925, 18.

62. Myrtle Gebhart, "The Discovery of Vilma Banky," *Picture Play*, February 1926, 34.

63. Donnell, "Lessons in Love," August 1929, 18–19.

64. Banner, *Women in Modern America*, 142.

65. Karen Sternheimer, *Celebrity Culture and the American Dream: Stardom and Social Mobility* (London: Routledge, 2011), 19.

66. Shelley Stamp, "An Awful Struggle between Love and Ambition: Serial Heroines, Serial Stars and Their Female Fans," in *Silent Cinema Reader*, ed. Lee Grieveson and Peter Krämer (New York and London: Routledge, 2004), 222.

67. Brouwers, "Letters from a Well-Known Woman," 440.

68. Biery, "Companionate Stardom," 92.

69. Francesca Sawaya, *Modern Women, Modern Work: Domesticity, Professionalism, and American Writing, 1890–1950* (Philadelphia: University of Pennsylvania Press, 2004), 1.

70. Biery, "Companionate Stardom," 92.

71. The phrase is used by Negra in reference to a different movie star, but it is applicable here. See Negra, *Off-White Hollywood*, 88.

72. Simon Dixon, "Ambiguous Ecologies: Stardom's Domestic Mise-en-Scène," *Cinema Journal* 42, no. 2 (Winter 2003): 83.

73. Dixon, "Ambiguous Ecologies," 82.

74. The exotic appeal of Negri's persona is extended to and visualized in her surroundings, which include Chinese vases and decorative parasols. See "When Pola Rests," *Picture Play,* March 1925, 80.

75. "In a Little Love Nest for Two," *Motion Picture Magazine*, April 1925, 72.

76. Negra, *Off-White Hollywood*, 3.

77. Antonella Palmieri, "Passport to the Dream Factory: Hollywood and the Exotic Allure of Female Italian Ethnicity" (PhD thesis, University of East Anglia, 2011), 164.

78. Dorothy Donnell, "Their Country, *Tis of Thee*," *Motion Picture Classic*, July 1929, 16–17.

79. William McKegg, "She Refuses to Glitter," *Picture Play*, June 1929, 112.

80. See Heiner Gillmeister, *Tennis: A Cultural History* (London: Leicester University Press, 1997), 194; and Richard Moorhead and Nick Wynne, *Golf in Florida 1886-1950* (Chicago: Arcadia Publishing, 2008), 7.

81. Arne Lunde, *Nordic Exposures: Scandinavian Identities in Classical Hollywood Cinema* (Seattle: University of Washington Press, 2010), 172.

82. John Highson, David Inglis, and Marcus Free, *The Uses of Sport: A Critical Study* (London: Routledge, 2005), 15–19.

83. Kathleen Drowne and Patrick Huber, *The 1920s* (Westport, CT: Greenwood Press, 2005), 154.

84. Edwin Schallert and Elza Schallert, "Hollywood Highlights," *Picture Play,* June 1927, 64.

85. "News and Gossip of All the Studios," *Photoplay*, May 1927, 108.

86. William H. McKegg, "*Must* They Become American?," *Picture Play*, May 1928, 66.

87. McKegg, "She Refuses to Glitter," 64.

88. "Uncle Sam" signifies the popular personification of American government, although it is notable that it could also apply to Samuel (Sam) Goldwyn. See "Last Minute News," *Motion Picture Classic*, January 1929, 6.

89. One of the articles upholding that view is McKegg's, "She Refuses to Glitter," 112.

90. McKegg, "She Refuses to Glitter," 64.

91. Palmieri, "Passport to the Dream Factory," 26.

92. Gladys Hall, "Can They Stay Retired?," *Motion Picture Classic*, October 1930, 86. Interestingly, Bánky and La Rocque never had children.

93. Schildgen, *More Than a Dream*, 207.

94. Richard Dyer, *Stars* (London: BFI, 1998), 26; and John Ellis, *Visible Fictions: Cinema, Television, Video* (London: Routledge, 1982), 91–108.

95. Freedman, "New Woman," 377; and Banner, *Women in Modern America*, 150.

CHAPTER 6 — JETTA GOUDAL AND EXOTICISM

Chapter subtitle: "She looks like a beautiful Cossack. She looks like an Oriental princess," Harry Carr, "Jetta and Her Temperament," *Motion Picture Classic*, October 1924, 20.

1. "A Picturesque Newcomer," *Picture Play*, July 1923, 80. It is worth noting that Pola Negri also incarnated a half-Chinese woman in one of her vehicles, *East of Suez* (1925).

2. Edwin Schallert, "A Forecast for 1924," *Picture Play*, February 1924, 21.

3. "Martinique" was a working title for the film released as *The Bright Shawl*. See "Greenroom Jottings," *Motion Picture Magazine*, January 1924, 115.

4. The term "wicked half-caste" was used by *Picture Play*. See Malcolm H. Oettinger, "A Gesture from Jetta," *Picture Play*, October 1927, 34.

5. Goudal was cast as a French woman in *Paris at Midnight* (1926), *Open All Night* (1924), *The Forbidden Woman* (1927), and *The Lady of the Pavements* (1929). She portrayed a Russian aristocrat in *The Coming of Amos* (1925), an Italian woman (Donna Vittoria) in *Fighting Love* (1927), and an Indian character in *Green Goddess* (1923). She was cast as a German heroine in *Her Man O' War* (1926) and as a Spanish woman in *The Spaniard* (1925), although the former film was set in Germany and the latter in Spain, with all the characters being of either German or Spanish origin.

6. Ella Shohat, "Gender and Culture of Empire: Toward a Feminist Ethnography of the Cinema," *Quarterly Review of Film and Video* 13, nos. 1–3 (1991): 63.

7. Edward Said, "Orientalism," in *The Post-Colonial Studies Reader*, ed. Bill Ashcroft, Gareth Griffiths, and Helen Tiffin (London: Routledge, 1995), 87.

8. Karla Rae Fuller, *Hollywood Goes Oriental: CaucAsian Performance in American Film* (Detroit: Wayne State University Press, 2010), 2.

9. Dorothy Donnell, "The Mistress of Mystery," *Motion Picture Classic*, February 1929, 22.

10. One of the studio's publicity pieces also used the association between the Orient and femininity by calling Goudal "orchid-like." Advertising of Pathé Exchange Inc., *Picture Play*, January 1928, 9.

11. William McKegg, "Uncensored Observations," *Picture Play*, December 1926, 87.

12. Antonia Lant, "The Curse of the Pharaoh, or How Cinema Contracted Egyptomania," in *Visions of the East: Orientalism in Film*, ed. Matthew Bernstein and Gaylyn Studlar (London: I.B. Tauris Publishers, 1997), 89.

13. Goudal had a nose that "one might term Mongolian." See Myrtle Gebhart, "Why Their Roles Fit Them," *Picture Play*, June 1928, 70–71. *Motion Picture Classic* discussed the potential Javanese heritage in Goudal's bloodline (and that she might be the lost daughter of Mata Hari): "Jetta Goudal has told one or two friends in Hollywood that her grandfather was in the consular service in Java for some years. Which might explain that haunting strangeness of hers that is not quite European and certainly not bred on Wisconsin farms or in the East Side Ghetto." Donnell, "Mistress of Mystery," 22.

14. Carr, "Jetta and Her Temperament," 20.

15. Margaret Reid, "A Persecuted Lady," *Picture Play*, May 1926, 74. Historically, the term "Hindu" stretched beyond religion and tended to be used as a geographical or ethnical identifier. See Brian K. Pennington, *Was Hinduism Invented? Britons, Indians, and the Colonial Construction of Religion* (Oxford: Oxford University Press, 2007), 111–118.

16. Fuller, *Hollywood Goes Oriental*, 2.

17. Carol Van Wyck, "Girl's Problems," *Photoplay*, February 1929, 92.

18. Myrtle Gebhart, "Never an Emerald without a Flaw," *Picture Play*, February 1928, 108.

19. Gebhart, "Never an Emerald without a Flaw," 108.

20. Vron Ware, "Perfidious Albion: Whiteness and the International Imagination," in *The Making and Unmaking of Whiteness*, ed. Brigitte Branden Rasmussen, Eric Klinenberg, Irene J. Nexica, and Matt Wray (Durham, NC: Duke University Press, 2001), 191.

21. Richard Dyer, *White: Essays on Race and Culture* (London: Routledge, 1997), 45.

22. M. M. Edgelow, "What Fans Think," *Picture Play*, May 1927, 115.

23. Reid, "A Persecuted Lady," 74.

24. The quotes come from, consecutively, Doris Blake, "How to Win a Man—Vamp with a Soul Likes Them with Brains," *Sunday News*, March 18, 1923, 10; and Oettinger, "Gesture from Jetta," 34. The article that compares Goudal to Negri and Barbara La Marr is Carr's "Jetta and Her Temperament," 78. The comparison to Alla Nazimova is drawn in Malcolm H. Oettinger, "Sapristi!—How Foreign!," *Picture Play*, November 1923, 22.

25. Rebecca L. Epstein, "Sharon Stone in a Gap Turtleneck," in *Hollywood Goes Shopping*, ed. David Desser and Garth Jowett (Minneapolis: University of Minnesota Press, 2000), 180.

26. Laura Mulvey, *Visual and Other Pleasures* (London: Palgrave, 1989), 25.

27. Jackie Stacey, *Star Gazing: Hollywood Cinema and Female Spectatorship* (London: Routledge, 1994), 207.

28. Myrtle Gebhart, "Why Their Roles Fit Them," *Picture Play*, June 1928, 70–71.

29. Ella Shohat and Robert Stam, *Unthinking Eurocentrism: Multiculturalism and the Media* (London: Routledge, 2001), 169.

30. Marguerite Rippy, "Commodity, Tragedy, Desire: Female Sexuality and Blackness in the Iconography of Dorothy Dandridge," in *Classic Hollywood, Classic Whiteness*, ed. Daniel Bernardi (Minneapolis: University of Minnesota Press, 2001), 203.

31. Francesca T. Royster, *Becoming Cleopatra: The Shifting Image of an Icon* (New York: Palgrave Macmillan, 2003), 97.

32. Pam Cook, "Picturing Natacha Rambova: Design and Celebrity Performance in the 1920s," in "Women and the Silent Screen," special dossier, *Screening the Past*, no. 40, September 15, 2015, accessed August 19, 2019, http://www.screeningthepast.com/2015/08/picturing-natacha-rambova-design-and-celebrity-performance-in-the-1920s/.

33. Matthew Bernstein, introduction to *Visions of the East: Orientalism in Film*, ed. Matthew Bernstein and Gaylyn Studlar (London: I.B. Tauris Publishers, 1997), 3.

34. Gaylyn Studlar, "*Out-Salomeing Salome*: Dance, the New Woman, and Fan Magazine Orientalism," in *Visions of the East: Orientalism in Film*, ed. Matthew Bernstein and Gaylyn Studlar (London: I.B. Tauris Publishers, 1997), 100.

35. Stephen Gundle and Clino Castelli, *The Glamour System* (Basingstoke: Palgrave Macmillan, 2006), 88.

36. Naomi Rosenblatt, "Orientalism in American Popular Culture," *Penn History Review* 16, no. 2 (Spring 2009): 63.

37. Adam Geczy, *Fashion and Orientalism: Dress, Textiles and Culture from the 17th to the 21st Century* (London: Bloomsbury, 2013), 150–151.

38. Lucy Fisher, *Cinema by Design: Art Nouveau, Modernism and Film* (New York: Columbia University Press, 2017), 71.

39. David S. Shields, *Still: American Silent Motion Picture Photography* (Chicago: University of Chicago Press, 2013), 244–245.

40. Cook, "Picturing Natacha Rambova."

41. See, for instance, Maureen Turim, "Seduction and Elegance: The New Woman of Fashion in Silent Cinema," in *On Fashion*, ed. Shari Benstock and Suzanne Ferris (New Brunswick, NJ: Rutgers University Press, 1994), 140–158.

42. Anna Prophater, "Rodolph Valentino and Marriage," *Screenland*, October 1923, 22.

43. Malcolm H. Oettinger, "Sapristi!—How Foreign!," *Picture Play*, November 1923, 22.

44. Jean Pierrot, *The Decadent Imagination, 1880-1900* (Chicago: University of Chicago Press, 1981), 27.

45. Gundle and Castelli, *Glamour System*, 65.

46. Gundle and Castelli, *Glamour System*, 97. See also Camille Paglia, *The Birds* (London: British Film Institute Publishing, 1998), 28.

47. Films referred to are, consecutively, *Judith of Bethulia* (1914), *Cleopatra* (1917), and *Salomé* (1922). See also Petra Dierkes-Thrun, *Alla Nazimova's Salomé: An Historical Phantasy by Oscar Wilde* (Ann Arbor: University of Michigan Press, 2011), 144.

48. These attributes are listed by Antonia Lant in her "Cinema in the Times of the Pharaohs," in *The Ancient World in Silent Cinema*, ed. Pantelis Michelakis and Maria Wyke (Cambridge: Cambridge University Press, 2013), 53.

49. Cook, "Picturing Natacha Rambova."

50. Cook, "Picturing Natacha Rambova."

51. Ruth Overton, "Stills between Shots," *Motion Picture Magazine*, April 1923, 108.

52. Overton, "Stills between Shots," 108.

53. In the novel of the same title, on which the film was based, Joseph Hergesheimer goes on to describe Pilar's "Chinese attributes," particularly her face, as "evenly, opaquely, pale, . . . flat, an oval which held eyes with full, ivory-like lids, narrow eye brows, a straight small nose and lips heavily coated with a carmine that failed utterly to disguise their level strength." Joseph Hergesheimer, *The Bright Shawl* (New York: Alfred A. Knopf, 1922), page unknown, available at Project Gutenberg, accessed August 20, 2019, http://www.gutenberg.org/files/31898/31898-h/31898-h.htm.

54. "Films in Review," *Visual Education*, June 1923, 195.

55. Photograph of Jetta Goudal, *Motion Picture Classic*, June 1923, 21.

56. Richard Martin and Harold Koda, *Orientalism: Visions of the East in Western Dress* (New York: Metropolitan Museum of Art, 1994), 29.

57. The quoted phrase comes from Anzia Yezierska, *Salome of the Tenements* (Urbana: University of Illinois Press, 1995), 5. Goudal's first bigger role came in the form of a young Parisian in Paul Bern's satire *Open All Night* (1924). Because her role in the film is not a supporting one, I limit its analysis and description. Goudal's character, Lea, is desperately in love with an unfaithful cyclist called Petit Mathieu. To make him jealous, she decides to pretend she is romantically involved with another man. The film concentrates on the married couple whose lives are intertwined with that intrigue.

58. Alan Robert Ginsberg, *The Salome Ensemble: Rose Pastor Stokes, Anzia Yezierska, Sonya Levien, and Jetta Goudal* (New York: Syracuse University Press, 2016), 16.

59. Mordaunt Hall, "The Screen: Review of Salome of the Tenements," *New York Times*, February 24, 1925, accessed August 20, 2019, http://www.nytimes.com/movie/review?res=9F01E3D91038E233A25757C2A9649C946495D6CF.

60. "The Shadow Stage," *Photoplay*, May 1925, 47.

61. The phrase is used in "The Shadow Stage," 47.

62. This element of such stories is elaborated on in the context of Pola Negri and her on-screen incarnations of gypsy dancers. See chapter 2.

63. Catherine Rottenberg, "*Salome of the Tenements*, the American Dream and Class Performativity," *American Studies* 45, no. 1 (Spring 2004): 70; Emmett J. Winn, "Moralizing Upward Mobility: Investigating the Myth of Class Mobility in *Working Girl*," *Southern Communication Journal* 66, no. 1 (2000): 42–48.

64. Yezierska, *Salome of the Tenements*, 71.

65. Gay Wilentz, introduction to *Salome of the Tenements*, by Anzia Yezierska (Urbana: University of Illinois Press, 1995), xviii.

66. Marguerite Orndorff, "The Theatrical Field," *Educational Screen*, May 1925, 290.

67. Gundle and Castelli, *Glamour System*, 92.

68. Palmieri pays particular attention to two of Valli's American films: *The Miracle of the Bells* (1948) and *Walk Softly, Stranger* (1950). Although both films were made in the late 1940s, I see Palmieri's analysis as relevant to *The Coming of Amos*. See Antonella Palmieri, "Passport to the Dream Factory: Hollywood and the Exotic Allure of Female Italian Ethnicity" (PhD thesis, University of East Anglia, 2011), 119.

69. "From the Shadow Stage: A Review of the New Pictures," *Photoplay*, March 1926, 54.

70. "From the Shadow Stage," 54.

71. Sally Benson, "From the Shadow Stage," *Picture Play*, April 1926, 65.

72. Norbert Lusk, "The Screen in Review," *Picture Play*, February 1928, 67.

73. Larry Langman, *American Cycles: Silent Film* (London: Greenwood Press, 1998), 100.

74. Jetta Goudal Vintage Original Photo 1927 "Forbidden Woman" Headdress Portrait, accessed August 19, 2019, https://uk.pinterest.com/pin/217017275770468477/.

75. This quote from *Moving Picture World* is included in the advertisement for *The Forbidden Woman*. See "Jetta Goudal—A Positive Sensation in *The Forbidden Woman*," *Film Daily*, December 18, 1927, back of the cover page.

76. The quote comes from *N.Y. Morning Telegraph*, and it is included in the advertisement for *The Forbidden Woman*. See "Jetta Goudal—A Positive Sensation in *The Forbidden Woman*," back of the cover page.

77. "Photoplay Gets Its Reviews Months Ahead of All Other Magazines, Check Out and See," *Photoplay*, December 1927, 55.

78. Rosie White, *Violent Femmes: Women as Spies in Popular Culture* (London: Routledge, 2007), 1.

79. White, *Violent Femmes*, 1.

80. Julie Wheelwright, *The Fatal Lover: Mata Hari and the Myth of Women in Espionage* (London: Collins and Brown Limited, 1992), 5.

81. The figure of Mata Hari, a Dutch-born dancer and a supposedly "Oriental" spy, exemplifies the conflation of orientalism and espionage. See Wheelwright, *Fatal Lover*, 4–6.

82. Oettinger, "Sapristi!—How Foreign!," 22.

83. Oettinger, "A Gesture from Jetta," 34.

84. Walter Adolphe Roberts, "Confidences Off-Screen," *Motion Picture Magazine*, February 1925, 24.

85. Lawrence Napper, *The Great War in Popular British Cinema of the 1920s: Before Journey's End* (London: Palgrave, 2015), 94–95. Although Napper's discussion is largely limited to British cinema, he points out that war films were particularly popular in Hollywood between 1926 and 1928.

86. William Boyd, "A Confidential Guide to New Releases," *Picture Play*, January 1926, 65.

87. Norbert Lusk, "The Screen in Review," *Picture Play*, December 1926, 110.

88. Richard Koszarski, *Hollywood on the Hudson: Film and Television in New York from Griffith to Sarnoff* (New Brunswick, NJ: Rutgers University Press, 2010), 474.

89. Denise Lowe, *An Encyclopaedic Dictionary of Women in Early American Film* (New York: Routledge, 2013), 117. See also Mordaunt Hall, "The Sheep Rancher," *New York Times*, April 11, 1927, 11.

90. Jimmy Franco Sr., "Silent Images of Latinos in Early Hollywood," interview with Stephen Sariñana-Lampson, January 10, 2011, accessed August 19, 2019, https://cinesilentemexicano.wordpress.com/2011/06/10/silent-images-of-latinos-in-early-hollywood/.

91. Rayna Green, "Pocahontas Perplex," in *Unequal Sisters: A Multicultural Reader in U.S. Women's History*, ed. Ellen Carol DuBois and Vicki L. Ruiz (New York: Routledge, 1990), 17–18.

92. The sentence is a reworking of ideas developed by Mary-Kay Gamel in relation to *Chinatown* (1974) that I found applicable to *White Gold.* See Mary-Kay Gamel, "An American Tragedy: Chinatown," in *Classical Myth & Culture in the Cinema*, ed. Martin M. Winkler (Oxford: Oxford University Press, 2001), 160.

93. María Raquél Casas, *Spanish-Mexican Women and Interethnic Marriage in California, 1820-1880* (Reno: University of Nevada Press, 2007), 21.

94. The expression was originally used by *Motion Picture Classic.* See Carr, "Jetta and Her Temperament," 20.

95. Donnell, "Mistress of Mystery," 22.

CHAPTER 7 — JETTA GOUDAL AND MYSTERY

Chapter subtitle: "A riddle in the city of eager autobiographies," Margaret Reid, "A Persecuted Lady," *Picture Play*, May 1926, 74.

1. Myrtle Gebhart, "Does Popularity in Hollywood Bring Success on Screen?," *Picture Play*, August 1927, 18.

2. Margaret Reid, "A Persecuted Lady," *Picture Play*, May 1926, 74.

3. Antonella Palmieri, "Passport to the Dream Factory: Hollywood and the Exotic Allure of Female Italian Ethnicity" (PhD thesis, University of East Anglia, 2011), 78.

4. Ella Shohat, "Gender and Culture of Empire: Toward a Feminist Ethnography of the Cinema," *Quarterly Review of Film and Video* 13, nos. 1/3 (1991): 63.

5. Richard Dyer, *Stars* (London: British Film Institute, 1979), 24.

6. Ramirez uses the term "diva" in relation to the female stars of the silent period in Italy. For her, "the diva is a figure whose origins are located in the received repertory of images and themes from decadent novels and the Italian silent cinema." Joy Ramirez, "Silent Divas: The *Femme Fatales* of Italian *Cinema Muto*," in *The Femme Fatale: Images, Histories, Contexts*, ed. Helen Hanson and Catherine O'Rawe (London: Palgrave Macmillan, 2010), 61–63.

7. Michaela Krutzen, *The Most Beautiful Woman on Screen: Fabrication of the Star Greta Garbo* (Frankfurt am Mein: Peter Lang AG, 1992), 42. Some silent stars, such as Douglas Fairbanks, went crashing down from their transcendent status, as their speaking voices did not match their image.

8. DeWitt Bodeen and Gene Ringgold, *The Films of Cecil B. DeMille* (New York: Citadel Press, 1974), 452.

9. Sean P. Holmes, "No Room for Manoeuvre: Star Images and the Regulation of Actors' Labor in Silent Era Hollywood," in *Working in the Global Film and Television Industries: Creativity, Systems, Space, Patronage*, ed. Andrew Dawson and Sean P. Holmes (London: Bloomsbury Academic, 2012), 77.

10. The name of the publicist was Sig Schlager; he expressed this view in a letter to Goudal. See Anthony Slide, *Silent Players: A Biographical and Autobiographical Study of 100 Silent Film Actors and Actresses* (Lexington: University Press of Kentucky, 2002), 147.

11. Holmes, "No Room for Manoeuvre," 77.

12. Simon Dixon, "Ambiguous Ecologies: Stardom's Domestic Mise-en-Scène," *Cinema Journal*, 42, no. 2 (Winter 2003): 82.

13. Edwin Schallert, "How the Stars Stay Famous," *Picture Play*, December 1926, 95.

14. Francis Clark, "Jetta Lives Down Her Past," *Photoplay*, August 1927, 35.

15. Walter Ramsey, "The Hotbed of Whoopee," *Motion Picture Classic*, February 1929, 31.

16. Reid, "Persecuted Lady," 74.

17. Clark, "Jetta Lives Down Her Past," 35.

18. Holmes, "No Room for Manoeuvre," 75.

19. Dorothy Donnell, "The Mistress of Mystery," *Motion Picture Classic*, February 1929, 22.

20. The link between Garbo and the sphinx, on which the article also elaborated, was taken even further in the following years. In 1931, Clarence Sinclair Bull created a famous montage of Garbo's face on the top of the sphinx, thus creating a "Swedish Sphinx." Alexander Doty writes that the nickname was devised by MGM's publicity department. See his "Marlene Dietrich and Greta Garbo: The Sexy Hausfrau versus the Swedish Sphinx," in *Glamour in a Golden Age: Movie Stars of the 1930s*, ed. Adrienne L. McLean (New Brunswick, NJ: Rutgers University Press, 2011), 118. See also Michael Williams, *Film Stardom and the Ancient Past: Idols, Artefacts and Epics* (London: Palgrave Macmillan, 2017), 26.

21. William H. McKegg, "The Three Sphinxes," *Picture Play*, July 1929, 89.

22. Evelyn West, "Hidden Histories," *Motion Picture Magazine*, December 1928, 34.

23. Marquis Busby, "Overtime Acting," *Motion Picture Classic*, August 1928, 79.

24. Busby, "Overtime Acting," 79.

25. Myrtle Gebhart, "Have Foreigners a Chance Now?," *Picture Play*, October 1929, 113.

26. L. Bailey, "What the Fans Think," *Picture Play*, March 1929, 12.

27. Sumiko Higashi, "1927: Movies and the New Woman as Consumer," in *American Cinema of the 1920s: Themes and Variations*, ed. Lucy Fisher (New Brunswick, NJ: Rutgers University Press, 2009), 210.

28. Holmes, "No Room for Manoeuvre," 77.

29. Garbo portrayed Leonora Moreno in *The Torrent* (1926), her first American feature; a French woman in *The Temptress* (1926); and Anna Karenina in *Love* (1927). Later in her career, she was cast as Marie Walewska in *Conquest* (1937) and Queen Christina in the film of the same title, released in 1933. Both films in question were made in the 1930s and are not a subject of this work; however, I suggest that the trend of casting Garbo in roles of non-American heroines spanned across her entire career.

30. Ginette Vincendeau and Alastair Phillips, introduction to *Journeys of Desire. European Actors in Hollywood: A Critical Companion*, ed. Alastair Phillips and Ginette Vincendeau (London: British Film Institute Publishing, 2006), 96.

31. Berry's argument, however valid, does not account for Garbo, a Swedish star who portrayed a famous Swedish queen in *Queen Christina*. See Sarah Berry, "Hollywood Exoticism," in *Stars: The Film Reader*, ed. Lucy Fisher and Marcia Landy (London: Routledge, 2004), 189.

32. Laura Horak, "Queer Crossings: Greta Garbo, National Identity and Gender Deviance," in *Silent Film and the Politics of Space*, ed. Jennifer Bean (Bloomington: Indiana University Press, 2014), 271.

33. Doris Blake, "How to Win a Man—Vamp with a Soul Likes Them with Brains," *Sunday News*, PA, March 18, 1923, 10.

34. Blake, "How to Win a Man," 10.

35. My analysis of articles from *Picture Play, Motion Picture Classic, Motion Picture Magazine*, and *Photoplay* reveals that Goudal was not presented as Franco-Dutch as often as she was presented as French in the years after 1924. However, this was not a rule. For example, Margaret Reid of *Picture Play* described Goudal as both Dutch and French in May 1926.

36. Barbara Little, "Preserving an Illusion," *Picture Play*, May 1923, 74.

37. "A Picturesque Newcomer," *Picture Play*, July 1923, 80.

38. Blake, "How to Win a Man," 10.

39. Cal York, "Studio News and Gossip—East and West," *Photoplay*, August 1924, 92.

40. Harry Carr, "Jetta and Her Temperament," *Motion Picture Classic*, October 1924, 20.

41. Carr, "Jetta and Her Temperament," 78.

42. Evelyn West, "Hidden Histories," *Motion Picture Magazine*, December 1928, 34.

43. Stephen Gundle and Clino Castelli, *The Glamour System* (London: Palgrave Macmillan, 2006), 90.

44. Véronique Pouillard, "In the Shadow of Paris? French Haute Couture and Belgian Fashions between the Wars," in *Producing Fashion: Commerce, Culture, and Consumers*, ed. Regina Lee Blaszczyk (Philadelphia: University of Pennsylvania Press, 2008), 64.

45. Richard Marchand, *Advertising the American Dream: Making Way for Modernity, 1920–1940* (Berkeley: University of California Press, 1986), 196.

46. Dorothy Donnell Calhoun, "What Do the Film Stars DO with All Their Old Clothes?," *Motion Picture Magazine*, April 1925, 122.

47. Margaret Reid, "Do the Stars Dress Badly?," *Picture Play*, April 1929, 72.

48. S. Hillybues, "What the Fans Think," *Picture Play*, March 1927, 115.

49. Donnell, "Mistress of Mystery," 22.

50. McKegg, "Three Sphinxes," 89.

51. Mejuffrouw Van Deventer, "What the Fans Think," *Picture Play*, September 1928, 117.

52. Harold Hunt, "Actress Is Busy with Rehearsals," unsourced clipping, September 29, 1931, page unknown, Jetta Goudal Papers, Clippings 1923-1980, 19-f.191, Margaret Herrick Library, Los Angeles.

53. Donnell, "Mistress of Mystery," 22.

54. Rosie White, "*You'll Be the Death of Me*: Mata Hari and the Myth of Femme Fatale," in *The Femme Fatale: Images, Histories, Contexts*, ed. Helen Hanson and Catherine O'Rawe (London: Palgrave Macmillan, 2010), 73.

55. Nora Gilbert, "*She Makes Love for the Papers*: Love, Sex and Exploitation in Hitchcock's Mata Hari Films," *Film & History: An Interdisciplinary Journal of Film and Television Studies* 41, no. 2 (Fall 2011): 6.

56. See Julie Wheelwright, *The Fatal Lover: Mata Hari and the Myth of Women in Espionage* (London: Collins and Brown, 1992), 137; and Rosie White, *Violent Femmes: Women as Spies in Popular Culture* (London: Routledge, 2007), 34.

57. The vague geographical setting is notable here. See Donnell, "Mistress of Mystery," 22.

58. Donnell, "Mistress of Mystery," 22.

59. Donnell, "Mistress of Mystery," 22.

60. Donnell, "Mistress of Mystery," 22.

61. Wheelwright, *Fatal Lover*, 5.

62. Negri's romance with Charlie Chaplin attracted criticism for being a promotional tactic. See Agnes Smith, "Between Stars and You," *Picture Play*, November 1923, 20; and Harry Carr, "On the Camera Coast," *Motion Picture Magazine*, June 1923, 67.

63. Richard Dyer, "A Star Is Born and the Construction of Authenticity," in *Stardom: Industry of Desire*, ed. Christine Gledhill (London: Routledge, 1991), 136.

64. Gaylyn Studlar, "*Out-Salomeing Salome*: Dance, the New Woman, and Fan Magazine Orientalism," in *Visions of the East: Orientalism in Film*, ed. Matthew Bernstein and Gaylyn Studlar (London: I.B. Tauris Publishers, 1997), 99.

CHAPTER 8 — JETTA GOUDAL AND TEMPERAMENT

Chapter subtitle: "The most temperamental actress," Harry Carr, "Jetta and Her Temperament," *Motion Picture Classic*, October 1924, 21.

1. The company was called Famous Players-Lasky in 1925, and changed its name to Paramount Famous Players-Lasky in 1927. In the interest of consistency, I refer to it as Famous Players-Lasky. See also Jetta Goudal vs. Famous Players-Lasky Corporation, Case Nr. 166251, March 27, 1925, Superior Court of the State of California in and for the county of Los Angeles.

2. The first legal lawsuit against a producer was initiated by Goudal against Distinctive Picture Corporation after she was fired in November 1923. Because this case was not granted any press coverage—and my interest lies in media representation of such events—I do not discuss the court case here at length.

3. Anthony Slide, *Silent Players: A Biographical and Autobiographical Study of 100 Silent Film Actors and Actresses* (Lexington: University Press of Kentucky, 2002), 149.

4. A. L. Wooldridge, "Will the Stars Behave?," *Picture Play*, December 1927, 94.

5. The sum is cited by "Hollywood Highlights," *Picture Play*, June 1929, 59; it would be equivalent to approximately $425,682 in 2016.

6. Barry King, "Stardom as an Occupation," in *The Hollywood Film Industry*, ed. Paul Kerr (London: Routledge, 1986), 156.

7. Andrew Dawson and Sean P. Holmes, "New Perspectives on Working in the Global Film and Television Industries," in *Working in the Global Film and Television Industries: Creativity, Systems, Space, Patronage*, ed. Andrew Dawson and Sean P. Holmes (London: Bloomsbury Academic, 2012), 12.

8. The animosity between Goudal and DeMille was short-lived. The two managed to remain friends after the lawsuit. See Rachel A. Schildgen, *More Than a Dream: Rediscovering the Life and Films of Vilma Bánky* (Hollywood, CA: 1921 PVG Publishing, 2010), 91.

9. Sean Holmes, "No Room for Manoeuvre: Star Images and the Regulation of Actors' Labor in Silent Era Hollywood," in *Working in the Global Film and Television Industries: Creativity, Systems, Space, Patronage*, ed. Andrew Dawson and Sean P. Holmes (London: Bloomsbury Academic, 2012), 77.

10. In reality, Goudal was of Jewish ancestry and was born in Amsterdam as Henriette Goudeket. Nevertheless, she was promoted as French and/or Oriental throughout her career in Hollywood. See Matthew Isaac Cohen, "Representing Java and Bali in Popular Film, 1919–1954: Sites of Performance, Extra-Daily Bodies, Enduring Stories," in *Sites, Bodies and Stories: Imagining Indonesia History*, ed. Susan Légene, Bambang Purwato, and Henk Schulte Nordholt (Singapore: National University of Singapore Press, 2015), 135.

11. Richard Dyer, "A Star Is Born and the Construction of Authenticity," in *Stardom: Industry of Desire*, ed. Christine Gledhill (London: Routledge, 1991), 137.

12. Jan-Christopher Horak, "Sauerkraut & Sausages with a Little Goulash: Germans in Hollywood, 1927," *Film History: An International Journal* 17, nos. 2/3 (2005): 244.

13. Stephen Gundle and Clino Castelli, *The Glamour System* (London: Palgrave Macmillan, 2006), 65.

14. Gloria Swanson was American, but her image also relied on the notion of temperament. Other stars that were seen as prone to "inflammable situations" include Greta Garbo, John Gilbert, and Erich von Stoinhem. See Helen Bailey, "Please Keep Out!," *Motion Picture Classic*, February 1928, 87.

15. Ruth M. Tildesley, "The Temperamental Dumb," *Picture Play*, February 1929, 88.

16. Helen Louise Walker, "Spanking the Stars: High and Mighty TEMPERAMENTAL Geniuses Told Where to Get Off," *Motion Picture Magazine*, November 1927, 21.

17. Horak, "Sauerkraut & Sausages with a Little Goulash," 259.

18. Transcript of a meeting in St. Louis, undated, Jetta Goudal Papers, Miscellaneous 1924–1971, 11-f.133, Margaret Herrick Library, Los Angeles.

19. Malcolm H. Oettinger, "Sapristi!—How Foreign!," *Picture Play*, November 1923, 22–23.

20. Cal York, "Studio News and Gossip—East and West," *Photoplay*, August 1924, 92.

21. Carr, "Jetta and Her Temperament," 21.

22. Harry Carr, "On the Camera Coast," *Motion Picture Magazine*, June 1925, 75.

23. Dorothy Calhoun, "The Tamer of the Temperamental," *Motion Picture Classic*, June 1928, 33.

24. Cal York, "Studio News and Gossip—East and West," *Photoplay*, May 1926, 88.

25. *Los Angeles Times*, November 11, 1926, 14, cited in Lucy Fisher, "Greta Garbo: Fashioning a Star Image," in *Idols of Modernity: Movie Stars of the 1920s*, ed. Patrice Petro (New Brunswick, NJ: Rutgers University Press, 2010), 142. See also Carl York, "What's the Matter with Greta Garbo?," *Photoplay*, April 1927, 28.

26. "But there is always a limit to human capacity; and no one can be a great genius without having some decidedly weak side, it may even be, some intellectual narrowness. In other words, there will be some faculty in which he is now and then inferior to men of moderate endowments." Arthur Schopenhauer, "On Genius," in *The Art of Literature*, trans. T. Bailey Sanders (Adelaide, Australia: The University of Adelaide, 2014), accessed August 20, 2019, https://ebooks.adelaide.edu.au/s/schopenhauer/arthur/lit/chapter9.html.

27. Crosland is described as a director who "is always given the most difficult stars to handle." The article lists Conrad Veidt, Dolores Costello, John Barrymore, and Lionel Barrymore as some of the picture players he worked with. See Calhoun, "Tamer of the Temperamental," 33.

28. Calhoun, "Tamer of the Temperamental," 80.

29. Walker, "Spanking the Stars," 21.

30. "A Picture of Jetta Goudal," *Motion Picture Magazine*, March 1928, 23.

31. Immanuel Kant, *Critique of Judgement*, trans. Werner S. Pluhar (Indianapolis: Hackett Publishing, 1987), 308.

32. Homer Currie, "Cinderellas? Maybe!," *Motion Picture Magazine*, February 1926, 112.

33. William H. McKegg, "Their Actions Speak Louder Than Words," *Picture Play*, November 1929, 18–19.

34. Vera L. Zolberg, *Constructing a Sociology of the Arts* (Cambridge: Cambridge University Press), 115.

35. Richard Dyer, *Stars* (London: British Film Institute, 1998), 43.

36. Zolberg, *Constructing a Sociology of the Arts*, 116.

37. "Long Arm of Coincidence Replaces Goudal on High," unsourced clipping, June 21, 1931, in Goudal, Jetta, microfilmed clippings file, Margaret Herrick Library, Los Angeles, cited in Holmes, "No Room for Manoeuvre," 77.

38. Jetta Goudal to the Bystander, January 10, 1924, Jetta Goudal Papers, Miscellaneous 1924–1967, 19-f.192, Margaret Herrick Library, Los Angeles.

39. The Bystander, "Over the Teacups," *Picture Play*, February 1924, 47.

40. The Bystander, "Over the Teacups," *Picture Play*, April 1924, 59.

41. "Long Arm of Coincidence," unsourced clipping, cited in Holmes, "No Room for Manoeuvre," 77.

42. Holmes, "No Room for Manoeuvre," 78.

43. Michelle Tolini Finamore, *Hollywood before Glamour: Fashion in American Silent Film* (London: Palgrave Macmillan, 2013), 138.

44. Tolini Finamore makes a distinction between "modern" gowns and historical costumes. The studios gave some stars a degree of freedom in relation to the former, but by 1928 the latter could be furnished only by the wardrobe departments. See Tolini Finamore, *Hollywood before Glamour*, 139.

45. Goudal was on loan from her studio at the time. Her active involvement in supervising her costumes is suggested by both Charles C. Benham and Michelle Tolini Finamore. The additional clause added to the "Standard Form Artist Contract" stated that "supplementing out standard form contract executed on the 16 day of July, covering your services in our forthcoming production 'THE LOVE SONG' [working title for *Lady of the Pavements*], we hereby grant you the right of supervision of the design of the clothes necessary to be worn by you in your part in this production." See *Standard Form Artist Contract* between Jetta Goudal and Feature Productions Incorporated (signed by M. C. Levee), July 18, 1928, Jetta Goudal Papers, Miscellaneous 1924–1971, 11-f.133, Margaret Herrick Library, Los Angeles. See also Charles C. Benham, "Jetta Goudal: The Exotic," Classic Images, September 1999, accessed January 10, 2010, http://www.classicimages.com/1999/september99/goudal.htm; and Tolini Finamore, *Hollywood before Glamour*, 139.

46. Tolini Finamore, *Hollywood before Glamour*, 139.

47. Tolini Finamore, *Hollywood before Glamour*, 139.

48. Exhibit "A," Jetta Goudal v. Cecil B. DeMille Pictures Corporation, 3, District Court of Appeal, Second Appellate District, State of California, Division 2; 118, Cal. App. 407 (Cal. Ct. App. 1931); Appellate Court Case #2Civ6752, On appeal from Jetta Goudal vs. Cecil B. De Mille Pictures Corporation, Case No. 243415, Superior Court of the State of California, in and for the County of Los Angeles, Department 31.

49. Reporter's Transcript, Jetta Goudal v. Cecil B. DeMille Pictures Corporation, 455, District Court of Appeal, Second Appellate District, State of California, Division 2; 118, Cal. App. 407 (Cal. Ct. App. 1931); Appellate Court Case #2Civ6752, On appeal from Jetta Goudal vs. Cecil B. De Mille Pictures Corporation, Case No. 243415, Superior Court of the State of California, in and for the County of Los Angeles, Department 31.

50. Edward Hayward, "Keeping Tabs on Temperament," *Motion Picture Classic*, July 1927, 33, 72.

51. Reporter's Transcript, Jetta Goudal vs. Cecil B. DeMille Pictures Corporation, 437.

52. Benham, "Jetta Goudal," cited in Holmes, "No Room for Manoeuvre," 78. See also Hester Robinson, "The Secrets of the Stars: Interview with Ferdinand Joseph Graf," *New Movie Magazine*, July 1932, 18.

53. "Dagmar Wins a Cast with Valentino," *Photoplay*, October 1924, 36.

54. Robert Oberfirst, *Rudolph Valentino: The Man behind the Myth* (New York: Citadel Press, 1962), 240.

55. Oberfirst, *Rudolph Valentino*, 240.

56. See Alan Robert Ginsberg, *The Salome Ensemble: Rose Pastor Stokes, Anzia Yezierska, Sonya Levien, and Jetta Goudal* (New York: Syracuse University Press, 2016), 178; and Patricia King Hanson and Stephen L. Hanson, *Magill's Survey of Cinema*, vol. 2, *Silent Films* (Englewood Cliffs, NJ: Salem Press, 1982), 770.

57. Looking back at the incident, Rambova referred to insinuations regarding her jealousy as entirely false. See Natacha Rambova, *Rudy: An Intimate Portrait of Rudolph Valentino by His Wife Natacha Rambova* (London: Hutchinson, 1926), 133.

58. Alan Arnold, *Valentino* (New York: Library Publishers, 1954), 111.

59. Ginsberg, *Salome Ensemble*, 178.

60. Holmes, "No Room for Manoeuvre," 80.

61. "Complaint," Jetta Goudal vs. Distinctive Pictures Corporation, Appelste Division of the Supreme Court of New York, 215 App. 674, 212 N.Y.S 818, October 1925: 2. New York County Clerk Archives.

62. "Memorandum on Behalf of the Defendant in Support of a Motion to Strike Out Certain Matter in the Complaint," Jetta Goudal vs. Distinctive Pictures Corporation, Appelste Division of the Supreme Court of New York, 215 App. 674, 212 N.Y.S 818, October 1925: 21. New York County Clerk Archives.

63. Ginsberg, *Salome Ensemble*, 171.

64. Walker, "Spanking the Stars," 21.

65. Hayward, "Keeping Tabs on Temperament," 33.

66. "These Movie People," *Kokomo Daily Tribune*, IN, August 12, 1927, 19. The column lists Vilma Bánky, Pola Negri, and Jetta Goudal as well as Lya de Putti and Emil Jannings as popular émigré performers.

67. "I am not temperamental. . . . It is only that I am intolerant of stupidity, and yet I never expect more from people than I believe them capable of giving." See Margaret Reid, "A Persecuted Lady," *Picture Play*, May 1926, 112.

68. Carr, "Jetta and Her Temperament," 21.

69. Malcolm H. Oettinger, "A Gesture from Jetta," *Picture Play*, October 1927, 34.

70. Reid, "Persecuted Lady," 74.

71. William H. McKegg, "Sure, They Have Brains!," *Picture Play*, May 1928, 20.

72. Ginsberg, *Salome Ensemble*, 173.

73. Cal York, "Studio News and Gossip—East and West," *Photoplay*, May 1926, 88.

74. Walker, "Spanking the Stars," 21.

75. William McKegg, "Don't Believe All You Hear," *Picture Play*, September 1926, 45.

76. Francis Clark, "Jetta Lives Down Her Past," *Photoplay*, August 1927, 35.

77. Clark, "Jetta Lives Down Her Past," 34.

78. According to Ultimate Movie Rankings, the film grossed $1.14 million in the domestic box office, selling 3.9 million tickets. "Movie Box Office Grosses: 1925 through 1931," Ultimate Movie Rankings, accessed August 20, 2019, http://www.ultimatemovierankings.com/box-office-grosses-1925-through-1931/.

79. The correspondence between Goudal and DeMille shows that she indeed referred to him as "Papa DeMille." See Jetta Goudal to Cecil B. DeMille, undated, Jetta Goudal Papers, Miscellaneous 1924–1971, 11-f.133, Margaret Herrick Library, Los Angeles; "We Hear No More These Days of 'Goudal Temperament' . . . ," *Picture Play*, July 1927, 38; and Reid, "Persecuted Lady," 112.

80. King, "Stardom as an Occupation," 156.

81. Cecil B. DeMille to Jetta Goudal, February 14, 1927, Jetta Goudal Papers, Miscellaneous 1924–1971, 11-f.133, Margaret Herrick Library, Los Angeles.

82. Sig Schlager to Jetta Goudal, March 2, 1927, Jetta Goudal Papers, Miscellaneous 1924–1971, 11-f.133, Margaret Herrick Library, Los Angeles.

83. Helen Louise Walker, "The Little Poses of the Stars," *Picture Play*, May 1928, 18.

84. *Picture Play* reported that Goudal "is suing Pathé for one hundred and one thousand dollars back salary." See The Bystander, "Over the Teacups," *Picture Play*, May 1929, 30.

85. The phrase was used in Cal York, "Studio News and Gossip—East and West," *Photoplay*, March 1926, 92.

86. The financial aspect of DeMille's behavior toward Goudal was brought to my attention by Gaylyn Studlar, following my presentation at the Celebrity Studies conference in Amsterdam, 2016.

87. Ginsberg, *Salome Ensemble*, 193.

88. Cecil B. DeMille to Jetta Goudal, telegram, April 4, 1926, from Reporter's Transcript on Appeal, Jetta Goudal v. Cecil B. DeMille Pictures Corporation, 595.

89. Ginsberg, *Salome Ensemble*, 193.

90. DeWitt Bodeen and Gene Ringgold, *Films of Cecil B. DeMille* (New York: Citadel Press, 1974), 458–459.

91. Goudal to DeMille, 11-f.133, Margaret Herrick Library, Los Angeles.

92. Ginsberg, *Salome Ensemble*, 178.

93. According to the letter written by Goudal's publicity representative, Sig Schlager, the star sued DeMille for $90,000 of financial compensation. Schlager claims that she was paid $2,750 weekly at DeMille's studio before she was made redundant. Sig Schlager to W. I. Gilbert, February 12, 1928, Jetta Goudal Papers, Miscellaneous 1924–1971, 11-f.133, Margaret Herrick Library, Los Angeles.

94. Leonard Hall, "Reeling around with Leonard Hall," *Photoplay*, June 1929, 70.

95. Aileen St. John-Brennon, "Weighed in the Balance," *Picture Play*, August 1929, 112.

96. The Bystander, "Over the Teacups," *Picture Play*, May 1929, 30.

97. The Bystander, "Over the Teacups," 30.

98. Virginia Wright Wexman, *Creating the Couple: Love, Marriage, and Hollywood Performance* (Princeton, NJ: Princeton University Press, 1993), 45.

99. See, for instance, Diane Negra, *Off-White Hollywood: American Culture and Ethnic Female Stardom* (London: Routledge, 2001), 75.

100. Rosie White, *Violent Femmes: Women as Spies in Popular Culture* (London: Routledge, 2007), 2.

101. The Bystander, "Over the Teacups," 30.

102. Richard Dyer, "A Star Is Born and the Construction of Authenticity," in *Stardom: Industry of Desire*, ed. Christine Gledhill (London: Routledge, 1991), 136.

103. Clare Whatling, *Screen Dreams: Fantasising Lesbians in Film* (Manchester: Manchester University Press, 1997), 123.

104. Mordaunt Hall, "De Mille as Director Is Disciplinarian," *New York Times*, July 19, 1925, 140.

105. Tricia Welsch, *Gloria Swanson: Ready for Her Close-Up* (Jackson: University Press of Mississippi, 2013), 73.

106. The Bystander, "Over the Teacups," 30.

107. See Dorothy Calhoun, "Do Women Rule the Movies?," *Motion Picture Classic*, August 1928, 88.

108. "Hollywood Highlights," *Picture Play*, June 1929, 59.

109. Harry Carr, "The Untold Tales of Hollywood," *Smart Set Magazine*, 1929, issue and page unknown, cited in Michelle Vogel, *Lupe Vélez: The Life and Career of Hollywood's "Mexican Spitfire"* (Jefferson, NC: McFarland Publishers, 2012), 179.

110. Margaret Reid, "Goudal and Velez Fight to Draw," *Motion Picture Classic*, December 1928, 58.

111. McKegg, "Their Actions Speak Louder Than Words," 18–19.

112. As Goudal explained: "Were I to force myself to do something that went against every fiber of my artistic senses, I would be false to myself—no longer an artist but a puppet." McKegg, "Their Actions Speak Louder Than Words," 18–19.

113. McKegg, "Sure, They Have Brains!," 20.

114. Although Basinger's discussion of Hollywood's power dynamic starts in the 1930s, I find her argument to be applicable to the previous decade. See Jeanine Basinger, *The Star Machine* (New York: Alfred A. Knopf, 2007), 141.

115. Basinger, *Star* Machine, 141.

116. In 1951, Hortense Powdermaker published her pioneering effort to explain the American film industry through the lens of anthropology. Although not bereft of shortcomings, *Hollywood: The Dream Factory* can be understood as a predecessor to the field of star studies. See Hortense Powdermaker, *Hollywood: The Dream Factory. An Anthropologist Looks at the Movie-Makers* (London: Secker & Warburg, 1951), 327.

117. Holmes notes that Goudal's fluency in French was the only reason why she was not blacklisted by Hollywood producers. At the dawn of the talking pictures, studios started shooting foreign-language versions of their top-grossing releases to bolster their market share in Europe. Holmes, "No Room for Manoeuvre," 87.

118. Alan Hynd and Dorothy Calhoun, "News of the Camera Coast," *Motion Picture Magazine*, December 1927, 46.

119. Cal York, "Studio News and Gossip—East and West," *Photoplay*, March 1926, 92.

120. St. John-Brennon, "Weighed in the Balance," 112.

121. Harold Hunt, "Actress Is Busy with Rehearsals," unsourced clipping, September 29, 1931, page unknown, Jetta Goudal Papers, Clippings 1923–1980, 19-f.191, Margaret Herrick Library, Los Angeles.

CONCLUSION

1. "The New Films at a Glance," *New Movie Magazine*, March 1932, 62.

2. Richard Jewel, "RKO Film Grosses: 1931–1951," *Historical Journal of Film Radio and Television* 14, no. 1 (1994): 58.

3. In the 1930s, Negri relocated to Germany, where she was cast in seven feature films. She came out of retirement to appear in two American productions: *Hi Diddle Diddle* (1943) and *The Moon-Spinners* (1963).

4. Harry Waldman, *Beyond Hollywood's Grasp: American Filmmakers Abroad, 1914–1945* (Metuchen, NJ: Scarecrow Press, 1994), 130.

5. Cal York, "Cal York Announcing the Monthly Broadcast of Hollywood Goings-On!," *Photoplay*, May 1933, 39. For the discussion of Negri's accent, see James Cunningham, "Asides and Interludes," *Motion Picture Herald*, January 21, 1933, 25.

6. See Mordaunt Hall, "Will Rogers in Fine Form," *New York Times*, February 13, 1932, accessed August 15, 2019, http://www.nytimes.com/movie/review?res=9905E5D81E3FE633A25750C1A9649C946394D6CF.

7. Alma Whitaker, "Domestic or Foreign Charmers?," *Screenland*, December 1931, 24.

8. Diane Negra, *Off-White Hollywood: American Culture and Ethnic Female Stardom* (London: Routledge, 2001), 57.

9. Jeanine Basinger, *Silent Stars* (Middletown, CT: Wesleyan University Press, 1999), 474.

10. See Scott A. Berg, *Goldwyn: A Biography* (New York: Alfred A. Knopf, 1989), 167.

11. One concerned fan wrote, "I wonder whether she will ever have a director who has as much ability to direct as she has to perform. If Pola Negri ever does, we will have a perfection in motion picture entertainment." B. La Comber, "Brickbats and Bouquets," *Photoplay*, April 1925, 12.

12. Sean P. Holmes suggested that this strategy was partially inspired by Goudal's determination to keep her private affairs out of the spotlight. See Andrew Dawson and Sean P. Holmes, "New Perspectives on Working in the Global Film and Television Industries," in *Working in the Global Film and Television Industries: Creativity, Systems, Space, Patronage*, ed. Andrew Dawson and Sean P. Holmes (London: Bloomsbury Academic, 2012), 77.

13. Tom Rice, "Protecting Protestantism: The Ku Klux Klan vs. the Motion Picture Industry," *Film History: An International Journal* 20, no. 3 (2008): 367.

14. Aileen St. John-Brenon, "Manhattan Medley," *Picture Play*, May 1928, 52.

15. Virginia Wright Wexman, *Creating the Couple: Love, Marriage, and Hollywood Performance* (Princeton, NJ: Princeton University Press, 1993), 134.

16. For a discussion of Bánky, see Elza Schallert and Edwin Schallert, "Hollywood Highlights," *Picture Play*, October 1925, 72; and Marian Brownridge, "Brickbats and Bouquets," *Photoplay*, February 1926, 12. For Negri, see Rosa Shpetner, "What the Fans Think," *Picture Play*, December 1929, 113. For Goudal, see "A Picture of Jetta Goudal," *Motion Picture Magazine*, March 1928, 23.

17. Goudal played a half-Peruvian/half-Chinese woman in *The Bright Shawl* (1923), a Russian character in *The Coming of Amos* (1927), and a Mexican one in *The White Gold* (1927).

18. Miriam Hansen, "Adventures of Goldilocks: Spectatorship, Consumerism and Public Life," *Camera Obscura* 8, no. 22 (1990): 64.

19. Sabrina Qiong Yu, "Performing Stardom: Star Studies in Transformation and Expansion," in *Revisiting Star Studies: Cultures, Themes and Methods*, ed. Sabrina Qiong Yu and Guy Austin (Edinburgh: Edinburgh University Press, 2017), 2.

20. Both quotes come from Alex Bilmes, "The Irresistible Rise of Pénelope Cruz," *Esquire*, October 13, 2017, accessed August 15, 2019, http://www.esquire.co.uk/culture/film/longform/a17840/penelope-cruz-interview/. See also "Penelope Cruz Adding Exotic Sexiness to *Pirates of the Caribbean*," I Watch Stuff, February 11, 2010, accessed November 1, 2017, http://iwatchstuff.com/2010/02/penelope-cruz-adding-exotic-se.php.

21. Pat McGrath, Dolce & Gabanna creative adviser, described Bellucci as follows: "She is so effortlessly flawless and a true screen siren. I wanted to keep her make-up quite simple here—we didn't really use a huge selection of products, mainly because Monica's radiance and Italian spirit shines through so naturally." See Rebecca Gonsalves, "Facing Up to La Dolce Vita," March 18, 2017, accessed November 1, 2017, http://www.independent.co.uk/life-style/fashion/features/facing-up-to-la-dolce-vita-of-monica-bellucci-9200201.html.

22. Sally Williams, "Monica Bellucci on Life after Divorce and Finding Herself in Her 50s," *The Telegraph*, July 15, 2017, accessed November 1, 2017, http://www.telegraph.co.uk/films/2017/07/15/monica-bellucci-life-divorce-finding-50s/.

23. See Sean M. Smith, "Romantic Cruz," *The Guardian*, March 2, 2001, accessed August 15, 2019, https://www.theguardian.com/film/2001/mar/02/culture.features1; and Bilmes, "Irresistible Rise of Pénelope Cruz."

24. Gregg Barrios, "Legendary Vamp Takes a Final Bow: Pola Negri on Her Hollywood Heydays," *Los Angeles Times*, August 9, 1987, accessed August 26, 2019, http://articles.latimes.com/1987-08-09/entertainment/ca-2_1_pola-negri/3.

Index

About the Author

Agata Frymus is a Marie Curie postdoctoral fellow at Ghent University, Belgium. She received her doctoral degree from the University of York, UK, in 2018. Agata's research concentrates on the relationship between race and silent film. Her work has been published in *Early Popular Visual Culture*, *Celebrity Journal*, and *Cinema Journal* (forthcoming).